SURVIVING ON THE MOVE:
MIGRATION, POVERTY AND DEVELOPMENT
IN SOUTHERN AFRICA

Eds: Jonathan Crush and Bruce Frayne

Acknowledgements

We wish to thank the International Development Research Centre (IDRC) for its gener-ous support of SAMP's research and policy project on "Migration, Development and Poverty Reduction in the SADC." This particular publication was made possible with the support of that project. The chapters were first published in a special issue of the journal Development Southern Africa (DSA) 24(1) (2007)and are reprinted here with the permission of the publishers of DSA, Taylor & Francis Ltd (http://www.informaworld.com). The first chapter has been updated to take account of recent thinking about the migration-development relationship. We would like to thank the editors and editorial staff of DSA for their assistance. David Dorey, Christina Hughes and Ashley Hill provided invaluable assistance. We also wish to thank Jennifer Payne, Teresa Pires, Moira Levy and Bronwen Müller for their assistance in readying the manuscript for publication.

Published by Idasa and Development Bank of Southern Africa (DBSA)

© Southern African Migration Programme (SAMP) 2010
ISBN 978-1-920409-09-8

First published 2010
Produced by Idasa Publishing
Cover design: Welma Odendaal
Cover photos: Greg Marinovich/Africa Media Online

Bound and printed by LogoPrint, Cape Town

Contents

Tables

Figures

Contributors

Abel Chikanda is in the Department of Geography, University of Western Ontario, Canada.

Jonathan Crush is in the Department of Global Development Studies, Queen's University, Ontario, Canada, and the Department of Environmental and Geographical Science, University of Cape Town.

Fion de Vletter is an Independent Consultant in Maputo, Mozambique.

Bruce Frayne is an associate of the Southern African Research Centre, Queen's University.

Miriam Grant is the Department of Geography, University of Calgary, Canada.

Loren Landau is in the Forced Migration Studies Programme, University of Witwatersrand.

Robert Mattes is in the Department of Political Studies and Centre for Social Science Research, University of Cape Town.

France Maphosa is in the Department of Sociology at the National University of Lesotho.

Namhla Mniki is in the Department of Political Studies and Centre for Social Science Research, University of Cape Town.

Samuel Owuor is in the Department of Geography & Environmental Studies, University of Nairobi.

Theresa Ulicki is in the Department of International Development Studies, Dalhousie University, Halifax, Nova Scotia, Canada.

Natalya Dinat is in the Department of Medicine, University of the Witwatersrand.

Sally Peberdy is in the Department of Geography at the University of Western Cape.

Prerna Banati is with the Global Fund to Fight AIDS, TB and Malaria.

France Maphosa is in the Department of Sociology, Anthropology and Social Work at the National University of Lesotho.

1 SURVIVING ON THE MOVE

JONATHAN CRUSH AND BRUCE FRAYNE

1. Introduction

Since 2000, the so-called 'migration–development nexus' has become a central item on the global development agenda (Gundel, 2002; Nyberg-Sørensen et al., 2002; Van Hear & Nyberg Sørensen, 2003; Haque, 2004; Sriskandarajah, 2005; de Haas 2009). Hardly a month now passes without a major international policy conference or workshop on the subject. In September 2006, the United Nations held its first High-Level Dialogue on International Migration and Development, signalling the full arrival of this critical issue on the global stage. In preparation for this event, the UN Population Division sponsored a series of expert technical workshops on various facets of the subject in 2005 (UN, 2004c, 2005a,b). Also in 2005, the UN-endorsed Global Commission on Migration published a seminal report following an intensive process of global consultations with governments and other stakeholders (GCIM, 2005). The UN's own 2004 World Economic and Social Survey was devoted entirely to International Migration (UN, 2004b). The World Bank has taken a particular interest in the financial implications of international migration and it dedicated its most recent World Economic Survey entirely to this subject (World Bank, 2006). Other multilateral agencies such as the International Organisation for Migration (IOM, 2005) and the International Labour Organisation (ILO, 2004) have recently focused their attention on the migration and development nexus. The Global Forum on International Migration and Development is now an annual fixture on the international conference circuit. The UNDP's 2009 Human Development Report focuses on the relationship between mobility and human development (UNDP, 2009).

At the regional scale, the links between migration, poverty and development are also increasingly being recognised and debated. The dramatic growth of Regional Consultative Processes (RCPs) on migration is indicative of the increased recognition by regional groupings of states that they share common interests in the management of this issue (von Koppenfels, 2001; Klein Solomon, 2005). Within RCPs, regional responses to the development implications of migration are now high on the agenda. The Migration Dialogue for Southern Africa (MIDSA) process, jointly hosted by the IOM and the Southern African Migration Programme (SAMP), has recently held several intergovernmental forums relating to issues of migration and development.

Until recently, discussions of migration and development tended to focus on the impact of the movement of migrants from the South to the North. More recently, South-South migration has garnered increasing attention in the debate (Ratha & Shaw, 2007; Castles and Wise, 2008.) However, policy responses to the challenge and opportunities of South-South migration have been much more limited, especially within Africa (Gundel, 2002; Crush, 2003; Ammasarri, 2005; Bloch, 2005, Landau & Segatti 2009). In most African and other developing countries, migration and development are seen as largely separate policy spheres. Development policies and plans do not normally integrate the realities of internal and international population mobility in any substantive manner. Poverty Reduction Strategy Papers (PRSPs) in southern Africa, for example, largely ignore migration, despite its demonstrable importance as a survival strategy for large numbers of households (Roberts, 2006). Similarly, national immigration and migration policy is generally disconnected from development planning. Migrants who leave are pervasively seen as undermining national economic plans and those who arrive are more often seen as a threat to citizens' rights and welfare. Migration policy is the preserve of states, and most are still focused primarily on sovereignty issues of management, enforcement and border control. Many migrant-receiving countries do not explicitly or implicitly recognise the value of immigrants and migrants to their own future national, regional and local economic development. Migrants are more commonly viewed by states and citizenries as a threat to their economic and social interests. In some southern African countries – particularly South Africa, Botswana and Namibia – opposition to migration has spilled over into intolerance and xenophobia (Crush, 2000; Crush & Pendleton, 2004; Nyamnjoh, 2006; SAMP, 2008). Similar responses to migrants are evident elsewhere in the South (Crush & Ramachandran, 2009).

On the other hand, there is a growing recognition, within the SADC region at least, that a community of states with common interests needs to facilitate the intra-regional movement of people, not just trade and investment, to further the process of economic integration and balanced regional development. As early as 1995, the SADC Secretariat moved to implement, first, a Protocol on the Freedom of Movement of Persons and then, when that failed, a Protocol on the Facilitation of Movement of Persons. As Oucho and Crush (2002) point out, opposition to both protocols within South Africa, Botswana and Namibia was particularly strong and effectively killed off any chance of ratification by 2000. However, in the last two years the Facilitation Protocol has been revived and ratified by a number of states, including South Africa. The unanswered question is what the implications, developmental and otherwise, would be for the countries of southern Africa if there was greater freedom of movement within the Community.

2. Perspectives on Migration and Development

An analysis of migration trends indicates the emergence of a new global migration system in the past 50 years, or what Castles and Miller (2003) refer to as the 'age of migration.' Since the end of the colonial period, international migration has become a truly global phenomenon. Migration has seen 'a great increase in the magnitude, density, velocity and diversity of global connections' (Nyberg-Sorenson et al., 2002). The globalisation of migration means that all parts of the world are now affected, to a greater or lesser degree, by international migration. There is hardly a village, town or city, much less a country, that is untouched by international migration, either as a sender or recipient of migrants or, in many cases, both. All of the major regions and continents, and many countries, have experienced growth in their 'migrant stock' over the last 30 years.

The absolute number of international migrants has increased dramatically in the last 50 years and is likely to continue to expand in the future. Most observers predict that the absolute and proportional numbers of global migrants will continue to increase, since the structural forces driving international migration will intensify (Papademetriou, 2001; Cohen, 2004). Measuring global migration flows has proven to be very difficult given current systems of data collection. The most common proxy measure of international migrant flows is the UN concept of 'migrant stock' – defined as the number of foreign-born residents in the population at the time of the most recent census.

The global migrant stock increased from 75,9 million in 1960 to 190,6 million in 2005 (Table 1.1). In the developed world, the increase was from 42 to 115 million and in the developing world from 49 to 86 million. All of the major geographical regions, with the notable exception of Latin America, experienced significant growth in their migrant stock. As the UN (2004b, p. viii) notes, 'reflecting the increasingly global nature of migration, there has been greater diversity both in the countries from which international migrants originate and in their countries of destination.' In 1960, there were 43 countries where the share of international migrants in the population exceeded 10 per cent. By 2000, this number had risen to 70 (UN, 2004b:28). There has still been a growing concentration of international migrants in the major receiving countries (the US, France, Germany, the UK, Italy and Canada), up from 26,6 per cent of the 1960 total to 37 per cent in 2000.

Table 1.1: Global Migration Stock by Region of Destination, 1960–2005						
Region	1960	1970	1980	1990	2000	2005
World	75.5	81.3	99.3	154.9	176.7	190.6
Developed countries	32.3	38.4	47.5	82.4	105.0	115.4
Developing countries	49.5	50.2	60.9	83.5	81.5	85.7
Regional						
Africa	9.1	9.9	14.1	16.3	16.5	17.1
Asia	28.5	27.8	32.1	49.9	50.3	53.3
Latin America and the Caribbean	6.0	5.7	6.1	7.0	6.3	6.6
Northern America	12.5	13.0	18.1	27.6	40.4	44.5
Oceania	2.1	3.0	3.7	4.8	5.1	5.0
Europe	14.2	18.8	21.9	49.4	58.2	64.1
Source: UNDESA, 2005.						

South–South migration has increased significantly in recent decades (Ratha & Shaw, 2007). In 2000, the major receiving countries in the South were the members of the Gulf Cooperation Council (migrant stock of 9,6 million), India (6,3 million), Pakistan (4,2 million), Iran (2,3 million), Jordan (1,9 million) and the United Arab Emirates (1,9 million). In Africa, major receiving countries include South Africa, Nigeria and Côte d'Ivoire. Most South–South migration is temporary and driven primarily by economic motives. As Skeldon (1997: 9) notes: 'Migration is not a simple move from an origin to a destination ... but is far more likely to consist of a complex sequence of moves that may involve several destinations and regular contact with the origin, which may eventually involve return migration.' Where well-regulated and managed, migration is organised using contract labour schemes. Most developing countries do not encourage permanent immigration. While many developing countries bemoan the loss of skills through the so-called 'brain drain' (Tanner, 2005), others actively export migrant labour as a matter of policy (such as the Philippines, Bangladesh and, locally, Mozambique and Lesotho) (Rozario & Gow, 2003; Ogena, 2004).

Researchers have attempted to explain the growth in international migration using a wide variety of theoretical perspectives and explanatory frameworks (Massey et al., 1998; Brettell & Hollifield, 2000; Castles & Miller, 2003; Massey & Taylor, 2004; Tamas, 2004; Toro-Morn & Marixsa, 2004; Bommes & Morawska, 2005). In the final analysis, these explanations are pitched at either the macro or micro level. Macro explanations focus on the broader structural changes that precipitate migration (usually economic but sometimes environmental or social); micro ones focus on individual and household decision-making processes and the reasons why decision-makers respond in different ways to the same push and pull factors. Ultimately, the causes of migration are multiple, variable, scale-dependent and often country-specific. No one explanation will suit all situations. The same applies to the relationship between migration and development. For every global generalisation about the impact of migration on development, or vice versa, there will be myriad local exceptions.

If the primary reason for examining the relationship between migration and development is to work out ways in which 'development' may act as a brake on migration, then it would be important to understand the root causes of migration (Gent, 2002). For example, one line of argument is that poverty causes migration and that poverty alleviation will dampen it (de Haan, 2000; Waddington & Sabates-Wheeler, 2005). Certainly, within particular countries, there is strong evidence that poverty (which may have a variety of local and general causes) is a major impetus for migration (Litchfield & Waddington, 2002; Kothari, 2003; Siddiqui, 2003). At the international scale, however, this causal connection is less obvious. In fact, analysts now tend to feel that the poorest, lacking the necessary resources, are least likely to migrate. Hence, as Skeldon (1997) counter-intuitively concludes, poverty alleviation may actually increase rather than decrease migration. The idea that development aid might be a lever to decrease migration thus seems increasingly misplaced (Gent, 2002).

Three distinct general perspectives on the migration–development nexus can be identified in the research literature and contemporary policy debates: (a) migration has positive implications for development and poverty reduction; (b) migration has a negative impact on development and increases poverty; and (c) the relationship between migration and development is both complex and place-specific. Advocates of migration as a positive force in development favour more migration and freedom of movement. They include the World Bank, which has recently concluded that international migration 'often generates great benefits for migrants and their families' and 'can generate substantial welfare gains for migrants, their countries of origin, and the countries to which they migrate' (World Bank, 2006: 25). These gains can be seen in three interlinked areas: remittances, the migration of skilled workers and global welfare.

First, with regard to remittances, the advocates of migration as a positive force in development point primarily to the massive increase in remittance transfers to developing countries in recent years (see, for example, Sander, 2003; Sander & Maimbo, 2003; Adams & Page, 2005; Maimbo & Ratha, 2005; Schiff & Özden, 2006). Globally, remittances have more than doubled in value in the past decade, easily outstripping Official Development Assistance (ODA) and closing in on Foreign Direct Investment (FDI) (Figure 1.1). Estimates of the volume of remittances are most likely on the low side since they do not include informal transfers, often thought to be up to 50 per cent of the total flow. Worth over US$170 billion per annum, remittances form the backbone of many developing economies and link many diasporan communities to their countries of origin. Remittance flows have increased dramatically in all six regions of the developing world (Table 1.2).

Remittances are thought to flow predominantly from North to South, from developed to developing nations. However, the World Bank has recently estimated that 35-40 per cent of remittances received in the developing world originate in other developing countries (World Bank, 2006: xxx). In the developing world as a whole, remittance receipts are equivalent to 6,7 per cent of imports and 7,5 per cent of domestic investment. Remittances make up significant percentages of many nations' GDP. In several Asian countries they are larger than the earnings from any single commodity export and are recognised as having important impacts on family, community, regional, and even national economies. The World Bank is

Figure 1.1: A Comparison of Remittance Growth with ODA and FDI

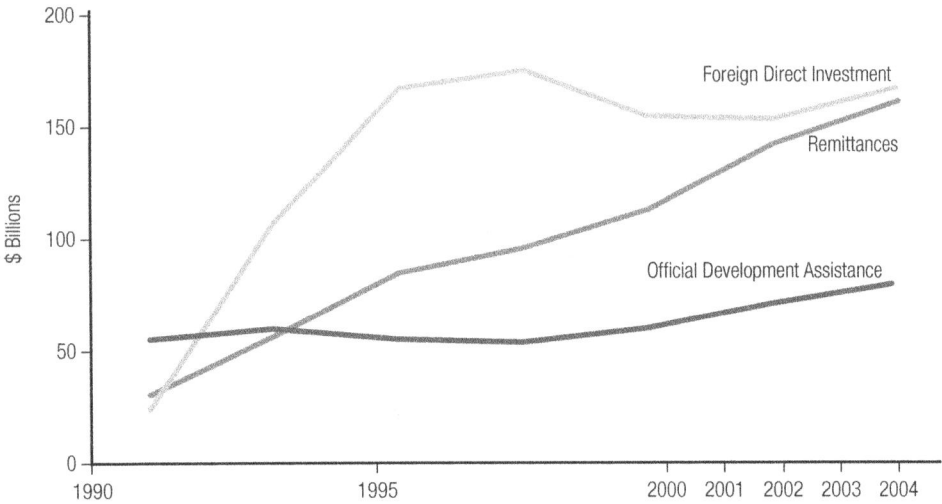

Table 1.2: Workers' Remittances to Developing Countries

	1990	1995	2000	2001	2002	2003	2004	2005	Change (%) 2001-05
Latin America and the Caribbean	5.8	13.4	20.1	24.4	28.1	34.8	40.7	42.4	74
South Asia	5.6	10.0	17.2	19.2	24.2	31.1	31.4	32.0	67
East Asia and the Pacific	3.3	9.7	16.7	20.1	27.2	35.8	40.9	43.1	114
Middle East and North Africa	11.4	13.4	13.2	15.1	15.6	18.6	20.3	21.3	41
Europe and Central Asia	3.2	8.1	13.4	13.0	13.3	15.1	19.4	19.9	53
Sub-Saharan Africa	1.9	3.2	4.9	4.7	5.2	6.8	7.7	8.1	72
Developing countries total	31.2	57.8	85.6	96.5	113.4	142.1	160.4	166.9	73

Source: Adapted from World Bank, 2006: 88.

a particularly firm proponent of the developmental value of remittances, pointing out that recorded remittance flows easily outweigh FDI in many countries of the developing world (Goldin & Reinert, 2006).

Secondly, with regard to skills migration, the World Bank suggests that the positive elements of migration for developing countries are often overlooked. According to the World

Bank, increasing the emigration of low-skilled workers would significantly reduce poverty in developing countries (World Bank, 2006). High-skilled migration can greatly benefit migrants and their families and help relieve labour market pressures. Well-educated diasporans can improve access to capital, technology, information foreign exchange and business contacts in the country of origin. Even the impacts of the brain drain are exaggerated, according to proponents of this view (Lowell, 2002; Wickramasekara, 2003; Lowell et al., 2004). Although the temporary or permanent loss of high-skilled workers can admittedly reduce growth, compromise good governance and impair service delivery in some countries, the countervailing advantages of migration must be acknowledged.

Thirdly, the World Bank's (2006) 'linkage' model is designed to measure and predict the impact of international migration on global welfare and development. The model predicts that (a) migration will produce a sizeable global gain in adjusted real incomes of $356 billion by 2025. All except old migrants in developed countries will gain – new migrants by $481 billion, non-migrant residents of developing countries by $143 billion and non-migrant residents of high-income countries by $139 billion. The highest gains will accrue to migrants from sub-Saharan Africa; (b) global incomes will rise owing to migration; (c) increased remittances will provide developing countries with the opportunity to import more and export less; (d) easing restrictions on migration could provide a significant boost to the world economy as a whole; (e) the gains from an increase in migration are greater for developing than developed countries; and (f) overall migrants have no impact, or very limited impact, on the wages or employment of the vast majority of non-migrant residents.

Those who suggest that migration has a negative impact on development include many governments (particularly in developing countries) and citizenries, as well as some researchers. Three arguments are usually advanced in support of this position. First, skills migration and the loss of human resources have a major negative impact on a country's development prospects. Costs include the pure loss of talent and state investment in training and education that effectively subsidise the destination country; fiscal costs through loss of tax revenue; and the possibility of crippling entire institutions and sectors of the economy (Lowell, 2002; Lowell & Findlay, 2002). The impact is obviously worst in countries with a weak human resource base (Kapur & McHale, 2005a,b; Tanner, 2005). Emotive images of 'brain drains' and 'poaching' are used to critique the policies of the governments of the countries to which skills migrate (Al-Samarrai & Bennell, 2003; Chikanda, 2005; Awases et al., 2005; Mensah et al., 2005). No less a personage than Nelson Mandela accused skilled migrants who leave his country of being 'traitors' and 'unpatriotic' (McDonald & Crush, 2002).

A highly charged debate has ensued at many international gatherings, with insistent demands from sending countries for monetary compensation and calls for bilateral and multilateral agreements restricting the movement of skilled people from developing countries. Very few of the countries which lament the loss of their own skills base are themselves active in the global market place for skills as buyers (Cornelius et al., 2001; Crush, 2002). Outdated and highly restrictive immigration policies make it extremely difficult for skilled people from other countries to live and work and settle. Only a handful of developing countries, notably the Gulf States, have developed policies that encourage the inflow of skills.

Secondly, with regard to remittances, those who view migration as a negative force in development certainly do acknowledge the magnitude of remittance flows. However, they question the developmental value of remittances in the sending country. Newland (2004: 194-5) suggests three basic reasons why remittance flows are often seen as failing to improve the development prospects of a country of origin: (a) there is the difficulty in many countries of converting remittances into sustainable productive capacity; (b) remittance income is rarely used for productive purposes: it is primarily used for direct consumption and very little is directed to income-earning, job-creating investment; and (c) remittances increase inequality, encourage import consumption and create dependency. In short, as Hamilton suggests, it is 'a distant hope that remittances could help families, communities and countries remain permanently out of poverty' (Hamilton, 2003: 2).

A third element in the argument that migration is bad for development is heard increasingly in recipient countries in the North and South. The argument here is that foreign migrants, legal or unauthorised, undermine citizens' economic and social development. Migrants are said to deprive citizens of already limited employment opportunities, depress wages, compete for scarce public resources (such as land, services, health, housing) and outcompete local business. This is usually a zero sum game in which every job occupied by a migrant is a job lost to a citizen. The belief that migrants undermine development for citizens is extremely pervasive in migrant-receiving countries, often shading into attitudes and acts of intolerance and xenophobia.

The 'balance sheet' approach to migration and development suggests that there are developmental pros and cons associated with migration and that these accrue to both developed and developing countries. One classification, shown in Table 1.3, suggests that the impacts of migration can be summarised through listing the positives and negatives on either side of a ledger (UN, 2004b: x).

A second element of the balance sheet approach is to see the impact of migration on development as scale-dependent. According to Skeldon (1997: 4), the implications of migration for development can vary according to the level of analysis – individual, family, community, nation or state, micro or macro level. Migration from a poor to a rich country generally benefits the individual migrant and sending household. However, do the benefits to individuals (and families left behind) aggregate to a general benefit to the home country? For example, large-scale out-migration may simultaneously be very good for the individual households involved (because of the subsequent flow of remittances) and very bad for the national economy as a whole (because of the loss of skilled, productive labour). The challenge for policy-makers is how to provide an environment that maximises the benefits and minimises the costs of migration at all levels.

Thirdly, the relationship between migration and development is country-specific, and even varies within countries. It is commonly argued, for example, that a small developing country with a limited human resource base will feel the impact of the loss of engineers, doctors and teachers much more acutely than a large country (Tanner, 2005). The issue of specificity, however, goes much further than the question of size. Whether migration and development are positively or negatively correlated in a specific country will depend on a variety of social, demographic, economic and political characteristics. In general, developing countries with strong economies are less likely than weak or fragile states to experience skills out-migration or to be negatively affected by loss of skills. Ironically, therefore, states that tend to suffer most from the 'brain drain' are those that are economically weak, non-diversified or under-developed.

Table 1.3: Effects of International Migration	
Positive effects	Negative effects
• Provides opportunities to workers not available in home country	• Loss of highly skilled workers reduces economic growth and productivity
• Eases the effect of unemployment and labour surplus in sending countries	• Reduced quality of essential services especially health, education, governance
• Inflow of remittances and foreign exchange	• Lower returns from public investment in education
• Poverty reduction	• Increased disparities in wealth
• Skills, technology transfer, investment by diasporas	• Loss of fiscal revenue from taxation of workers
• Increased trade flows between sending and receiving countries	• Dependence on remittances
• Stimulus to investment in domestic education and individual human capital investments	• Remittances may diminish over time
• Return of skilled workers increases local human capital, skills transfer and foreign linkages	• Social problems from prolonged family separation
	• Increased vulnerability to disease, e.g., HIV/AIDS
• International student migration increases local skills base on return	• Intolerance of migrants from other countries
Source: Adapted from UN, 2004b: x	

3. Addressing the Nexus

Three factors impede the easy resolution of the migration and development debate. The first is the tendency in much of the literature to separate international from internal migration and to try to assess the impact of the former without any consideration of the latter. There is a tendency to treat internal and cross-border migration as discrete processes, even though they are not only interconnected but often mimic each other in form and impact. The vast majority of global migrant movements are internal and often involve greater distances and more disruption than cross-border movements. The interconnectedness of internal and international migration needs to be recognised because it has profound consequences for development (Adepoju, 1998; Deshingkar & Grimm, 2005). A rural household struggling to survive may, for example, receive both internal and international remittances. To isolate the two paints a misleading picture of the survival strategies and options available to the household. This collection therefore recognises the importance of linking internal and international migration in thinking about the migration–development nexus.

Secondly, the argument is increasingly advanced that development needs to be 'main-streamed' in migration policy, and vice versa. In practice, there are few examples of what mainstreaming actually means and how it might be achieved. Take the internationally accepted Millennium Development Goals (MDGs), for example. There is no specific reference to migration in the MDGs, possibly because (a) the MDGs were formulated before migration was recognised as a critical international development issue; (b) while all nations signed on to and support the MDGs, it would be far more problematic for them to formulate a mutually acceptable migration goal given the real and perceived conflicts of interest between origin and destination countries when it comes to migration; and (c) the MDGs are target-based and it would be difficult to formulate and agree on common migration targets in terms, for example, of numbers, types of migration, policies, rights or remittance flows (Skeldon, 2005). The UN's Road Map to the Millennium Declaration does mention the need for 'dialogue on specific policies dealing with migration issues and their implications' (UN General Assembly, 2001: 39). However, the Millennium Project Task Force Reports view migration as having a primarily negative effect on development (Usher, 2005).

Migration can be seen as a cross-cutting issue which has a bearing on most, if not all, of the MDGs (Skeldon, 2005). Migration can either facilitate the attainment of some MDGs or, in some circumstances, actively undermine them. For example, if a developing country loses most of its health professionals and teachers to out-migration, this could make the achievement of the targets in Goals 2 to 6 virtually impossible (Table 1.4). On the other hand, these migrants could remit funds home in such quantities that the same country could make some progress towards achieving Goal 1. Further complicating the issue, migration can actually be a consequence of the attainment of some of the MDGs. For example, the achievement of Goal 2 (universal primary education) will almost certainly lead to increased migration to urban areas and even to other countries (Skeldon, 2005). There is therefore a need to mainstream migration into the MDGs and understand how policies on migration might constrain or enable achievement of targets. Mainstreaming migration into the MDGs in this way helps identify points of leverage for both developing and developed countries, NGOs, migrant organisations and the private sector (Table 1.4). By pursuing any of these points of leverage, SADC could potentially make an important contribution to the fulfilment of MDG targets.

Thirdly, discussions of migration and development consistently complain about the lack of reliable information and data on the subject, particularly in Africa. The UN (2004b: 8) notes that migration is a field in which the data are often incompatible and sparse and observes that the challenges of data collection require coordination and cooperation between states. Newland (2004: 193) points out that the evidence is contradictory and fragmentary and that much of the research about costs and benefits is 'micro' and cannot conclusively demonstrate the validity of 'macro' conclusions: 'Understanding the causal relationship between rich country immigration policy and poor country development is a frustrating pursuit, hamstrung by the absence of data, frequently inaccurate data, and a lack of comparable data.' Castles (1999: 14) concurs on the 'deficiencies of data sources and lack of uniformity in statistical categories' and says: 'National monitoring is frequently inadequate and cross-national comparability in data often lacking.'

Table 1.4: Mainstreaming Migration in the Millennium Development Goals
1. Eradicate extreme poverty and hunger
Reduce by 50% the proportion of people living on less than $1 per day
Remittances • Increase transfers to developing countries • Facilitate more cost-effective transfers and financial products • Better opportunities for investment of remittances in productive, employment-generating activities (SMMEs, agriculture, trade) • Reduced need to use remittances for consumption/survival • Redistribution of remittances to poor
Migrant Rights • Eliminate super-exploitation of vulnerable migrant workers • Adherence to principles in ILO and UN Migrant Workers Conventions • Control irregular migration, trafficking and illegal employment • Ensure greater legal access to temporary employment in other countries • Facilitate cross-border movements for economic gain (informal trading)
Reduce by 50% the proportion of people who suffer from hunger • Encourage investment of remittances in agricultural production • Minimise costs of foodstuffs purchased with remittances • Encourage urban agriculture amongst rural–urban migrants • Facilitate transfers of foodstuffs from rural to urban areas • Target food aid at vulnerable migrant groups
2. Achieve universal primary education
Ensure that all boys and girls complete a full course of primary schooling • Encourage recipient investment of remittances in primary education • Encourage diasporan involvement in primary education delivery • Inventory numbers of children who migrate to access education • Remove obstacles to children/families migrating to access education • Eliminate use of migrant child labour
3. Promote gender equality and empower women
Eliminate gender disparity in primary and secondary education preferably by 2005, and at all levels by 2015 • Facilitate women's empowerment through control of remittances • Encourage recipient investment of remittances in women's education • Identify and address obstacles to girls' migration for education • Increase access to educational opportunities for girls in migrant households and communities • Address gender discrimination in migrant households • Eliminate use of female migrant child labour

4. Reduce child mortality
Reduce by two-thirds the mortality rate of children under 5 years
• Encourage remittance investment in primary healthcare
• Reduce health professionals' out-migration from vulnerable countries
• Promote diasporan and other exchanges of health-care personnel between countries
• Address health needs of pregnant women migrants and newborns
• Reduce mother-to-child transmission of HIV/AIDS in migrant communities by two-thirds
• Develop special programmes of care for orphans of migrants

5. Improve maternal health
Reduce by three-quarters the maternal mortality ratio
• Ensure access to health care for migrants in home and destination countries
• Encourage remittance investment in primary healthcare
• Reduce health professionals' out-migration from vulnerable countries
• Promote exchanges of healthcare personnel between over- and under-serviced countries
• Eliminate gender-based violence against migrant women

6. Combat HIV/AIDS, malaria and other diseases
Halt and begin to reverse the spread of HIV/AIDS
• Understand role of migration in spread of HIV/AIDS
• Reduce vulnerability of migrants and other mobile people to infection
• Promote safe sex practices amongst migrants and in migrant communities
• Eliminate migration systems that forcibly separate migrants from spouses/partners
• Develop and implement strategies targeted at specific circumstances of migrants including workers, truckers, orphans, people living with Aids (PLWAs)
• Ensure access of anti-retroviral (ARV) treatment for migrant men and women
• Eliminate informal cross-border trade in ARV medication by migrants
Halt and begin to reverse the incidence of malaria and other major diseases
• Understand role of migration in spread of malaria and other major diseases
• Improve access of migrants and other mobile people to healthcare and drugs
• Reduce health professionals' out-migration from vulnerable countries
• Promote exchanges of healthcare personnel between over- and under-serviced countries
• Improve living and working conditions of migrants

7. Ensure environmental sustainability
Integrate the principles of sustainable development into country policies and programmes; reverse loss of environmental resources
• Acknowledge role of migration in supporting or undermining sustainable development policies and programmes
• Address situations where migrants are involved in unsustainable resource exploitation or where exploitation leads to unnecessary population migration
• Avoid resettlement of people in marginal or unsustainable environments
• Reduce development-related resettlement

Reduce by half the proportion of people without access to safe drinking water
• Ensure access to safe, affordable drinking water in migrant-sending areas and receiving communities
Achieve significant improvement in lives of at least 100 million slum dwellers by 2020
• Understand role of migration in rapid urbanisation and pressure on resources
• Eliminate all discrimination against migrants in access to land, housing, urban services
• Encourage use of remittances in job creation and micro-credit for slum dwellers
• Upgrade slum dwellings without destroying livelihoods and shelter for slum dwellers including migrants
• Provide affordable alternatives to slum housing for migrants and families
8. Develop a global partnership for development
Develop further an open trading and financial system that is rule-based, predictable and non-discriminatory. Includes a commitment to good governance, development and poverty eradication – nationally and internationally
• Ensure that the financial system for migrant remittances is open and fair, provides good value and maximises the flows of remittances through official and unofficial channels
• Liberalise movement of people as per Mode 4 of GATS
• Promote good governance of global migration through commitments to policy development, harmonisation and capacity-building
• Strengthen multilateral and regional efforts to manage migration in the best interests of developing countries
More generous official development assistance to countries committed to poverty reduction
• Ensure that migration is mainstreamed in all global, regional and national development and poverty reduction plans
• Provide technical expertise and resources to develop capacity for managed migration and good governance
• Direct ODA towards special needs of migrants and migrant communities e.g. migrant women, AIDS orphans, informal traders
Address the special needs of landlocked and small island states
• Facilitate access of migrants to regional labour markets and facilitate return flow of remittances
• Provide opportunities for productive investment of remittances
• Maintain skills base of economy in sectors vulnerable to out-migration (health, education)
Develop decent and productive work for youth
• Eliminate migrant child labour
• Provide training and employment opportunities for young migrants
Make available the benefits of new technologies
• Encourage return migration of skilled nationals
• Encourage transfer of knowledge, ideas and technologies through diaspora groups
• Facilitate access of developing country students and institutions to developed country technologies and training

Russell (2003) notes that 'much of the current discussion lacks an adequately updated and expanded knowledge base from which to derive meaningful, prescriptive guidance to developing (and developed) countries.' Multilateral agencies and organisations in particular are still loath to make policy recommendations and programmatic statements. This has resulted in a fundamental disjuncture between policy and research. Policy prescriptions are informed by a research and information base that is either nonexistent or certainly inconsistent and often directed at answering questions that are of limited interest to policy-makers (Parker, 2005). Data gathering and research on migration and development tends to be supply rather than demand driven. Official datasets are generally of little value for explaining the causes, consequences and impacts of migration. A recent survey of migration data collection systems in SADC confirms that official data is spotty, unsystematic and often unreliable (Williams, 2005).

The research literature long predates the current policy concern with migration and development (Papademetriou & Martin, 1991; Ghosh, 1992; Taylor et al., 1996; Skeldon, 1997). While it provides very useful information it also has several limitations. The first is that researchers often pose and answer questions that are of limited interest to policy makers. Policy-makers often ask questions to which researchers cannot supply answers. The second is that, primarily because of funding limitations, much research continues to be of a case-study character, which prompts serious questions about the extent to which findings are representative or generalisable, and does not allow for cross-national comparisons. And the third limitation is that research is only rarely conducted in both sending and receiving countries within a single study. A recent trend has been the emergence of multi-country, multi-partner research networks. These are generally better funded and permit collaborative cross-national comparisons and conclusions. Nevertheless, there is clearly a need for well-funded national and regional research networks.

SAMP has been conducting qualitative and quantitative research on migration issues in southern Africa since the mid-1990s. Increasingly, its research agenda has focused on the migration–development nexus. It has recently conducted major cross-national household surveys of migration and remittances and migration and poverty in six SADC countries. This data, once analysed, will provide an unprecedented picture of the relationship between migration and development at local household level. SAMP has also been pursuing and encouraging complementary case study research of a more in-depth character. In addition, the Programme is aware that many individual researchers are conducting their own research for projects and theses on aspects of the migration–development nexus. This collection intends to move the debate on migration and development forward in the southern African context in three ways: (a) by collaboratively presenting the results of policy oriented research by SAMP and non-SAMP researchers; (b) by combining the results of large-scale representative surveys with in-depth local case studies; and (c) by presenting the results of research on international and internal migration.

4. Migration, Poverty and Development in Southern Africa

Cross-border migration in southern Africa dates back over 150 years. The whole continent has been profoundly shaped by migration. Scholars have studied in considerable depth the changing reasons for migration and its cumulative impact, particularly on rural areas. The most influential school of historical thought – associated primarily with underdevelopment theory – argues that migration in southern Africa was primarily a function of colonial coercion, including land dispossession, heavy taxation and support of white settlers at the expense of black peasants (Palmer & Parsons, 1977; Bundy, 1979). Productive, independent peasant communities were destroyed because their labour was needed more than their produce. The result was 'labour reserve economies' in which the rural areas experienced declines in production and productivity and acted to subsidise low wages in the mines and on the farms. Deep within most thinking about migration in southern Africa is the belief that it has been a cause of underdevelopment rather than development.

Contemporary official and public policy discourse in southern Africa continues to view migration as essentially a bad thing. Contemporary migration trends have given added impetus to the naysayers. First, many countries in southern Africa have become the 'victims' of the brain drain of talent to the North. South Africa, Zimbabwe, Zambia and Malawi have been hardest hit but none have escaped completely. With the exception of Botswana, and latterly South Africa, countries have not viewed the import of skilled migrants as a good thing. Secondly, there is a pervasive and misleading view that every job occupied by a foreign migrant, at whatever level, is one job less for a citizen. Thirdly, most countries of the region grapple with the problem of 'irregular migration.' The numbers are usually vastly exaggerated and illegal status is conflated with criminality. Indeed, many people feel that without migrants there would be no crime. The prevailing emphasis is on how to control and stop migration. This can be done in one of two ways: by pouring resources into an essentially fruitless and frustrating effort to seal borders or by encouraging 'development' in the source areas.

Researchers have recently begun to challenge this essentially negative view of migration. This too has historical precedents in southern Africa. In the 1980s, social historians took issue with the prevailing negative view of the relationship between migration and development (Beinart, 1982; Crush, 1989). They argued that the causes and consequences of migration were far more complex and nuanced. While the overall impact of migration on a region may have been negative, some migrant-sending households were able to use migration as a strategy for accumulating resources and reinvesting in local development.

The contemporary rethinking of the migration–development policy nexus has begun in relation to remittances, poverty reduction and the brain drain. One argument is that the exodus of skilled SADC citizens may not be an unmitigated disaster for the region. The African Union (AU) has been at the forefront in arguing that citizens overseas may constitute an untapped resource. Already, many migrants are remitting sizeable sums of cash to their families within the region. But the development potential of the SADC diaspora has hardly been recognised to date. Whether this be in the form of financial support to development projects and communities, knowledge transfer, temporary home visits and sabbaticals, or a range of other potential activities and impacts, the countries of the region need to develop programmes to actively court the diaspora and involve these migrants in development. A first step in this process is to identify the physical locations of the diaspora. A first approximation can be achieved by identifying the SADC 'migrant stock' resident outside the region (Table 1.5). As this data shows, a few countries, particularly the UK, the US, Canada, Australia and Portugal, are the predominant destinations for SADC migrants. Data needs to be collected on the diaspora's demography, socio-economic profile, skills levels and existing contacts with home. Such an exercise could also provide valuable insights into what kinds of diaspora mobilisation programmes would have the greatest chance of success.

Migrants in southern Africa are reputedly fond of saying that there is only one thing worse than being a migrant worker, and that is not being a migrant worker. For households and individuals throughout the region, migration is not a 'bad' or a 'good' thing; it is an essential thing. It is a household strategy, at its most abject, to stave off poverty and hunger. But it is also a developmental resource. Migration means cash for children's education, for health services, for shelter, for starting small businesses and, yes, for small luxuries. This is not to say that migration is not a disruptive and often demeaning necessity. Rather, from the point of view of the migrant and his or her sending household, it is simply a viable household-level development strategy. This is as true of the uneducated woman who crosses the Caledon to work on a Free State farm as it is of the nurse who goes to work in Saudi Arabia or the doctor who emigrates to the UK. In other words, as a number of scholars point out, at the micro-level, migration can have positive outcomes and benefits. Indeed, most migrants are not desperate people. They are usually the most innovative, independent and resourceful members of a household, community or society.

As the chapters in this collection suggest, migration should not be viewed as unremittingly negative. It should be acknowledged as a reality, an inevitability. The people of southern Africa are becoming more and more mobile, both within and between countries. The real policy challenge is not to devise means to stop the unstoppable; it is to devise managed migration systems that encourage legal migration and do not push migrants into the shadows – and the sweatshops. It is also to take the development potential of migration seriously.

The chapters in this collection address several recurrent themes in the migration and development literature relevant to South-South migration. The first is the 'brain drain.' Two studies discuss the push and pull factors influencing the cross-border migration of skilled workers. In the case of Zimbabwe, Abel Chikanda argues that its medical brain drain shows no signs of slowing down. However, the more affluent countries to which Zimbabwean healthcare professionals are moving cannot be accused of poaching; rather, it is the ongoing economic and political crisis in Zimbabwe that is driving healthcare professionals from the country. While South Africa is proving an increasingly important destination for Zimbabwean healthcare professionals, Robert Mattes and Namhla Mniki show that South Africa is itself experiencing a significant brain drain. Their chapter suggests that this is likely to continue and even accelerate since the emigration potential of

Table 1.5: The Southern African Diaspora, 2000

Country of destination	Migrant stock (Country of origin by birth)														
	Angola	Bots-wana	DRC	Lesotho	Malawi	Mauritius	Mozam-bique	Namibia	Sey-chelles	South Africa	Swazi-land	Tanzania	Zambia	Zimb-abwe	SADC region
Australia	353	708	267	53	486	16962	552	437	2448	79425	205	1714	3070	11734	118414
Austria										1929					1929
Belgium	2281	21	49885	8	53	2672	278	23	77	2722	59	290	218	318	58905
Canada	2500	200	10200	165	430	6720	910	305	1035	37680	195	19960	2380	4185	86865
Czech Republic	135	2	33	5	19	4	4	7	2	154	2	20	20	21	428
Denmark	117	53		40	49	114	124	32	20	1008	40	814	357	261	3029
Finland	112	3	329		2	26	21	29	2	208	7	172	70	23	1004
France	8563	171	25670	24	85	30096	877	102	383	2993	8	574	280	350	70176
Greece	19	3	1226	2	20	52	66	7	33	5546	13	402	242	448	8079
Hungary	36	1	19			5	11	1		94		19	4	13	203
Ireland	587	121	100	52	91	132	34	53	16	6260	27	183	569	1462	9687
Italy	1124	21	2129	12	121	5727	496	68	778	4638	22	980	639	665	17420
Japan	3	7	99	1	18	20	3	2	6	248	1	186	70	44	708
Luxembourg	354		575		5	87	149	4	1	171		3	10	28	1387
Mexico	38		10	1	2	5	7	2	3	75	2	9	2	4	158
Netherlands	4646	185	3239	88	234	299	475	174	83	11286	91	1180	880	1018	23878
Norway	130	93		8	28	141	88	66	13	783	17	588	224	172	2351
New Zealand	18	75	60	24	144	162	48	231	57	26061	39	276	945	2886	31026
Poland	27		33	3	3	9	15	3	3	267	3	51	36	27	480
Portugal	174210	34	1617	2	191	12	76017	132	2	11197	165	166	113	1352	265210
Slovakia	31		6				2			16		2	2	1	60
Spain	2423	11	770	15	27	142	639	37	25	1372	5	146	97	123	5832
Sweden	511	56	1226	21	47	144	228	56	53	1408	15	1012	289	320	5386
Switzerland	4253	23	3600	91	49	1974	800	144	196	4542	50	590	188	522	17022
Turkey	2	13		9	4	7	6	3	1	296	77	223	12	11	664
United Kingdom	5914	2051	8569	331	12340	27078	3353	1230	2905	141405	863	32630	21529	49524	309722
United States	4560	1555	5975	320	1770	1550	2070	975	680	68290	620	12225	6395	11740	118725
Total	212947	5407	115637	1275	16218	94140	87273	4123	8822	410074	2524	74415	38641	87259	1158748

Source: Development Research Centre on Migration, Globalisation and Poverty, University of Sussex

postgraduate and final year undergraduate students at South Africa's tertiary educational institutions is high.

The South African government, concerned that young people with skills intend to emigrate in large numbers, thus adversely affecting the country's economic prospects, is considering measures to stem this flow of skilled workers to other countries. However, South African students and professionals believe that sound economic and social development in the country would be the biggest incentive to staying, and that draconian measures to restrict emigration would only increase people's determination to leave. These two chapters agree that governments can best stem the brain drain by offering skilled workers positive (economic and other benefits) rather than negative (setting up barriers to leaving, which may only increase out-migration) incentives to stay.

The second theme addressed in this collection is internal and international migration and poverty reduction, in particular migrant urban livelihood and food security strategies. The four chapters on this theme discuss the emerging complexity of migration to cities, and agree that while increased mobility is a challenge to social, economic and political institutions, it is essential for migrant household economies. Unless governments find ways to understand and support the livelihoods of urban migrants, the social, economic and political welfare of society as a whole may be undermined. For example, Loren Landau demonstrates in his chapter that the consequences of not proactively accepting international migrants include irregular policing and insecurity, threats to public health, lack of investment and job creation, and less accountable institutions. In her chapter, Miriam Grant shows how changes in the social and economic conditions of migrants in Gweru, Zimbabwe, affect household composition, shelter, economic coping mechanisms, and the overall vulnerability of migrants in urban centres. The chapters by Bruce Frayne and Samuel Owuor examine in detail the role of urban–rural linkages in the food security strategies of urban migrants in Namibia and Kenya and demonstrate that these linkages are important livelihood strategies not only for rural households but also increasingly for poorer urban ones.

The third theme is remittances and their rural impact. Although the scale of remittances to rural households in southern Africa as a whole is unknown, this component of rural livelihoods remains important in the context of stagnant off-farm wage alternatives. In particular, the potential role of cross-border remittances for rural development today has not been fully understood or explored. In their chapters, France Maphosa and Fion de Vletter demonstrate that wages remitted by migrants in neighbouring counties have resulted in positive economic and welfare gains in the sending communities in Zimbabwe and Mozambique. Both authors recognise that for the developmental potential of remittances to be fully realised there is need for collaborative effort involving a wide range of stakeholders, not least of whom are the migrants and their sending communities.

The fourth theme is the re-gendering of migration flows. Here, two chapters show how the historically dominant role of rural males in the labour migrant system in southern Africa is changing, and how women are increasingly on the move. Theresa Ulicki and Jonathan Crush show that migrants from Lesotho who work across the border on South African farms are predominantly older women (some of the poorest citizens of Lesotho) who generally see farm work in South Africa as the only option available to them. The authors argue that while commercial farming is sometimes heralded as one of the success stories of the post apartheid economy, much of South Africa's economic 'success' in this area relies heavily on migrants from neighbouring countries who generally work in exploitative and abusive conditions.

While commercial farming may still rely largely on migrants in post-apartheid South Africa, the mining industry has seen its traditionally male migrant labour force reduced over the past ten years. Xola Ngonini, focusing on the sending communities of the Eastern Cape, argues that as a result of this large-scale downsizing the migrant identity of mineworkers, developed over the better part of a century, is being lost. Women seem better equipped than men to deal with a social economy that is changing as a result of male migrant retrenchments – the men appear to have been unable to adapt to the new circumstances and women are now emerging as the new migrants.

The final theme addressed here is the relationship between mobility and vulnerability to HIV/AIDS. The two chapters on this theme agree that migrants are at significantly higher risk of exposure to the disease than non-migrants. Prerna Banati demonstrates how urban informal settlements, as focal receiving areas of migrants, are magnifiers of HIV risk, amplifying the vulnerability of migrants living in these areas. She argues for a context-specific approach to understanding and addressing the HIV/AIDS risk for migrant workers, and for consequent HIV and AIDS programming within the broader development context. In the second chapter, context is again shown to be important for another distinct group of migrants. In Johannesburg, domestic work is the largest employment sector for black women in the area studied by Natalya Dinat and Sally Peberdy, and most of these domestic workers are migrants. The authors show that although these women's working conditions may mean that their risk of becoming infected could be lower than that of their non-migrant counterparts, their migrant status itself, as well as separation from partners and, for many, restrictions on when and where they can see their partners and friends, are factors that increase their vulnerability.

5. Conclusion

The current international debate on migration and development is framed by a particular understanding and conception of both entities. "Migration" generally means movement from developing to developed countries (so-called South-North migration). "Development" consists of finding ways of making the South more like the North. South-South migration has received very little attention to date primarily because it does not fit very easily within the dominant paradigm (Ratha and Shaw 2007; Bakewell, 2009). The North only becomes interested in South-South migrants if they turn North. With some exceptions, governments and citizenries in the South view migrants from other developing countries with suspicion, if not outright hostility (Crush and Ramachandran, 2009). This is generally because many South-South migrants are poorer, less-skilled and more marginalized. Their movements are motivated by everyday struggles for survival; they survive by being on the move. Yet, as the essays in this volume show, to dismiss their activities as parasitic or non-developmental would be a serious mistake. They contribute both to countries of origin and countries of destination. Their role is under-valued and denigrated and their lives are often blighted by exploitation, abuse and ill-treatment by employers and state officials. Yet they remain highly energetic and enterprising people whose activities and contributions need to be highlighted as a positive contribution to poverty reduction and genuine development.

Acknowledgements

We wish to thank the IDRC, DFID and CIDA for its support of the Southern African Migration Programme (SAMP).

References

ADAMS, R & PAGE, J, 2005. Do international migration and remittances reduce poverty in developing countries? *World Development*, 33(10): 1645–69.

ADEPOJU, A, 1998. Linkages between internal and international migration: the African situation. *International Social Science Journal*, 50(157): 387–95.

AL-SAMARRAI, S & BENNELL, P, 2003. *Where has all the education gone in Africa?* Brighton: Institute for Development Studies.

AMMASARRI, S, 2005. *Migration and development: new strategic outlooks and practical ways forward – the cases of Angola and Zambia.* Migration Research Series No. 21, IOM, Geneva.

AWASES, M, GBARY, A, NYONI, J & CHATORA, R, 2005. *Migration of health professionals in six countries: a synthesis report.* Brazzaville: World Health Organisation Regional Office for Africa.

BAKEWELL, O, 2009. *South-South migration and human development: reflections on African experiences.* Human Development Research Paper 2009/07, UNDP, New York.

BEINART, W, 1982. *The political economy of Pondoland 1860 to 1930.* Cambridge: Cambridge University Press.

BLOCH, A, 2005. *The development potential of Zimbabweans living in the diaspora.* Migration Research Series No. 17, IOM, Geneva.

BOMMES, M & MORAWSKA, E (eds), 2005. *International migration research.* Aldershot: Ashgate.

BRETTELL, C & HOLLIFIELD, J (eds), 2000. *Migration theory: talking across disciplines.* New York: Routledge.

BUNDY, C, 1979. *The rise & fall of the South African peasantry.* London: Heinemann.

CASTLES, S, 1999. International migration and the global agenda: reflections on the 1998 UN Technical Symposium. In Appleyard, R (ed.), *Migration and development.* Geneva: International Organisation for Migration, pp. 5–20.

CASTLES, S, 2000. International migration at the beginning of the twenty-first century. *International Social Science Journal*, 52(3): 269–81.

CASTLES, S & MILLER, M, 2003. *The age of migration.* 3rd Ed. New York: Palgrave Macmillan.

CASTLES, S & WISE, R, (eds), 2008. *Migration and development: perspectives from the South*. Geneva: International Organisation for Migration.

CHIKANDA, A, 2005. *Medical leave: the exodus of health professionals from Zimbabwe*. Southern African Migration Programme (SAMP), Migration Policy Series No. 34, Cape Town.

COHEN, R, 2004. What will drive international migration in the next 50 years? Presentation to Migration Futures Workshop, Oxford.

CORNELIUS, W, EPENSHADE, T & SALEHYAN, I, 2001. *The international migration of the highly skilled: demand, supply, and development consequences for sending and receiving countries*. Boulder, Colorado: Lynne Rienner Publishers.

CRUSH, J, 1989. *The struggle for Swazi labour, 1890–1920*. Kingston and Montreal: McGill-Queen's Press.

— 2000. The dark side of democracy: immigration, xenophobia and human rights in South Africa. *International Migration*, 38(6): 103–34.

— 2002. The global raiders: nationalism, globalisation and the South African brain drain. *Journal of International Affairs*, 56(1): 147–72.

— 2003. Migration and development in post-apartheid South Africa. In Sakia, A (ed.), *Population, environment and the challenge of development*. New Delhi: Akansha Publishing House, pp. 201–26.

CRUSH, J & PENDLETON, W, 2004. *Regionalizing xenophobia? Citizen attitudes to immigration and refugee policy in Southern Africa*. Southern African Migration Programme (SAMP), Migration Policy Series No. 30.

CRUSH, J. & RAMACHANDRAN, S. 2009. Xenophobia, international migration and human development. Human Development Research Paper 2009/47, UNDP, New York.

DE HAAN, A, 2000. Migration and livelihoods: case studies in Bangladesh, Ethiopia and Mali. IDS Research Report no. 46, University of Sussex.

DE HAAS, H. 2009. *Mobility and human development*. Human Development Research Paper 2009/01, UNDP, New York.

DESHINGKAR, P & GRIMM, S, 2005. *Internal migration and development: a global perspective*. Migration Research Series No. 19, IOM, Geneva.

GENT, S, 2002. *The root causes of migration: criticising the approach and finding a way forward*. Working Paper No. 11, Centre for Migration Research, Sussex University.

GHOSH, B, 1992. Migration–development linkages: some specific issues and practical policy measures. *International Migration*, 30: 423–52.

GLOBAL COMMISSION ON INTERNATIONAL MIGRATION (GCIM), 2005. *Migration in an interconnected world: new directions for action*. Geneva: GCIM.

GOLDIN, I & REINERT, K, 2006. *Globalisation for development: trade, finance, aid, migration, and policy*. Washington: Palgrave Macmillan.

GUNDEL, J, 2002. The migration–development nexus: Somalia case study. *International Migration*, 40(5): 255–77.

HAMILTON, K, 2003. Migration and development: blind faith and hard-to-find facts. Migration Policy Institute, Washington, Feature Story, 1 November.

HAQUE, S, 2004. The nexus between migration, globalisation and development. In Mitra, P (ed.), *Orderly and humane migration: an emerging development paradigm*. Geneva: IOM.

INTERNATIONAL LABOUR ORGANISATION (ILO), 2004. *Towards a fair deal for migrant workers in the global economy*. Geneva: ILO.

INTERNATIONAL ORGANISATION FOR MIGRATION (IOM), 2005. *World migration 2005: costs and benefits of international migration.* Geneva: IOM.

KAPUR, D & McHALE, J, 2005a. The global migration of talent: what does it mean for developing countries? Center for Global Development Brief, Washington.

— 2005b. *Give us your best and brightest.* Washington: Center for Global Development.

KLEIN SOLOMON, M, 2005. International migration management through inter-state consultation mechanisms. Paper presented at the United Nations Expert Group Meeting on International Migration and Development, New York, 6–8 July 2005.

KOTHARI, U, 2003. Staying put and staying poor? *Journal of International Development,* 15(5): 645–57.

LANDAU, L. & WA KABWE SEGATTI, A, 2009. Human Development impacts of migration: South Africa case study. Human Development Research Paper 2009/05, UNDP, New York.

LITCHFIELD, J & WADDINGTON, H, 2002. Migration and poverty in Ghana: evidence from the Ghana Living Standards Survey. Centre for Migration Research, Sussex University.

LOWELL, L, 2002. *Some developmental effects of the international migration of highly skilled persons.* International Migration Paper No. 46, International Labour Organisation, Geneva.

LOWELL, L & FINDLAY, A, 2002. *Migration of highly skilled persons from developing countries: impact and policy responses.* International Labour Organisation, Geneva.

LOWELL, L, FINDLAY, A & STEWART, E, 2004. *Brain strain. Optimising highly skilled migration from developing countries.* Asylum and Migration Working Paper 3, Institute for Public Policy Research, London.

MAIMBO, S & RATHA, D, 2005. *Remittances: development impact and future prospects.* Washington: World Bank.

MASSEY, D et al., 1998. *Worlds in motion: understanding international migration at the end of the millennium.* New York: Oxford University Press.

MASSEY, D & TAYLOR, J (eds), 2004. *International migration: prospects and policies in a global market.* Oxford: Oxford University Press.

MCDONALD, D & CRUSH, J, 2002. Thinking about the brain drain in Southern Africa. In McDonald, D & Crush, J (eds), *Destinations unknown: perspectives on the brain drain in Southern Africa.* Pretoria: Africa Institute, pp. 1–16.

MENSAH, L, MACKINTOSH, M & HENRY, L, 2005. *The skills drain of health professionals from the developing world: a framework for policy formulation.* London: Medact.

NEWLAND, K, 2004. Migration as a factor in development and poverty reduction: the impact of rich countries' immigration policies on the prospects of the poor. In Picciotto, R & Weaving, R (eds), *Impact of Rich Countries' Policies on Poor Countries.* New Brunswick, NJ: Transaction.

NYAMNJOH, F, 2006. *Insiders & outsiders: citizenship and xenophobia in contemporary southern Africa.* London: Zed Press.

NYBERG SØRENSEN, N, VAN HEAR, N & ENGBERG-PEDERSEN, P, 2002. The migration–development nexus: evidence and policy options. *International Migration,* 40(5): 3-47.

OGENA, N, 2004. Policies on international migration: Philippine issues and challenges. In Ananta, A & Nurviya Arifin, E (eds), *International migration in Southeast Asia.* Singapore: ISEAS.

OUCHO, J & CRUSH, J, 2002. Contra free movement: South Africa and SADC migration protocols. *Africa Today,* 48(1): 139–58.

PALMER, R, & PARSONS, N (eds), 1977. The roots of rural poverty in central and southern Africa. London: Heinemann.

PAPADEMETRIOU, D, 2001. Reflections on international migration and its future. J. Douglas Gibson Lecture, School of Policy Studies, Queen's University.

PAPADEMETRIOU, D & MARTIN, P (eds), 1991. *The unsettled relationship: labour migration and economic development.* Westport: Greenwood Press.

PARKER, J, 2005. International migration data collection. Paper prepared for the Policy Analysis and Research Programme of the GCIM, Geneva.

RATHA, D & SHAW, W, 2007. *South–South migration and remittances.* World Bank Working Paper No. 102, World Bank, Washington.

ROBERTS, B, 2006. *Shifting boundaries: a migration audit of poverty reduction strategies in Southern Africa.* SAMP Migration Policy Series No. 44, Cape Town.

ROZARIO, S & GOW, J, 2003. Bangladesh: return migration and social transformation. In Iredale, R, Guo, F & Rozario, S (eds), *Return migration in the Asia Pacific.* Northampton, MA: Edward Elgar, pp. 47-87.

RUSSELL, S, 2003. Migration and development: reframing the international policy agenda. Migration Policy Institute Feature Story, 1 June.

SAMP (SOUTHERN AFRICAN MIGRATION PROGRAMME), 2008: The perfect storm: the realities of xenophobia in contemporary South Africa. SAMP Migration Policy Series No. 50, Cape Town.

SANDER, C, 2003. *Migrant remittances to developing countries: a scoping study.* London: Bannock Consulting.

SANDER, C & MAIMBO, S, 2003. *Migrant labour remittances in Africa: reducing obstacles to developmental contributions.* African Region Working Paper Series No. 64, World Bank, Washington.

SCHIFF, M, & ÖZDEN, C (eds), 2006. *International migration, remittances, and the brain drain.* Washington: World Bank & Palgrave Macmillan.

SIDDIQUI, T, 2003. Migration as a livelihood strategy of the poor: the Bangladesh case. Working Paper Series WP-C1, Development Research Centre on Migration, Globalisation and Poverty, Sussex University.

SKELDON, R, 1997. *Migration and development: a global perspective.* Geneva: IOM.

— 2005. Linkages between migration and poverty: the Millennium Development Goals and population mobility In UNFPA, *International Migration and the Millennium Development Goals: selected papers of the UNFPA Expert Group meeting* (New York: UN, 2005), pp. 55–66.

SRISKANDARAJAH, D, 2005. Migration and development. Paper prepared for the Policy Analysis and Research Programme of the GCIM, Geneva.

TAMAS, K, 2004. *Mapping study on international migration.* Stockholm: Institute for Futures Studies.

TANNER, A, 2005. *Emigration, brain drain and development: the case of sub-Saharan Africa.* Helsinki: East–West Books.

TAYLOR, J, ARANGO, J, HUGO, G, KOUAOUCI, A, MASSEY, D & PELLEGRINO, A, 1996. International migration and national development. *Population Index,* 62(2): 181-212.

TORO-MORN, M & MARIXSA, A (eds), 2004. *Migration and immigration: a global view.* Westport: Greenwood Press.

UNITED NATIONS (UN), 2004a. *Review and appraisal of the progress made in achieving the goals and objectives of the Programme of Action of the International Conference on Population and Development: the 2004 report.* New York: UN Department of Economic and Social Affairs.

— 2004b. *World economic and social survey.* New York: UN Department of Economic and Social Affairs.

— 2004c. Third coordination meeting on international migration and development, New York, 27–28 October.

— 2005a. Expert group meeting on international migration and development, New York, 6–8 July.

— 2005b. Fourth coordination meeting on international migration and development, New York, 26–27 October.

UNDESA (UN DEPARTMENT OF ECONOMIC AND SOCIAL AFFAIRS – Population Division), 2005. World Migrant Stock: The 2005 Revision Population Database,

UNDP, 2009. *Overcoming barriers: human mobility and development.* Human Development Report 2009, New York.

UN GENERAL ASSEMBLY, 2001. Road map towards the implementation of the United Nations Millennium Declaration. Report of the Secretary-General, 6 September.

USHER, E, 2005. The millennium development goals and migration. Migration Research Series No. 20, IOM, Geneva.

VAN HEAR, N & NYBERG SØRENSEN, N (eds), 2003. The migration–development nexus. Geneva: IOM.

VON KOPPENFELS, A K, 2001. The role of Regional Consultative Processes in managing migration. Migration Research Series No. 3, IOM, Geneva.

WADDINGTON, H & SABATES-WHEELER, R, 2005. How does poverty affect migration choice? A review of the literature. Working Paper T3, Development Research Centre on Migration, Globalisation and Poverty, Sussex University.

WICKRAMASEKARA, P, 2003. *Policy responses to skilled migration: retention, return and circulation.* Geneva: International Labour Office.

WILLIAMS, V, 2005. Migration data harmonisation in SADC. SAMP Report for Migration Dialogue for Southern Africa (MIDSA), Cape Town.

WORLD BANK, 2006. Global economic prospects 2006: economic implications of remittances and migration. Washington: World Bank.

2 RESTLESS MINDS: SOUTH AFRICAN STUDENTS AND THE BRAIN DRAIN

ROBERT MATTES AND NAMHLA MNIKI

1. Introduction

As they near graduation, highly educated young adults begin to make important decisions about employment, career, marriage and family. In the early 21st century, increasing numbers of students around the world must also decide where they want to pursue these plans. Things are no different in South Africa. Since the end of apartheid, young South Africans have been able to look beyond the country's borders to find employment. Yet while greater opportunities and a wider range of choice may be good news for South Africa's talented tertiary students, it may be bad news for the country as a whole, robbing the country of considerable investments in training and education, as well as depriving the economy of needed skills and upper-end consumers.

Virtually all South African analyses of the 'brain drain' have focused on the negative aspects of skilled people emigrating (Haffajee, 1998; Van Rooyen, 2001; Bhorat et al., 2002; Crush, 2002; Dumont & Meyer, 2004). Yet some analysts argue that the word 'loss' is misguided since emigration also brings gains (Meyer, 2001; Khadria, 2002; Martin & Widgren, 2002; Commander et al., 2003). Emigrés not only remit income while abroad but also tend to return home and pass on advanced skills to their colleagues. This has led to the increasing use of terms such as skills 'transfer', 'exchange' and 'circulation' (Abella, 1997; Stalker, 2000; Wimaldharma et al., 2004). In fact, some argue that skills migration is not only a reality but is also necessary for industrial growth and cultural exchange in highly specialised socie-ties (Khadria, 2002). But, regardless of whether skilled emigration includes gains as well as losses, a brain drain is likely to be particularly damaging to an economy when skilled people leave relatively soon after training and the country fails to receive any appreciable return on its direct investments.

Yet while the past ten years have seen a great deal of debate on the South African government's immigration policies, there is still no precise estimate of the extent of emigration from South Africa, or its causes. For example, Statistics SA estimated total emigration from 1989 to 1997 at approximately 82 000, including 11 000 'professionals.' Yet a study of South Africans living in just five countries abroad put the total number at 232 000, of whom 42 000 were 'professionals' (a category narrower than that of 'skilled') (Brown et al., 2002). Using census data, another study argued that at least one million white South Africans emigrated between 1985 and 1996 (Van Rooyen, 2001). In a more predictive mode, an analysis of a 1998 nationally representative survey of skilled adults estimated that approximately 2 per cent (or 30 000 adults) had a 'very high' probability of leaving within the next five years, and another 160 000 had a 'high' probability (Mattes & Richmond, 2000). Thus, this study attempts to look into the future and assess potential emigration among South Africa's potential skills base: that is, young adults in tertiary training institutions. It also tests competing arguments that purport to explain the reasons behind South Africa's brain drain.

2. Methodology

This chapter is based on data collected by the Southern African Migration Programme (SAMP) about the region's potential skills base. Conceptually, the target population for the SAMP Potential Skills Base Survey was South Africa's skills in training. Skilled persons are defined as those who have received specialised training and possess key competencies and skills vital to the functional core of the economy (Mattes & Richmond, 2000). Thus, a country's potential skills base consists of those people currently training to fill positions critical to that functional core.

This study defined South Africa's current potential skills base as consisting of students (a) studying at a South African tertiary institution (university, technikon or college); and (b) in the final year of an undergraduate or postgraduate degree programme. However, no national database of tertiary student numbers exists, especially of final year students. Thus, in mid-2002, the authors collected this data from registrars at each tertiary institution across the country. On the basis of this definition, South Africa's potential skills base in 2002 was estimated at approximately 150 000 students (see Table 1).

At the first stage of sampling, a list was compiled of all teaching faculties at all tertiary institutions across the country and the numbers of their final year students. This list of faculties was then stratified according to (a) the type of institution (historically black or historically white); (b) the level of institution (university, technikon or college); (c) the type of degree (undergraduate or postgraduate); and (d) type of faculty. A sample of faculties was drawn from the entire list, with the probability proportionate to population size. Altogether, 74 undergraduate university faculties were selected, along with 92 postgraduate university faculties, 37 technikon faculties, and 3 nursing college faculties. At the second stage of sampling, one class was chosen from each randomly selected faculty (or for each time that a large faculty was selected). While the sample was based on an expectation of eight interviews per class, it turned out to be more efficient to administer the questionnaire to all the students in each selected class. Thus the actual unweighted sample size was 4 784. All cases were then weighted back to intended sample targets so that the weighted data was based on a sample of 2 400.

3. The Potential Skills Base

On the basis of this sample, South Africa's potential skills base is more female (54 per cent) than male (46 per cent) and more black (48 per cent) than white (40 per cent), coloured or Asian (12 per cent each) (Table 2.1). Just under half of the students use an African language at home, the largest proportion being Xhosa (14 per cent). A quarter of the students said they speak English and another quarter use Afrikaans. While there is no time series data with which to draw a direct comparison, this seems to suggest dramatic changes at the country's tertiary institutions. The 1998 SAMP survey of skilled adults found a sample that was over-whelmingly male (61 per cent) and white (72 per cent) with most speaking Afrikaans (45 per cent) (Mattes & Richmond, 2000).

A quarter of the students described their family's socio-economic status as 'upper-class' or 'upper middle-class', and one third 'middle-class.' One-fifth said they came from a 'working-class' background and 15 per cent classified their family as 'lower-class.' Half of the final year students said they lived in a rural area, either in a rural farming area (25 per cent) or a small town (26 per cent). The rest said they came from a large town (13 per cent) or city (36 per cent).

Just over one-third were completing a certificate or diploma (36 per cent), and 38 per cent were completing a bachelor's degree. One-fifth of final-year students were engaged in postgraduate study pursuing an honours degree (10 per cent), master's degree (12 per cent) or a doctorate (less than 1 per cent). The low number of PhD candidates may reflect a bias in the classroom-based setting of the sample, given that most PhDs in the South African system are obtained through individualised study. Four per cent were pursuing some other form of degree.

Table 2.1: 2002 Final Year South African Tertiary Population and Sample				
Type of student	2002 population	2002 population (%)	Unweighted 2003 sample (%)	Weighted 2003 sample (%)
Level of education				
Undergraduate	97,285	62	62	59
Postgraduate	59,810	38	38	41
Total	157,095	100	100	100

Type of institution				
University	100,118	64	63	63
Technikon	56,195	36	35	34
Nursing colleges	782	0.5	2	3
Total	157,095	100	100	100
Faculty				
Commerce	42,500	27	35	26
Law	5,750	4	3	3
Engineering	20,517	13	14	14
Science & Tech	15,744	10	8	9
Humanities	19,820	13	8	12
Education	22,178	14	13	13
Health Sciences	14,948	10	10	10
Management & IT	11,228	7	6	5
Medical/Dentistry	1,653	1	1	2
Theology	802	1	1	1
Architecture	1,173	1	1	1
Nursing	782	0.5	2	3
Total	157,095	100	100	100
University background				
Historically white	81,048	81	80	78
Historically black	19,070	19	20	22
Total	100,118	100	100	100
N=			4,784	2,400
Note: Final year student population data collected by authors from registrars.				

4. Measuring Emigration Potential

What is the potential for skills loss from final-year students emigrating? For a person to have a high emigration potential, they should – at a minimum – have given extensive thought to emigrating, they should want to emigrate, and they should consider it likely that they will do so. While four in ten final-year students say they have given 'a great deal' of consideration to moving to another country to live and work, it is clear that as more demanding questions about commitment and probability of leaving are asked, the numbers drop (Figure 2.1).

To measure emigration potential, the students were first asked which countries they would most likely go to if they ever left South Africa (their 'most likely destination' or MLD). They were then asked a series of questions about possible movement to that country. Just over a quarter (28 per cent) said they wanted 'to a great extent' to move to their MLD to live and

Figure 2.1: Measuring Emigration Potential

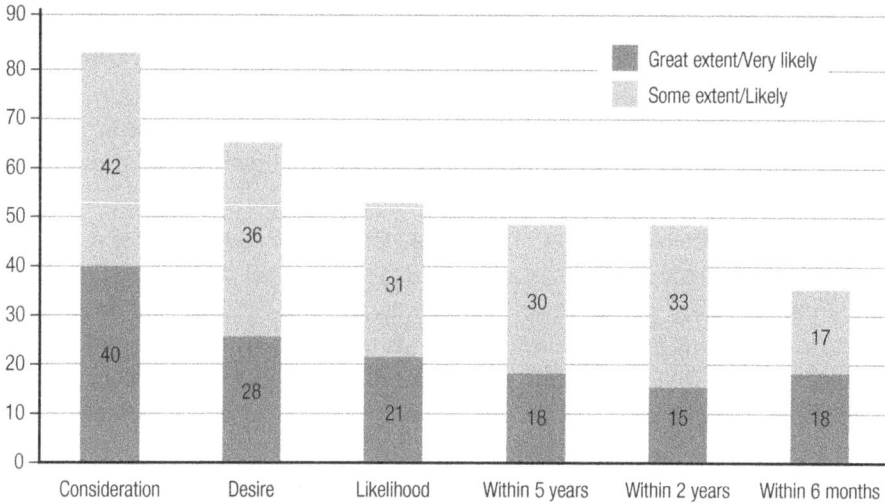

work for two years or more. One in five (21 per cent) said it was 'very likely' that they would actually do this. Short-term emigration potential appears to be even higher. Four in ten said they wanted 'to a great extent' to go to their MLD to live and work for less than two years. A quarter said it was 'very likely' they would actually go. About one in five said it was 'very likely' that they would leave the country within six months of graduation. Smaller numbers said they would leave within two years (15 per cent) and within five years (18 per cent).

Table 2.2: Statistics for Emigration Potential

	Mean (0-3 Scale)	Standard deviation	Factor loading (structure matrix)
1. To what extent do you want to move to your MLD to live and work for a long period (longer than two years)?	1.67	1.10	.79
2. How likely or unlikely is it that you would move to your MLD to live and work for a long period (two years or longer)?	1.47	1.08	.77
3. How much consideration have you given to moving to another country to live and work?	1.82	1.10	.49
4. How likely or unlikely is it that you would move from South Africa within five years after graduation?	1.34	1.10	.38
5. How likely or unlikely is it that you would move from South Africa within two years after graduation?	1.32	1.03	.35
N=3907			
Note: The unrotated factor has an Eigenvalue of 2.37 and explains 47.3 per cent of common variance. Reliability (Cronbach's Alpha) = .72			

Statistical methods of factor and reliability analysis were used to test which of these indicators best helped tap the underlying concept of 'emigration potential' in a valid and reliable way (as well as for all subsequent indices). The analysis indicated that the indicator on leaving within six months should be dropped. An average Index of Emigration Potential was then created which yields an emigration potential score for each respondent by summing responses across the five items listed in Table 2.2 and dividing by five. Because all items had four point response scales (0 to 3), the index produces a decimalised average index score for each respondent ranging from 0 to 3.

While these scores may be helpful in making fine-grained distinctions in emigration potential amongst students, broader categories are needed to help analyse broad differences among respondents (Mattes & Richmond, 2000). Those who gave the most extreme responses to each item in terms of emigration were coded either as having a 'very high' emigration potential (3) or 'no potential' (0). Students with a score between 2.1 and 2.8 were deemed to have a 'high' emigration potential. Those between 2 and 1.5 have a 'moderate' potential. Those scoring less than 1.5 have a 'low' potential.

Compared to a 1998 SAMP survey of skilled South African adults, the proportion of students with a 'very high' emigration potential is exactly the same (2 per cent). However, twice as many students have a 'high' emigration potential (20 per cent) as the adult sample, with a further quarter (25 per cent) having a 'moderate' potential (Mattes & Richmond, 2000). As many as 20 per cent of skilled adults had 'zero' emigration potential, compared to only 3 per cent of the students (Figure 2.2). In other words, emigration potential is higher among students than among people already pursuing their chosen profession.

Figure 2.2: Emigration Potential of Final Year Students and Skilled Adults

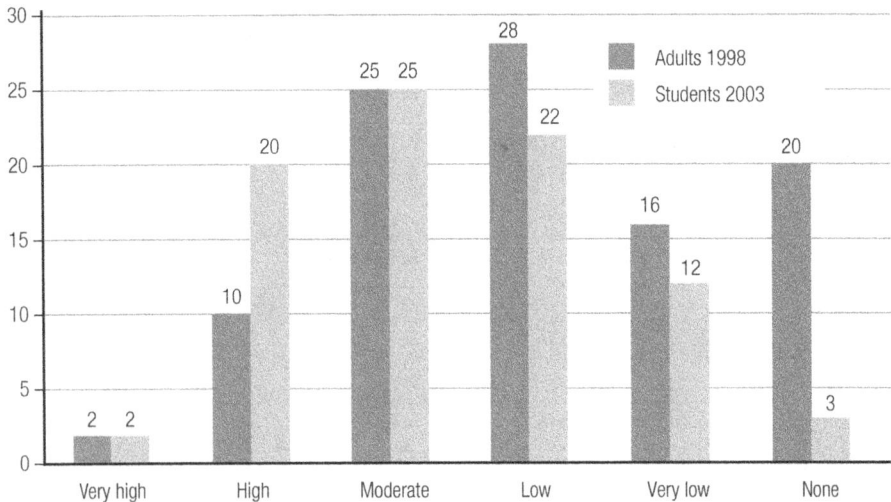

5. The Nature of Potential Skilled Emigration

This section now investigates the nature of these emigration plans. Where do students want to go? How long do they want to stay? Will they return? What will they take with them? Students were first asked: 'If you were ever to leave South Africa, in which country[s] would you most prefer to go to live?' (being allowed to list up to three destinations). At over 40 per cent, Europe was the most popular potential destination. Realising that a variety of reasons may prevent people from going to their most preferred destinations, the students were then asked, 'If you had to leave South Africa, which country would you most likely end up living in?' Amongst all respondents, the UK was the leading preferred destination, selected by almost three in ten respondents (24 per cent said UK or England, and another 4 per cent specifically said London). This was followed by the US (19 per cent), Australia (15 per cent), Europe (7 per cent), and Canada (5 per cent). In total, 44 per cent gave a European destination (including the UK), 25 per cent North American, 19 per cent Australasian, and just 7 per cent southern African (Figure 2.3).

Figure 2.3: Most Likely Destination (all students)

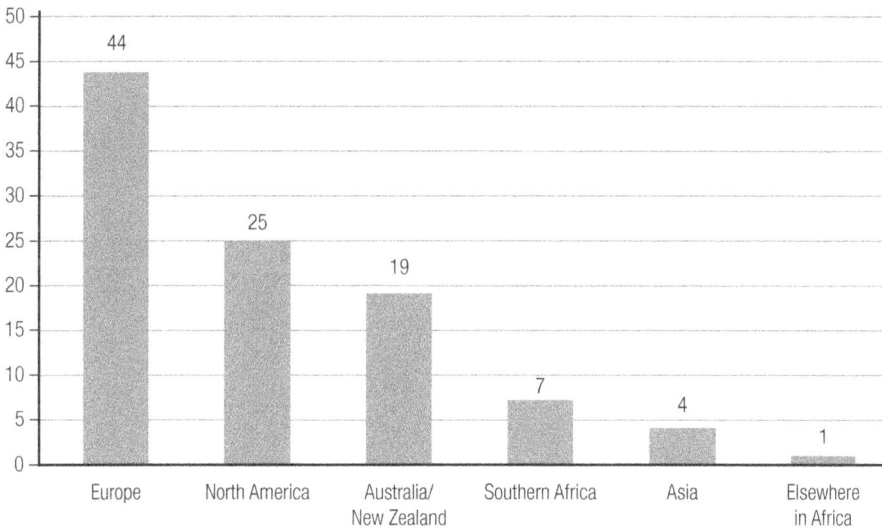

There are a few important racial differences. Black, white and coloured respondents all agreed that they would most likely end up in Europe, though Indian respondents are significantly less likely to say so. Black respondents were slightly more likely to think they would end up in North America or southern Africa than other students. White students were more likely than others to see Australasia as a likely destination (Table 2.3).

Table 2.3: Most Likely Destination (by race) (%)				
	Black	White	Coloured	Asian / Indian
Southern Africa	13	3	3	2
Elsewhere in Africa	1	<1	0	0
Europe	46	44	50	32
North America	29	21	21	19
Australia/ New Zealand	8	31	20	24
Asia	4	2	7	23
Total	100	100	100	100
Note: Totals may be more than 100% due to rounding.				

At this stage of their career development, high emigration potential amongst students does not automatically translate into a permanent skills loss for the country. Among the 2 per cent of all students who definitely want to leave (those with 'very high' emigration potential), three-quarters (74 per cent) say they want to stay in their most likely destination for more than five years. However, among the one-quarter with 'high' emigration potential, students seem to envisage a more limited stay, at least at first: although one-third (34 per cent) of these students said they want to stay more than five years, 44 per cent said they plan on a stay of 2 to 5 years (Figure 4).

Figure 2.4: Length of Intended Stay (by emigration potential)

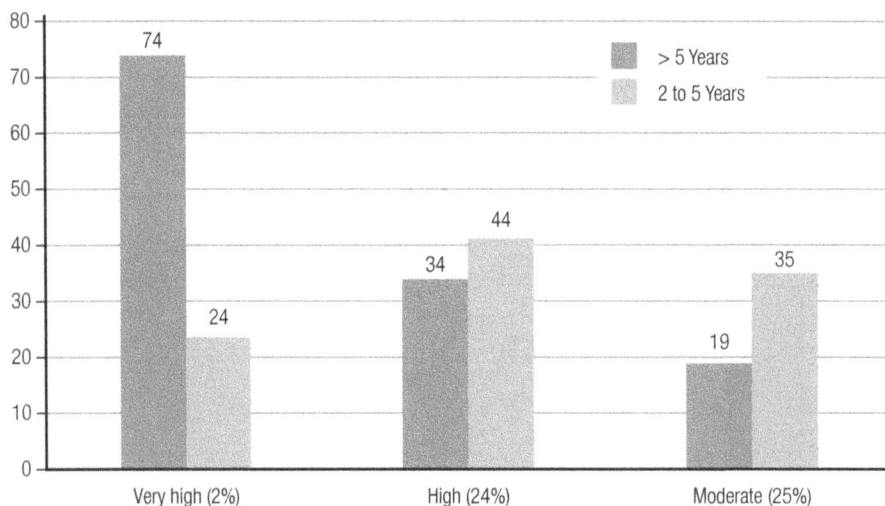

In addition, most respondents with either high or very high emigration potential plan on returning to South Africa on an annual basis. And those most likely to leave still plan on sending money home on a monthly basis (Figure 2.5).

Figure 2.5: Frequency of Return and Remittance (by emigration potential)

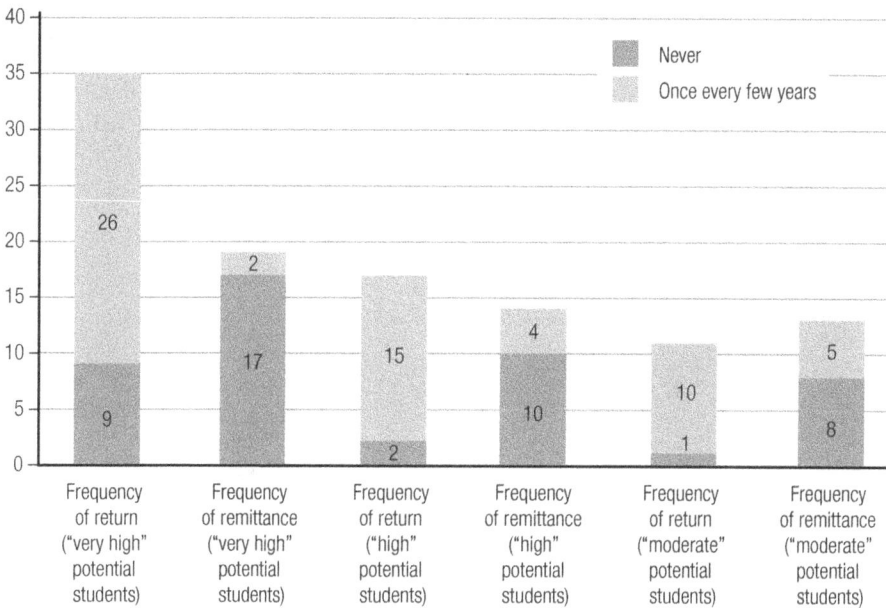

Possibly because younger people have not yet put down firm roots of their own, a large proportion of those students most likely to emigrate appear ready to give up any assets they might have in the country (Figure 2.6). Two-thirds of very high potential respondents said they would be willing to give up their home in South Africa, as did almost half of the high potential students. Most very high emigration potential respondents would be willing (32 per cent) or very willing (32 per cent) to take all their possessions out of South Africa. High potential students are evenly split on the matter, but all lower categories of emigration potential would be unwilling to do this if they had to relocate. Roughly the same patterns emerged when the question turned to taking all assets out of South Africa, with two-thirds of very high emigration potential respondents willing to do this, compared to only 40 per cent of high potential and 37 per cent of moderate potential students. Finally, while half of the very high emigration potential students said they would be willing to give up citizenship, only 24 per cent of the high probability students would do so, and far fewer in all other categories.

While students may be willing to pull up roots that are not yet deeply planted in South African soil, there are only moderate levels of desire among likely emigrants to put down deep roots in other countries. There is no overwhelming desire for citizenship or permanent residence, and even less for other indicators of a long-term stay. Differences by emigration potential are pronounced, especially when asked about longer duration stays in the most likely destination. Six in ten very high potential respondents expressed a strong desire to retire in that country, whereas the average respondent in all other categories of emigration potential said they want this hardly at all (Figure 2.7). Less than half of the very high potential respondents would want to be buried in their most likely destination (40 per cent), indicating that even among this group most students cannot envisage a total break with South Africa. Most high potential and moderate potential students do not want this at all.

Figure 2.6: Willingness to Give up Assets in South Africa (by emigration potential)

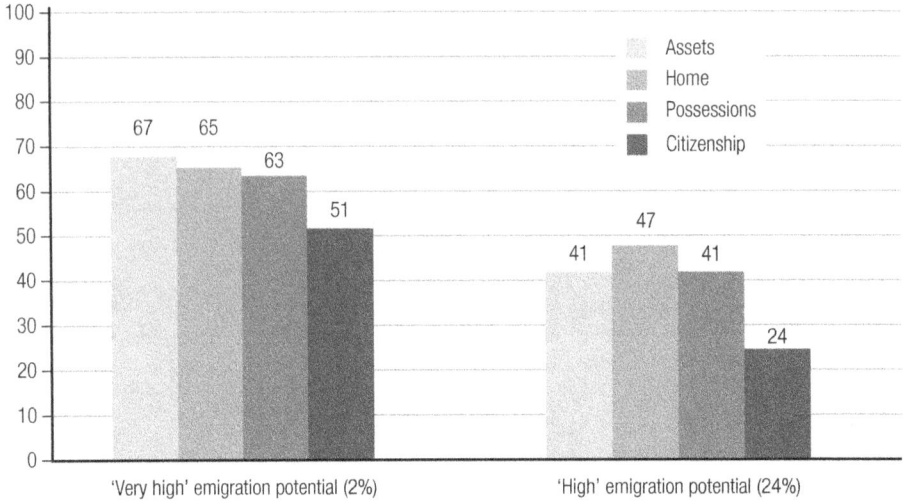

Legend:
- Assets
- Home
- Possessions
- Citizenship

'Very high' emigration potential (2%): Assets 67, Home 65, Possessions 63, Citizenship 51
'High' emigration potential (24%): Assets 41, Home 47, Possessions 41, Citizenship 24

Figure 2.7: Willingness to Put Down Roots in New Country (by emigration potential)

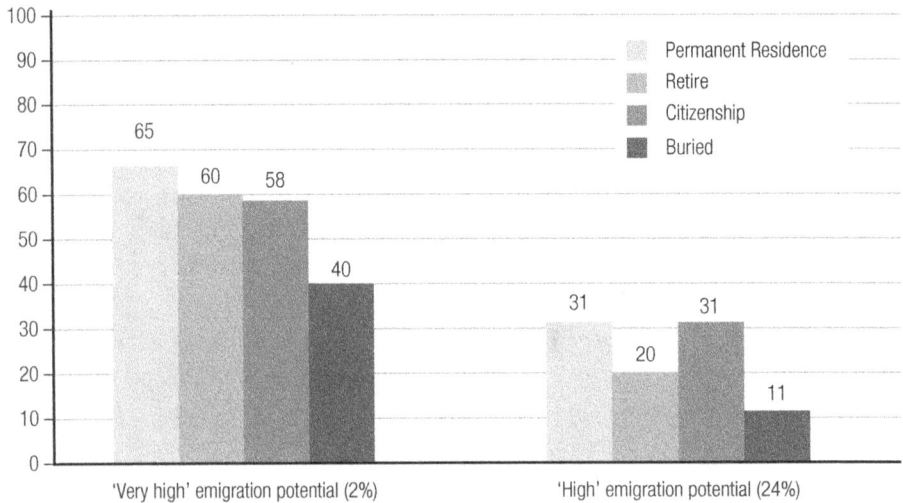

Legend:
- Permanent Residence
- Retire
- Citizenship
- Buried

'Very high' emigration potential (2%): Permanent Residence 65, Retire 60, Citizenship 58, Buried 40
'High' emigration potential (24%): Permanent Residence 31, Retire 20, Citizenship 31, Buried 11

6. Explaining Emigration Potential

This section examines the causal factors that may increase or decrease emigration potential. Five different 'theoretical families' of explanations were tested. First, a series of demographic variables was measured to test whether emigration potential is primarily a function of a student's place in the social structure. For example, are student behaviours and predispositions shaped simply by their racial or ethnic background, their gender or their socio-economic status? Secondly, a set of measures related to social identity was developed, specifically looking at national identity and patriotism and particularly whether emotional ties to South Africa constitute a type of social glue that may inhibit emigration. Thirdly, the impact of a wide range of economic evaluations was tested. Regardless of how strongly they feel about their country, will new graduates leave because of intense dissatisfaction with personal and national conditions? What are students' expectations of their future in South Africa, and their relative comparisons of South Africa with their most likely destination? Fourthly, a series of factors related to experience and information about emigration and the outside world was also tested. Are students who have more contact with émigrés or who gather more information about emigration more likely to leave? Fifthly, and finally, the role of logistical factors was examined: to what extent is emigration related simply to the ability to move?

6.1   Social structure

To what extent is emigration potential simply a function of a person's place in South Africa's social structure? Given the country's history, the most obvious starting point is race. Owing to their loss of dominant political and economic power and perceptions of reduced employment opportunities because of affirmative action, it is widely assumed that white South Africans are much more likely to leave than blacks. A previous SAMP study of skilled professionals found that there was no significant racial difference in the proportions of skilled adults with a very high emigration potential (2 per cent of each group), though there was a noticeable difference amongst those with a high probability (11 per cent of whites compared to only 6 per cent of blacks) (Mattes & Richmond, 2000). Given the racially skewed make-up of South Africa's skilled population, the absolute number of black respondents was relatively small in that study. The present study provides a larger and more robust sample.

This study found that black emigration potential among students was slightly lower than the midpoint of 1.5 and white emigration potential slightly higher (Figure 2.8). This difference was statistically significant, meaning that the difference in the sample can be generalised to the larger population of all students. However, given that the emigration potential scale runs from 0 to 3, these differences are substantively trivial. In comparison with the many different factors reviewed throughout this chapter, a respondent's racial background is of little help in distinguishing between those with high and low emigration potential.[1]

Figure 2.8: Emigration Potential by Race

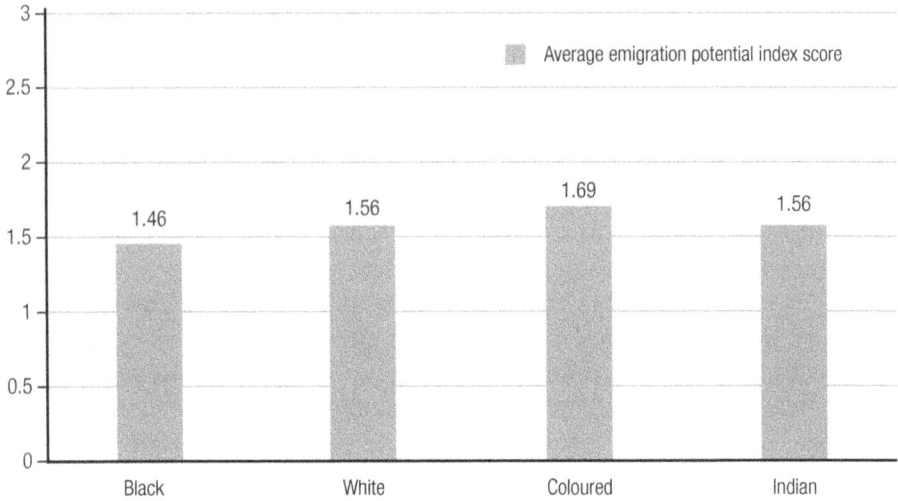

There was also a statistically significant difference according to home language, with English speakers (1.64) registering the highest emigration potential and Shangaan speakers the lowest (1.29) (Figure 2.9). But again, these substantive differences between different language groups are very small.[2]

Figure 2.9: Emigration Potential by Home Language

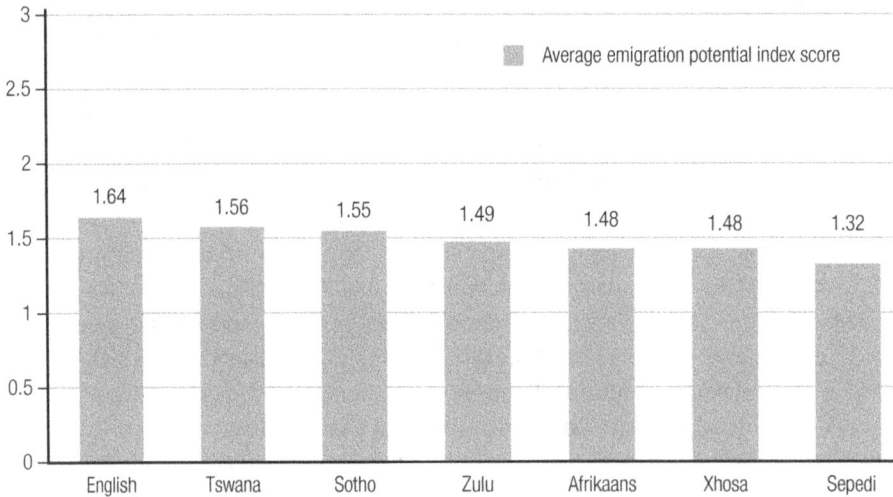

In fact, there are few meaningful differences across a range of demographic factors, including gender.[3] And while one might expect that students from wealthier backgrounds would have more economic freedom to leave, there were only small differences according to self-reported class background. Students who said they were from 'upper middle class' families have a significantly higher emigration potential (1.59 on a scale of 0 to 3) than those from 'working-class' (1.52) or 'lower-class' (1.47) backgrounds.[4] Students from rural backgrounds (1.43) or small towns (1.43) are less likely to emigrate than those who come from urban areas (1.61), but again the difference is not very large.[5]

There is some evidence that particular courses of study make some students think they are more attractive on the international job market. Popular perception is that medical students are the most likely to leave. However, the results demonstrate that those pursuing final-year studies in computer science/information technology at technikons (1.73) and studying in medical or dental faculties at technikons (1.74) are the most likely to want to leave. Students in nursing training colleges display the lowest emigration potential (1.29). Students studying in university faculties of medicine or pharmacy (1.53) have an average emigration potential. However, these differences across degree paths are again not very large.[6] Finally, students at technikons have a significantly higher emigration potential (1.63) than university (1.48) or nursing college (1.29) students.

6.2   National identity

Common wisdom holds that South Africa's brain drain would be much lower if skilled South Africans were more patriotic, with higher levels of national identity. This study found that the bulk of South African tertiary students actually exhibit a high degree of national identity and patriotism. Eight in ten agreed they were proud to be called South African (83 per cent) and had a strong desire to help build South Africa (79 per cent). Over two-thirds wanted their children to think of themselves as South African (76 per cent) and felt they had a duty to contribute their talents and skills to the growth of South Africa (73 per cent). Seven in ten agreed that being a citizen of South Africa was a very important part of how they see themselves. At the same time, these levels of national identity were substantially lower than those measured amongst ordinary adult South Africans, where more than 90 per cent have consistently registered strong levels of national identity since 1994 (Mattes, 2003). Whether younger, more educated people are inherently less likely to exhibit very high levels of patriotism, or whether these results portend a slow, secular decline in patriotism in the future, is a subject for future research.

The pattern of responses to these questions can be used to form a single reliable index that measures 'patriotism.'[7] While there was little difference by race group in terms of emigration potential, the study did find substantial differences between racial groups, with white final-year tertiary students exhibiting far lower levels of patriotism (3.74 on a scale of 1 to 5) than black students (4.43), with coloured (4.07) and Indian (3.98) students in between.[8] Yet responses to two other questions suggest that even though they feel patriotic towards South Africa, students in a globalising world have competing loyalties. Just 17 per cent disagreed with the statement that you 'have more in common with people from other countries working in your profession than with people from South Africa.' Only 38 per cent agreed, with the balance saying they neither agreed nor disagreed. Six in ten agreed that 'it really does not matter where you are a citizen as long as you have a good quality of life,' and just one in five disagreed.

Figure 2.10: Levels of Patriotism and National Identity among Students

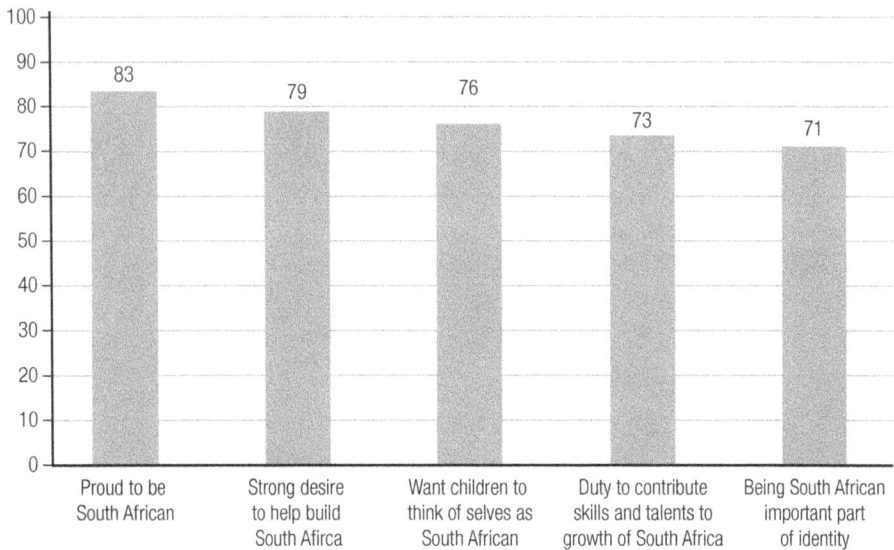

Some maintain that South Africans from minority groups (white, coloured and Indian) will leave the country because although they personally feel strongly about their South African identity, they also feel that they do not have a real role to play in the new South Africa. However, just 3 per cent said that people of their race, people who speak their language, or they themselves have 'no role at all' to play in the future of South Africa and another 9 to 10 per cent answered that they have only a 'minor role.' Because these three items tap a common underlying dimension, they were combined to create an index of 'Perceptions of a future role in South Africa.'[9] While students across all racial groups tend to see a role for themselves in the future of the country, black students are more enthusiastic (a mean of 2.62 on a scale of 0 to 3) than coloured (2.34), white (2.23) or Indian (2.21) students.[10]

Each of these sets of attitudes matters in terms of emigration potential. Respondents with higher levels of patriotism have substantially lower emigration potential (Pearson's r – a product-moment correlation coefficient = -.235). The more a student feels he or she has a role to play in the future of the country, the lower the emigration potential (r = -.130). Whether students feel closer to their national than their professional identity (-.121), or emphasise national identity over quality of life (-.171), also contributes to lower emigration potential.[11]

6.3   Economic evaluations

The study measured student perceptions of a range of features of life in South Africa by asking about present satisfaction with personal and national economic conditions, and then asking students whether they thought conditions in South Africa would be better or worse in five years' time across a wide range of specific features of national life. Finally, they were asked to assess whether each factor would be better in South Africa or in their most likely destination.

Almost half of all students (47 per cent) were dissatisfied with their present personal economic conditions. However, 82 per cent expected that their personal economic conditions would be better or much better in five years. About half felt that their level of income would be better. Six in ten were dissatisfied with current national economic conditions, but 47 per cent felt things would get better in five years' time. Only 27 per cent said they would get worse.

However, once the students were asked what they thought things would look like in South Africa in five years' time across a broad range of factors, perceptions were decidedly more pessimistic. For example, 80 per cent said the HIV/AIDS situation would be worse and two-thirds felt the cost of living would get worse. In terms of their ability to find the job they want, their personal safety, and their family's safety, 58 per cent predicted that all would be worse than they are today. Half foresaw deterioration in the upkeep of public amenities and 40 per cent expected things to deteriorate with regard to availability of affordable quality products, job security, level of taxation and children's future.

On no single item was there a preponderance of optimistic expectations, but there was more variation with regard to expectations about finding the house they want (36 per cent said things would be worse in five years, but 28 per cent said they would be better), a good school for their children (35 per cent worse, 32 per cent better), medical services for their family (36 per cent worse, 31 per cent better), the future quality of customer service (32 per cent worse, 31 per cent better), and their own prospects for professional advancement (31 per cent worse, 30 per cent better). Perhaps most important of all, only 41 per cent felt that it would be easy or very easy for them to find a job in their field of study after graduation. Eighty-one per cent felt the government had not done enough to create jobs for graduates.

The responses to fifteen of these items followed a sufficiently similar pattern to allow for the creation of a single index that measures 'Pessimistic expectations of quality of life.'[12] The two items on safety obtained different patterns of response and were used to construct a separate index of 'Pessimistic expectations of safety.'[13]

The study found that pessimistic expectations of quality of life are indeed positively correlated to higher degrees of emigration potential (r =.181), as are pessimistic expectations of safety (r = .160).[14] However, emigration potential is only weakly associated with personal economic dissatisfaction (r = .061)[15] and national economic dissatisfaction (r = .063).[16] There is no statistically significant link between emigration likelihood and whether or not he or she thinks it will be easy to find a job,[17] personal economic pessimism,[18] or dissatisfaction with government efforts to create jobs.[19]

Regardless of whether students expect conditions in South Africa to get worse, they would have no reason to leave if they consider that conditions are still are better than elsewhere.

Thus the students were asked whether conditions would be better in South Africa or in their most likely destination. Overall, the results indicate that a large number of final-year students indeed see the grass as much greener on the other side. A massive three-quarters are certain that they would enjoy a higher income in their most likely destination. Solid majorities said things would be better elsewhere in terms of their prospects for professional advancement (59 per cent), their ability to find a desired job (56 per cent), and their job security (54 per cent). Forty-one per cent felt that the cost of living would be better elsewhere and they would also pay a fairer level of tax. These six items form a scale that measures 'Relative comparisons of financial prospects.'[20]

About half of the students consider that their ability to find good quality medical services for their family (55 per cent) and a good school for their children (50 per cent) would be better elsewhere. Opinion is more evenly divided when it comes to their expected ability to find a good house (37 per cent say it would be better elsewhere, but 27 per cent say it would be better in South Africa). Overall, just under half felt that their children would have a better future in their most likely destination than in South Africa. Responses to these four items form a separate scale that measures 'Relative comparisons of family prospects.'[21] Around two-thirds felt that public amenities would be better maintained elsewhere (65 per cent), and that the HIV/AIDS situation would also be better (63 per cent). Majorities also expected to have an easier time finding affordable quality products (57 per cent) and quality of customer service (54 per cent) in their most likely destination. These four items form a scale that measures 'Relative comparisons of quality of life.'[22] Finally, two-thirds thought that they (66 per cent) and their family (65 per cent) would be safer elsewhere. These items form a separate index of 'Relative comparisons of safety.'[23]

Students' emigration potential increases predictably as they conclude that they would enjoy better financial prospects ($r = .280$), better family prospects ($r = .261$) and a better quality of life ($r = .220$), and be safer in their most likely destination ($r = .179$). Finally, emigration potential increases sharply to the extent students believe that émigrés lead better lives in their new countries ($r = .271$) but less so in terms of feeling that émigrés' skills have been optimised ($r = .147$).[24]

6.4   Information and experience

Beyond people's emotional attachment to their own country, or their rational assessments of conditions in their own country and their target destinations, another factor that may shape emigration potential is simply their level of information about and contact with the act of emigration.

6.4.1   Personal experience with emigration

Large numbers of the students interviewed reported at least some direct or indirect experience with emigration. Fifty-eight per cent said that they knew at least one fellow student or colleague or close friend who had left the country permanently. Roughly half of all students had had at least one member of their extended family (46 per cent) emigrate, with a quarter saying that someone in their Immediate family (24 per cent) had done so. These four items tap a single underlying dimension of 'Personal contact with emigration.'[25] Emigration potential is modestly related to the extent that students know people who have already emigrated (r = .219).[26]

6.4.2   Personal experience abroad

Do students make their decision on the basis of an idealised or romanticised vision of what life is like on the other side, or have they actually spent meaningful time in the countries they say are their most likely destination? To what extent are these students' views of emigration and the outside world based on real experience (through travel) rather than vicarious experience via the stories they hear from departed friends and families, or through the news media?

In their 1998 study of skilled adults, Mattes and Richmond (2000: 33) found that South Africans tended to form preferences about emigration that had little do to with whether or not they themselves had ever been out of the country to visit the places to which they dreamt of moving. Their study found that extremely small proportions travelled regularly (once a year or more) to other African countries (3 per cent), Europe (7 per cent), North America (3 per cent), Australia and New Zealand (2 per cent) or Asia (1 per cent). In contrast, South Africa's tertiary students have far higher levels of regular contact with Africa (34 per cent travel to southern Africa at least once a year, and 8 per cent do so elsewhere in Africa). But regular contact with frequently listed likely destinations such as Europe (4 per cent), North America (2 per cent), or Australia or New Zealand (1 per cent) is just as low as it was for the adults.

These items form two distinct scales of 'African travel' (southern Africa, and elsewhere in Africa)[27] and 'Overseas travel' (to Europe, North America, Australasia and Asia).[28] Perhaps, contrary to expectations, emigration potential is only weakly related to the extent to which students travel in Africa (.068)[29] or overseas (.077).[30]

6.4.3   Information about the outside world

A number of questions were asked about various ways of acquiring information, which created three composite measures. A quarter of the students interviewed say they 'often' obtain information about job opportunities from family (23 per cent) or co-workers (24 per cent) and one-third say they 'often' do so from fellow students (37 per cent). Approximately one in three say they get information about living conditions from co-workers (30 per cent) or their family (33 per cent) while half get it from friends or fellow students (48 per cent). These items form a valid and reliable scale of 'Obtaining information about life abroad through personal networks.'[31] While half say they 'often' get information about job opportunities from newspapers and magazines (48 per cent), less than one in five get it from television or radio (17 per cent). Half often obtain information about living conditions from newspapers and magazines (53 per cent). But, in contrast to job opportunities, six in ten say they 'often' get information about living conditions in other countries through television or radio (60 per cent). These four items form a separate scale of 'Obtaining information: Life abroad through news media.'[32]

Finally, 45 per cent seek information about job opportunities and 44 per cent about living conditions through the internet. These two items form a distinctive composite scale of 'Obtaining information about life abroad through the internet.'[33] There is a modest relationship between higher levels of emigration potential and higher frequency of seeking out information about conditions abroad via the internet (r = .216), personal networks (r = .213) and news media (r = .149).

6.5.   Logistics

Finally, to what extent does emigration hinge on the simple issue of whether people are able to plan to move or afford to move? Large numbers do seem to think that emigration would not present insurmountable obstacles. Over half of all final students believe that it would be 'easy' or 'very easy' to get a job (54 per cent) in their most likely destination if they wanted to. Forty-three per cent say it would be easy to leave the country to work in their most likely destination. And one-third (32 per cent) believe that the costs of moving to that destination and finding a good home would be affordable; notably, half (52 per cent) say it would be unaffordable or very unaffordable. These three items tap a common underlying dimension that can be called 'Ease of leaving.'[34] A psychological element of logistics would simply be the extent to which people may feel they have the support of loved ones in making this move. Forty-five percent of final-year students say that their family would encourage them to leave South Africa; just one in five (19 per cent) say their families would discourage emigration. As was expected, those who feel that leaving South Africa would be easy and affordable have considerably higher emigration potential than those who think the effort would be daunting (r = .236).[35] Emigration potential increases sharply to the extent that students say their families would encourage them to leave South Africa (r = .394).

7. Multivariate Analysis

We have reviewed the bivariate connections between the possible factors that may help us account for and explain variations in emigration potential. We will now use multivariate regression to test which of these factors remain important predictors when we consider all other factors simultaneously. We use 'blockwise entry' and enter in theoretical 'families' of variables in groups to help us understand which set of factors contributes most to our understanding of emigration potential.

We arrive at a relatively parsimonious model that explains 31 per cent of emigration potential, a relatively strong result given that we are measuring the experiences of widely varying types of students across very different types of educational institutions. The single strongest predictor of emigration potential is simply whether or not students feel that their families would encourage or discourage their decision to move (Beta – the standardised regression coefficient = .289, explaining on its own 19 per cent of the variance of emigration potential). Students' perceptions about the fortunes of those who have already moved are the second strongest set of predictors; particularly the belief that émigrés lead better lives (B = .127) and that they are working in the areas for which they were trained (B =.095) (see Table 2.4).

Relative economic assessments and national identity have approximately equal impacts on emigration potential, though they work in the opposite directions. The belief that family prospects would be better in a student's most likely destination than in South Africa increases emigration potential (B = .132), while a sense of patriotism (-.098) and a belief that where you live is more important than qualify of life (-.056) serves to decrease emigration potential.

Table 2.4: OLS Estimates of Predictors of Emigration Potential						
	r	B	S.E.	Beta	Adj. R² (Block)	Adj. R² (Cumul.)
Constant		.025	104			
Social structure					.000	.000
National identity					.078	.078
Index of patriotism	-.258	-.093	.015	-.098		
National identity more important than quality of life	-.179	-.034	.009	.056		
Economic evaluations					.152	.198
Relative comparisons of family prospects	.298	.109	.013	.132		
Believes emigrants do better	.283	.105	.013	.127		
Believes emigrants' skills optimised	.189	.136	.021	.095		
Information and experience					.059	.223
International travel	.099	.067	.021	.047		
Obtains information via internet	.224	.098	.010	.139		
Logistics					.209	.308
Ease of leaving	.249	.070	.013	.084		
Family support	.430	.198	.011	.289		
St. error of estimate						.6114
Adjusted R2						.308

Notes: All variables significant =/<.001
N = 3386
1. The dependent variable is the Index of Emigration Potential (an average score composed of six different indicators of emigration).
2. Ordinary least squares regression estimates.

Finally, logistic and informational factors have about equal impact. The more one seeks out information from the internet about the living conditions and job opportunities abroad (B = .139) and regularly travels internationally (.047), the greater one's probability of emigrating.[36]

And the more one thinks that emigration would be manageable and affordable (.084), the more likely one is to emigrate.

Once all these factors are taken into consideration, no structural factor (such as race, gender, language, or social class) has any statistically significant impact. Moreover, there was virtually no evidence of any of the so-called 'push factors' widely supposed to be propelling South Africans out of the country, such as crime, economic pessimism, falling standards, mismanagement, or HIV/AIDS (for example, Van Rooyen, 2001). While this is usually based on popular wisdom, some systematic attempts have reached the same conclusions because they have only asked those who have already left the country and thus miss the fact that those who have not left also mention the same problems (Haldenwag, 1996; Statistics SA, 1998).

Rather it seems they are being 'pulled' out by some factors in their identified target destinations. However, these factors are not primarily the simple material gains of better jobs, higher salaries and living standards often supposed by migration theorists (for example, Aderinto, 1978) or the fulfilment of occupational or professional aspirations (Weis, 1986). It is true that students are much more likely to emigrate if they believe that émigrés lead better lives abroad (B=.127) and that their skills are being optimised (B=.095). But the most important factors are students' forecasts of whether their family's prospects would be better elsewhere than in South Africa in terms of such things as finding good schools and houses and good-quality medical services.

8. Policy Implications

What kinds of investments does the South African government stand to lose if likely emigrants do in fact leave? According to students' present dispositions, the South African government would lose about 1 to 2 per cent of final year students with bursaries that require no repayment, and approximately 5 per cent of those that require some repayment (Figure 2.11). Universities and technikons also stand to lose about 5 per cent of their investments in bursaries. However, these numbers would rise dramatically to as high as one-quarter to one-third of government bursaries if the 'high' potential emigrants also left.

With regard to investments in specialised technical training, a great deal of public attention has focused on the impacts of skilled emigration on the medical profession. The survey results indicated that the greatest losses may in fact be amongst certain sectors of technikon-trained students, especially those training in information technology (IT) (Figure 2.12).

Faced with significant emigration, it is understandable that governments are inclined to try and limit emigration through restrictive policies. Most analysts feel such policies are likely to hasten the rate of emigration even further. The data collected by this survey tends to support such conclusions. First of all, students with study bursaries were asked whether the conditions of those bursaries required them to remain in the country after they completed their studies and/or to work specifically in either the public or private sector. Twenty-two per cent of all students had such a bursary. While these students do have a lower emigration potential than others, the difference is very small, suggesting that these restrictions have a minimal effect on student plans and calculations.[37]

Figure 2.11: Potential Loss of State Investments by Type of Bursary

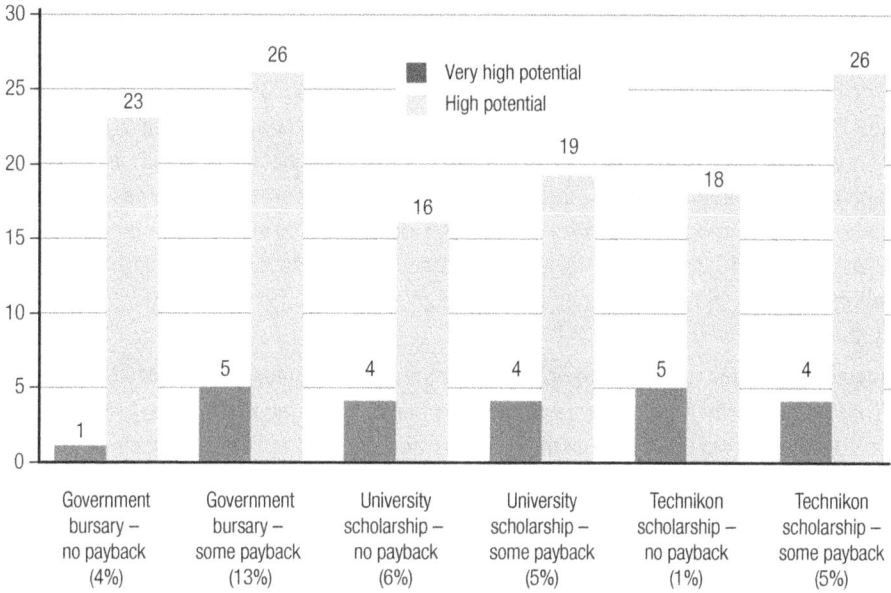

Figure 2.12: Potential Losses of State Investments by Course and Study

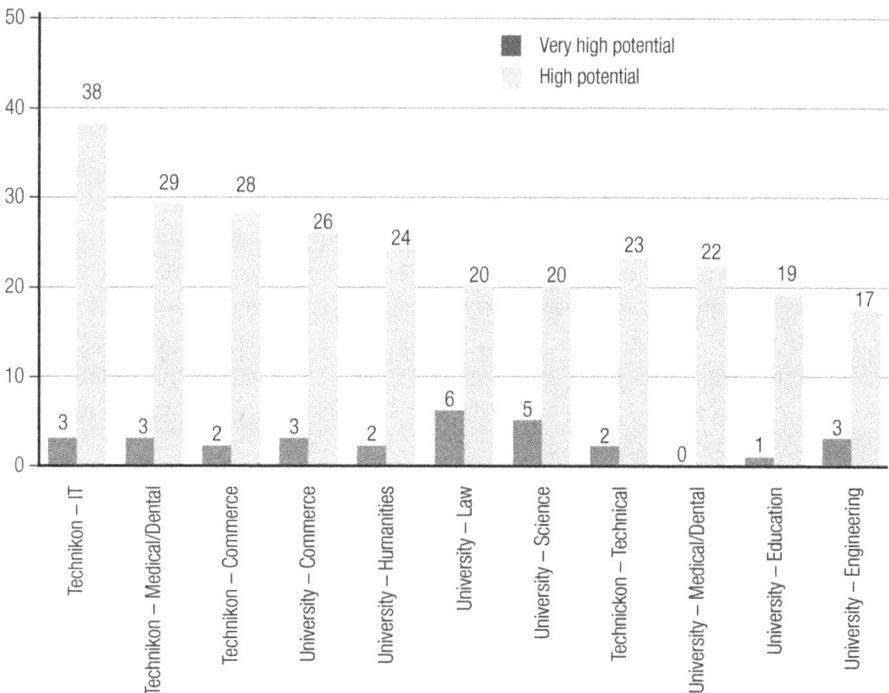

Secondly, they were asked whether they felt a range of potential government interventions to restrict emigration were justifiable. For example, one type of government intervention is a requirement that students perform some form of national service in return for their education. Since 2001, the Department of Health has required final year medical students to do a year of community work. The ANC argued in its 2002 Party Conference Manifesto that this should be broadened to include other healthcare professionals and those in higher education. The survey results suggest that if handled well, and if specifically required of those students who had received some form of bursary, restrictions would not meet with massive resistance, or make students more likely to leave. Just 18 per cent said the government would not be justified in requiring those who have received government bursaries to complete some form of national service in return for this funding. High emigration potential students were no more likely than others to think so.[38]

However, students are far more opposed to other types of interventions. Half of the students feel that requirements that students complete some form of national service before they began tertiary education would not be justified. Fifty-three per cent said requiring citizens to work in the country for several years after graduation was not justified, with higher emigration potential students especially opposed to it.[39] Nearly six in ten (57 per cent) said that limiting the amount of money they could send out of the country was not justified, with higher emigration students more likely to resent this.[40] And 60 per cent said that making people pay taxes on income earned outside the country was not justified, again with high emigration potential students especially opposed to it.[41]

Finally, students were asked whether some other possible interventions would make them less or more likely to leave. Their answers showed that requiring students leaving professional schools to do a year of national service in their area;[42] limiting people to one passport;[43] or increasing fees for emigration documents[44] would make it more, or much more likely that the very high and high emigration potential students would leave, as would any government steps to make emigration more difficult.[45]

In contrast, students feel there are far more effective ways to limit emigration. Three-quarters agreed that development and growth in South Africa would reduce emigration and six in ten agree that measures to encourage the return of skilled nationals living abroad would also reduce it. But only just over one-quarter think legislation limiting the ability of state-trained students to emigrate would actually reduce emigration, and students with higher emigration potential were even less likely to think so.[46] Just over one-fifth said that South Africa's efforts to discourage other governments from employing South African emigrants would reduce emigration. Finally, just 20 per cent think a legal prohibition on emigration would reduce the outflow of people.

9. Conclusions

Whether South Africa is able to retain its future skills base is a far more complex matter than simply reducing crime to satisfy 'whinging' white students or training more black (and presumably more patriotic) students. First of all, there are many factors that fall outside the government's direct control. Short of resorting to draconian measures, for example, there is no chance of limiting curious students' international travel or their use of the internet to find out about the quality of life in Australia, or of forbidding students to communicate with their relatives who have moved to the United States. Rather, the government must make proactive use of both its ability to set economic policy and the impressive resources of public communications at its command to demonstrate to highly skilled – and thus highly marketable – young South Africans from all backgrounds (as well as to their families who offer them valued advice and support) that the country offers people like themselves a bright future for their families, including good-quality schools and medical services and affordable housing, and that they will have ample opportunities to put their skills to full use and be rewarded accordingly. Such a positive approach promises to retain far more students than the negative, lecturing and restrictive approach that the government has adopted to date.

References

ABELLA, M, 1997. *Sending workers abroad.* Geneva: International Labour Organisation.

ADERINTO, A, 1978. Toward a better understanding of brain drain. In Damaci, UG & Diejomaoh, VP (eds), *Human resources and African development.* New York: Praeger, pp. 320-32.

BHORAT, H, MEYER, J-B & MLATSHENI, C, 2002. *Skilled labour migration from developing countries: study on South and Southern Africa.* International Migration Papers No. 52, International Labour Organisation.

BROWN, M, KAPLAN, D & MEYER, J-B, 2002. The brain drain: an outline of skilled emigration from South Africa. In McDonald, D & Crush J (eds), *Destinations unknown: Perspectives on the brain drain in southern Africa.* Pretoria and Cape Town: Africa Institute and Southern African Migration Programme, pp. 113–38.

COMMANDER, S, KANGASNIEMI, M & WINTERS, L, 2003. The brain drain: curse or boon? In Baldwin, R & Winters, L (eds), *Challenges to globalisation.* Chicago: University of Chicago Press.

CRUSH, J, 2002. The global raiders: nationalism, globalisation and the South African brain drain. *Journal of International Affairs,* 56: 147–72.

DUMONT, JC & MEYER, J-B, 2004. The international mobility of health professionals: an evaluation and analysis based on the case of South Africa. In OECD, *Trends in International Migration.* Paris: OECD Publishing.

HAFFAJEE, F, 1998. Exit the middle classes. *Mail & Guardian,* 22 September.

HALDENWAG, B, 1996. *Migration processes, systems and policies.* Stellenbosch: University of Stellenbosch Press.

KHADRIA, B, 2002. *Skilled labour migration from developing countries: study on India.* International Migration Papers No. 49, International Labour Organisation.

MARTIN, P & WIDGREN, J, 2002. International migration: facing the challenge. *The Population Bulletin,* 57 (1): 1-40.

MATTES, R, 2003. Towards an understanding of African identity. In Burgess, S (ed.) *SA tribes: who we are, how we think and what we want out of life.* Cape Town: David Philip.

MATTES, R & RICHMOND, W, 2000. The brain drain: what do skilled South Africans think? In McDonald, D & Crush, J (eds), *Destinations unknown: perspectives on the brain drain in southern Africa.* Pretoria and Cape Town: Africa Institute and Southern African Migration Programme, pp. 17–46.

MEYER, J-B, 2001. Network approach versus brain drain: lessons from the diaspora. *International Migration*, 39: 91–108.

STALKER, P, 2000. *Workers without frontiers: The impact of globalisation on international migration.* Boulder: Lynne Reiner.

STATISTICS SOUTH AFRICA (STATSSA), 1998. *Tourism and migration: 1994-1996.* Statistical Release. Pretoria: Statistics South Africa.

VAN ROOYEN, J, 2001. *The new Great Trek: The story of South Africa's white exodus.* Pretoria: Unisa Press.

WEIS, T, 1998. Addressing the brain drain: the return and reintegration of qualified African nationals programme. In Sachikonye, LM (ed.), *Labour markets and migration in southern Africa.* SAPES (Southern Africa Political Economy Series) Trust, Harare.

WIMALDHARMA, J, PEARCE, D & STANTON, D, 2004. Remittances: the new development finance? *Small Enterprise Development Journal*, 15(1): 1–8.

Notes

1 Eta = .087, p =.002.

2 Eta = .120; p =.003.

3 Eta = .041; p =.065.

4 Eta = .112; p =.000.

5 Eta = .109, p =.000.

6 Eta = .169; p =.000. Those studying IT at university are also more likely to leave (1.81) but there are only 20 cases in this category, insufficient for reliable analysis.

7 These five items have an Eigenvalue of 3.14 and explain 62.8 per cent of common variance. Reliability (Cronbach's Alpha) = .85.

8 Eta = .435; p =.000.

9 These three items have an Eigenvalue of 2.06 and explain 68.7 per cent of common variance. Reliability (Cronbach's Alpha) = .77.

10 Eta = .295; p =.000.

11 All correlations significant at p =.000.

12 The single scale composed of these 15 items has an Eigenvalue of 8.12 and explains 54.2 per cent of the common variance. Reliability (Cronbach's Alpha) = .94.

13 The correlation between these two items is an almost perfect .96, with reliability = .98.

14 Both correlations are significant at p =.000.

15 p =.006.

16 p =.005.

17 Pearson's r = -.061; p =.06.

18 Pearson's r = -.024; p =.282.

19 Pearson's r = .032; p =187.

20 The scale created by these six items has an Eigenvalue of 3.00 and explains 50 per cent of common variance. Reliability (Cronbach's Alpha) = .80.

21 The scale created by these four items has an Eigenvalue of 2.55 and explains 63.7 per cent of common variance. Reliability (Cronbach's Alpha) = .81.

22 The scale created by these four items has an Eigenvalue of 2.56 and explains 63.6 per cent of common variance. Reliability (Cronbach's Alpha) = .81.

23 The two items are almost perfectly correlated (.94) with a reliability (Cronbach's Alpha) of .97.

24 All correlations are significant at p =.000.

25 The scale created by these four items has an Eigenvalue of 2.28 and explains 60 per cent of common variance. Reliability (Cronbach's Alpha) = .75.

26 All correlations are significant at p =.000.

27 These two items are moderately correlated (.38) with reliability (Cronbach's Alpha) = .50.

28 The scale created by these four items has an Eigenvalue of 2.61 and explains 65.1% of common variance. Reliability (Cronbach's Alpha) = .80.

29 p =.003.

30 p =.001.

31 The scale created by these six items has an Eigenvalue of 3.21 and explains 53.5 per cent of common variance. Reliability (Cronbach's Alpha)=.83.

32 The scale created by these four items has an Eigenvalue of 1.99 and explains 49.8 per cent of common variance. Reliability (Cronbach's Alpha) =.66.

33 These two items are strongly related (.68) and form a very reliable construct (Alpha =.81).

34 The scale created by these three items has an Eigenvalue of 1.69 and explains 56.5 per cent of the common variance. Reliability (Cronbach's Alpha) = .66.

35 p =.000.

36 We could entertain plausible arguments that seeking information from the internet is as much a consequence of the decision to emigrate as a cause. If this variable is omitted, a third identity variable (whether people value national identity more than occupational identity) remains in the model, but the overall explanatory strength of the model is slightly weaker (Adj. R2 = .29).

37 Eta = .072; p =.001.

38 Tau b = .033; p =.073.

39 Tau b = .146; p =.000.

40 Tau b = .108; p =.000.

41 Tau b = .146; p =.000.

42 Tau b = .220; p =.000.

43 Tau b = .199; p =.000.

44 Tau b = .199; p =.000.

45 Tau b = .230; p =.000.

46 Tau b = -.090; p =.000.

3 MEDICAL MIGRATION FROM ZIMBABWE: MAGNITUDE, CAUSES AND IMPACT ON THE POOR

ABEL CHIKANDA

1. Introduction

The World Bank (2000) cites the migration of skilled professionals from developing to industrialised countries (the so-called 'brain drain') as one of the major forces shaping the landscape of the 21st century. Africa is faced with this large and growing problem (Mutizwa-Mangiza, 1996; Bloom & Standing, 2001). While a number of factors have been blamed for such movement, recent studies have shown that economic push factors are largely responsible for the outflow of skilled professionals from the continent (Gaidzanwa, 1999). This migration has been blamed for worsening the human capital crisis in Africa (Wadda, 2000). For instance, by the late 1980s Africa had lost nearly one-third of its skilled workers, with up to 60 000 middle- and high-level managers migrating to Europe and North America between 1985 and 1990 (World Bank, 2000). In the mid-1990s, Africa was losing about 23 000 professionals annually who were in search of better working conditions in the developed world (World Bank,

1995). The figures show a steady increase in the number of skilled professionals migrating from developing countries.

This migration is often a response to the lack of opportunity in the professionals' home country and the availability of opportunity and deliberate promotion of immigration in the other (Saravia & Miranda, 2004). Hence, a significant 'brain drain' of key professionals has been witnessed in Africa, such as engineers and information technologists (Johnson & Regets, 1998), doctors (Grant, 2004) and nurses (Buchan & Sochalski, 2004). These professionals are sometimes replaced by high-cost expatriate professionals: it is estimated that African countries spend nearly $4 billion annually on replacing the professionals lost through migration with expatriates from the west (Commission for Africa, 2005). Expatriates are more expensive to hire than locally trained professionals and the fact that they are prepared to work in the host country for only a limited period makes sustainable economic development even more difficult to achieve.

In Zimbabwe, the increase in the scale of migration of skilled professionals can partly be linked to the adoption of the Economic Structural Adjustment Programme (ESAP) by the government in the early 1990s (Republic of Zimbabwe, 1999). The widely acknowledged failure of this programme saw the standard of living of skilled professionals falling, as salary benefits could not keep pace with the escalating cost of living. Faced with this situation, most professionals adopted a wide range of livelihood strategies, with some resorting to long-distance international migration. However, no studies to date have attempted to establish the link between migration and poverty in the country. This study seeks to provide the missing link by showing how poverty is influencing the migration of healthcare professionals from Zimbabwe, and how such movement has affected the poor.

Zimbabwe's health sector has been badly affected by the brain drain, with unprecedented opportunities for mobility globally and a marked deterioration in working conditions and prospects at home. In particular, the country's prevailing political and economic situation is generally seen as a major factor precipitating out-migration. Most of the healthcare professionals who have left Zimbabwe have migrated to countries where their qualifications are recognised, such as the UK, South Africa and Botswana.

The relatively poor salaries that Zimbabwe's healthcare professionals in the country are paid compared to those offered to their counterparts in more developed countries have hastened the emigration of health staff. According to a report by a commission tasked to review the country's health services, salaries in the public sector are grossly uncompetitive (Republic of Zimbabwe, 1999). The report shows that a newly qualified doctor in South Africa earns more than twice the salary of the most senior doctor in Zimbabwe (Republic of Zimbabwe, 1999). On the national scale, the World Bank estimated in 1997 that the private to public sector salary ratios were about 2:1 for nurses and at least 6:1 for doctors (cited in Republic of Zimbabwe, 1999). Consequently, there have been huge outflows of healthcare professionals from public health institutions to the private sector and beyond the country's borders.

Healthcare professionals in Zimbabwe frequently express their dissatisfaction with their remuneration and working conditions by going on strike, but the government has not been able to effect the required salary hikes because of the current harsh economic climate. In

2001, former Health Minister Dr Timothy Stamps noted that Zimbabwe had been losing an average of 20 per cent of its healthcare professionals every year to other countries (*Daily News*, 17 September 2001). The minister pointed out that each of the country's five major hospitals was losing about 24 senior nurses and three doctors every month, leaving the hospitals in a desperate situation. In fact, most of the country's public health institutions are manned by a skeleton staff that is failing to cope with increased workloads in the face of the growing HIV/AIDS crisis. This has led to low morale and productivity among the workforce and little desire to serve beyond the call of duty.

This chapter draws on data obtained from a study conducted in 2002 that sought to establish the magnitude and causes of the migration of healthcare professionals from Zimbabwe and to document its impact on the quality of care.

2. Research Methodology

Five interlinked research instruments were developed in order to better understand the dimensions, causes, impacts and future course of the medical brain drain from Zimbabwe. The first questionnaire (A1) was administered to hospital authorities and to the Ministry of Health and Child Welfare (MoHCW). It asked about staffing patterns at Zimbabwean healthcare institutions over the past decade and the workload of the various healthcare worker categories at each healthcare institution. The A2 questionnaire was used to interview informants in key positions in the healthcare delivery system. The A3 questionnaire was administered to individual health workers from selected healthcare institutions. The A4 questionnaire was a guide for focus group discussions with key community stakeholders. The A5 questionnaire was administered to emigrant healthcare professionals. The methodologies used to select respondents for each research instrument are outlined below.

2.1   The health institution survey (A1)

Random sampling was used to select healthcare facilities. Zimbabwe has ten provinces, seven of which were randomly selected for sampling. In each of the selected provinces, a provincial hospital was selected as well as one district healthcare institution and one healthcare centre. One questionnaire was distributed to each institution for completion by the hospital superintendent. The provincial hospitals selected for the study are shown in Figure 3.1.

The selection of health centres was guided by the authorities interviewed at district centres. One health centre was targeted for each district hospital. Two schools of nursing and midwifery, located at Harare Central Hospital and Mpilo Central Hospital, Bulawayo, were also selected.

Figure 3.1: Location of Provincial Hospitals Selected for the Study

2.2 Professional informants (A2)

Interviews were held with professional informants in key positions in the healthcare system. These included personnel from MoHCW, members of professional councils and associations, and representatives of partner organisations and the private healthcare sector. The interviews sought to establish the causes of migration and the measures being implemented to reduce such movement.

2.3 Individual healthcare workers (A3)

The A3 questionnaire was administered in the healthcare institutions which had been randomly selected for the A1 questionnaire. It was not possible to obtain data on the number of healthcare professionals employed in each of the selected institutions from the MoHCW. This presented a problem in determining the target number of respondents for each of the institutions. The study thus relied on informal figures presented by people with expert knowledge of staffing patterns in the country's hospitals. In total, 312 people were identified for interviews, including 215 nurses and 59 doctors, and 231 completed questionnaires were returned (a return rate of 75 per cent). Nurses were the largest group of healthcare professionals inter-viewed, comprising almost 60 per cent of the respondents (Table 3.1). A smaller number of doctors (13 per cent) were also interviewed, with a smattering of pharmacists, midwives and dentists. Also interviewed were tutors and lecturers, drawn mainly from the nursing schools at Harare and Mpilo Central Hospitals, and some lecturers from the Medical School of the University of Zimbabwe.

Table 3.1: Employment Profile of the Respondents

	Frequency	Percentage
Category of health team		
Nurse	137	59.3
Midwife	20	8.7
Medical doctor	30	13.0
Pharmacist	10	4.3
Tutor/lecturer	17	7.4
Dentist	5	2.2
Any other category	12	5.2
Type of facility where employed		
District hospital	39	16.9
Provincial or regional hospital	117	50.6
Tertiary hospital	41	17.7
Rural health centre	9	3.9
Nursing school in a university	2	0.9
Nursing school not in a university	13	5.6
Medical school	10	4.3
N = 231		

Nearly half of the respondents were drawn from provincial hospitals, while others were from district hospitals (16,9 per cent) and tertiary hospitals (17,7 per cent). The rest were drawn from rural health centres (3,9 per cent), nursing schools (6,5 per cent) and from the Medical School of the University of Zimbabwe (4,3 per cent). The health professionals inter-viewed were highly qualified: the majority have tertiary diplomas (65,8 per cent) and 19,9 per cent have bachelors' degrees. Some 6,1 per cent have tertiary certificates and 1,3 per cent had other qualifications. Noteworthy are the 5,2 per cent who had masters' degrees and the 1,7 per cent who had doctorates.

2.4   Focus groups (A4)

The focus group discussions were held in Epworth, a suburb just outside the administrative boundary of Harare, the capital. Three focus groups were held with the participants identified in Table 3.2.

Table 3.2: Breakdown of Participants in Focus Groups	
Group	Composition
1 (n = 12)	• Religious leaders (2) • Senior teacher/teacher in charge (1) • Traditional healer/practitioner (1) • Community representatives/clubs (2) • Home-based caregivers (3) • Traditional midwives (2) • Village community worker (1)
2 (n = 12)	Adolescent users of health services (6 females, 6 males, ages 15–19 years)
3 (n = 12)	Adult users of health services (6 women of child-bearing age, 30+ years; 6 men, 30–50+ years)
N = 36	

2.5 Emigrant health professionals (A5)

The A5 research instrument was designed to survey doctors, nurses and pharmacists living outside the country. However, response rates were extremely low. Only 25 completed questionnaires were returned.

3. Staffing Zimbabwe's Healthcare Sector

The magnitude of migration from Zimbabwe's healthcare sector is difficult to establish because of the lack of reliable data. This is further compounded by the fact that departing healthcare professionals rarely declare their intention to migrate when they resign from public sector jobs. In 2002, in the UK alone, 2346 work permits were issued to nurses from Zimbabwe (Table 3.3). Zimbabwe was the UK's fourth largest supplier of overseas nurses, after the Philippines, India and South Africa.

To review trends in the migration of healthcare professionals, the study analysed changes in the number of registered professionals. The data was obtained from the Central Statistical Office and covered the period 1995–2000. The study also analysed the staffing trends in the public sector, which is the principal provider of healthcare services in Zimbabwe. This data was obtained from the MoHCW using the A1 questionnaire.

The number of registered medical practitioners countrywide increased slightly from 1575 in 1995 to 1629 in 2000 (a 3 per cent increase) (Figure 3.2). This small increase was despite the fact that the Medical School of the University of Zimbabwe trains between 80 and 90 doctors every year. There was an overall increase of only 54 doctors (rather than the expected 360 or so) over the four-year period, which suggests that emigration is at least partly responsible. The data also shows a general decline in the number of doctors employed in the public sector over time. For instance, the number of doctors employed countrywide in public healthcare institutions fell from 742 in 1997 to 692 in 1998 (a loss of nearly 7 per cent). The figure rose to 742 in 2000, a staffing level which had been attained three years previously.

Table 3.3: Work Permits Issued to Nurses in UK, 2002

Country	No. of work permits issued
Philippines	10 424
India	3 392
South Africa	2 835
Zimbabwe	2 346
Nigeria	1 501
Ghana	528
Australia	503
Pakistan	385
Kenya	354
Mauritius	351
Other	2 983
Total	25 602
Source: Dovlo, 2003: 9	

Figure 3.2: Medical Practitioners in Zimbabwe, 1995–2000

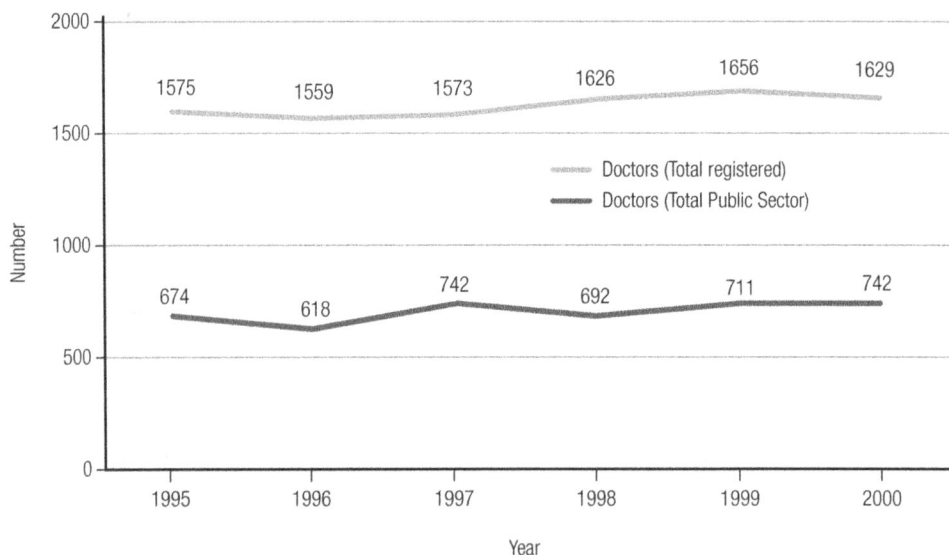

A comparison of the number of registered medical practitioners in the country and those employed in public healthcare institutions shows that the public sector is in crisis because of its failure to retain staff, leading to an internal brain drain to the private sector. In 1997, for example, there were 831 private and 742 public sector doctors. Two years later, the figures were 945 and 711 respectively, suggesting that the private sector has been growing at the expense of the public sector. Such movement has left most public healthcare institutions running on a skeleton staff. In fact, public healthcare institutions employed only 28,7 per cent of the required number of doctors in 1997 (Republic of Zimbabwe, 1999). In the same year, it was estimated that the public sector employed only 34 per cent of the medical doctors registered in the country (Republic of Zimbabwe, 1999). The rest were employed in the private sector.

The total number of registered nursing professionals in the country was stable up to the late 1990s, after which a significant decline was experienced (Figure 3.3). While there were 15 476 registered nurses in Zimbabwe in 1999, only 12 477 remained by 2001. Such a sudden decline is clearly the result of nurses emigrating from the country. On the other hand, the number of nurses employed in the public healthcare sector fell from a peak of 8662 in 1996 to 7007 in 1999 (a decline of 1655 or 19,1 per cent). This decline occurred during a period when 1370 nurses were produced by the country's public training institutions. While some of the nurses might have left the public sector through attrition (such as retirement and death) or moved to the private sector, a significant proportion of the loss may be blamed on emigration.

Figure 3.3: Nurses in Zimbabwe, 1995–2000

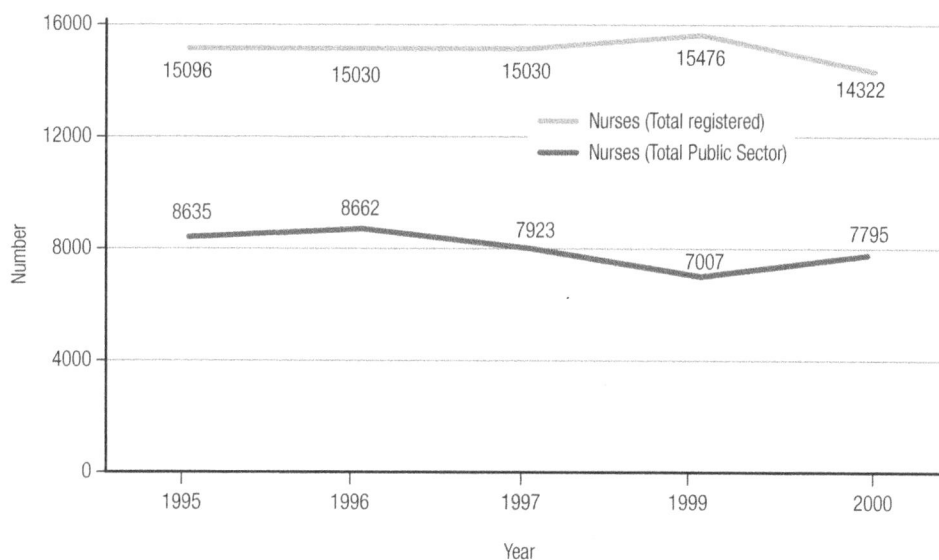

Further evidence that nurses were moving to the private sector is provided by the number of nurses registered nationally, which rose marginally from 15 096 in 1995 to 15 476 in 1999 (an increase of 2,5 per cent), while the number of nurses employed in public healthcare institutions declined from 8635 in 1995 to 7007 in 1999 (a decline of 19 per cent). Symptomatic of the growing staffing crisis in Zimbabwe's public health sector is the fact that only 28,7 per cent of the available posts for doctors were filled in 1997 (Table 3.4). Dentists, pharmacists and even nurses were also in short supply. Of the 1634 doctors registered in the country in 1997, only 551 (33,7 per cent) were employed in the public sector.

Table 3.4: Health Professionals Employed in the Public Sector, 1997				
	No. registered in the country	MoHCW requirement	Approved posts	Filled posts	% of require-ment filled
Doctors	1,634	1,851	676	551	28.7
Nurses	16,407	14,251	7,923	7,923	55.6
Pharmacists	524	198	59	37	18.7
Dentists	148	43	14	14	32.6
Source: Republic of Zimbabwe, 1999.				

4. Migration Intentions

An examination of Zimbabwean healthcare professionals' intentions to migrate provides a useful indication of likely future brain drain patterns. The migration intentions measured included migration to the private sector as well as long-distance international migration.

The survey results showed that 68 per cent of the healthcare professionals were considering leaving their public sector jobs in pursuit of better paying jobs in the private sector, for various reasons. Most of them argued that the public sector did not offer competitive salaries (87 per cent) (Table 3.5). They were finding it difficult to live on the salary they were receiving (68 per cent) and concurred that it was necessary for public health sector professionals to do two or more jobs to make ends meet (79 per cent). They would prefer to stay in the public sector if they were offered better salaries (87 per cent). The private sector clearly offers better fringe benefits than the public sector. The respondents also expressed fears about their social security in old age, with 81 per cent indicating that they were afraid they would not be adequately provided for when they retired. Hence, the public sector is largely left with people who are poorly paid and poorly motivated to perform their duties.

The survey results also show that the majority of the healthcare professionals interviewed (68 per cent) were considering leaving the country in the near future. In the case of nurses, the figure was 71 per cent, suggesting that the likelihood of nurses emigrating is high. The most likely destination is the UK (29 per cent) (Figure 3.4). However, a sizeable number prefer destinations within Africa (mostly South Africa, followed by Botswana). Other fairly popular intended destinations are Australia (6 per cent), the US (5 per cent), New Zealand (2 per cent) and Canada (2 per cent). Even though intentions do not automatically translate into action, the extent of dissatisfaction in the healthcare sector is clearly massive. This makes it imperative for policy-makers to implement policies that address the welfare and other concerns of healthcare professionals.

Table 3.5: Employment Benefits	
Do you agree with the following statements?	Yes (%)
The public health sector does not offer competitive salaries to healthcare workers in this country	87
If I received a better salary, I would be happy to stay in my present position	87
I worry that I will not be adequately provided for when I retire	81
If you work in the public health service, it is necessary to do two (or more) jobs to make ends meet	79
The private sector offers better fringe benefits to healthcare workers in this country than the public sector	78
I am considering moving to the private sector because I will receive a better salary	68
I find it difficult to live on the salary I receive	68
N = 231	

Figure 3.4: Most Likely Destinations of Zimbabwean Health Professionals

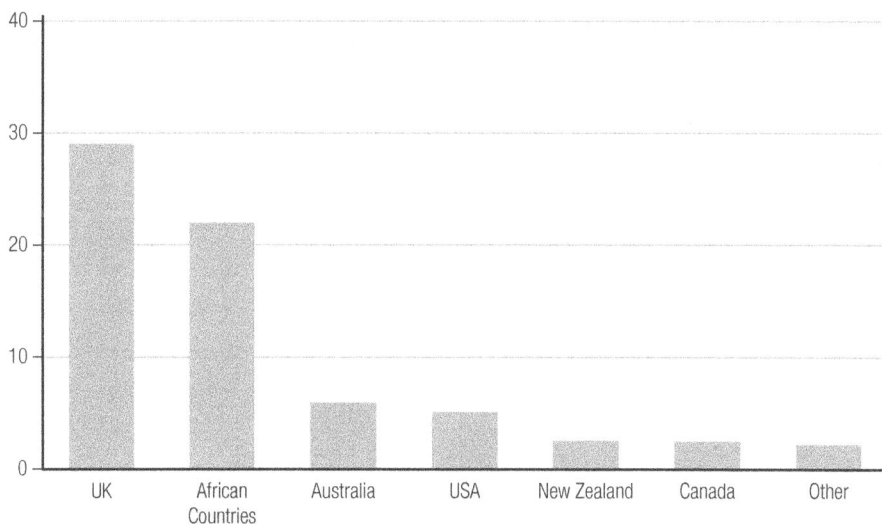

The survey also sought to establish the broad causes of healthcare professionals' disenchantment. These can be grouped into economic, political, professional and social factors, as shown in Table 3.6. More than half of the respondents (55 per cent) cited economic factors as a reason for wanting to leave the country. These included the desire to receive better remuneration in the intended country of destination (55 per cent) or to save money quickly for later use in the home country (54 per cent). Political factors cited included the general sense of despondency (24 per cent) and the high levels of crime and violence in the country (23 per cent). Professional factors influencing emigration included heavy workloads (39 per cent) and insufficient opportunities for promotion and self-improvement (32 per cent). Lastly, social factors cited included the desire to find better living conditions (47 per cent) and family-related reasons (10 per cent).

Table 3.6: Reason for Intention to Move	
Reason	Percentage
Economic	
Because I will receive better remuneration in another country	55
Because of a general decline in the economic situation in this country	55
To save money quickly to buy a car, pay off a home loan, or for a similar reason	54
Political	
Because I see no future in this country	45
Because there is a general sense of despondency in this country	24
Because of the high levels of violence and crime in this country	23
Professional	
Because of a lack of resources and facilities within this country's healthcare system	45
Because there is a general decline in the healthcare services of this country	43
Because the workload in the healthcare services of this country is too heavy	39
Because of insufficient opportunities for promotion and self-improvement	32
To gain experience abroad	32
Because of the poor management of the healthcare services in this country	31
Because I need to upgrade my professional qualifications due to the unsatisfactory quality of education and training in this country	23
Because I cannot find a suitable job in this country	11
Because of an unacceptable workload	10
Social	
In order to find better living conditions	47
Because the value systems in this country have declined to such an extent that I can no longer see my way clear to remain here	32
To ensure a safer environment for my children	25
In order to travel and see the world	15
In order to join family/friends abroad	14
Because of family-related matters	10
N = 231	
Note: Question is multiple response.	

Without question, economic factors have exerted the greatest influence on healthcare professionals' decision to migrate. This is in line with the general decline in the country's economic conditions since the late 1990s. Political factors also gained greater prominence as the country's major political parties fought fierce battles, first in the 2000 parliamentary elections, and then in the 2002 presidential elections. These campaigns were associated with widespread violence, which was more severe in rural areas. This saw many profession-als fleeing the countryside for their safety and that of their children. Still other healthcare professionals are migrating because of professional factors. Most of these factors relate to the poor economic conditions prevailing in the country, which have resulted in a general decline in healthcare services.

Interviews with emigrant healthcare professionals confirmed that economic and political factors were the main reasons they had left the country (Table 3.7). Economic factors cited included low remuneration (56 per cent) and the general decline in the economic situation at home (40 per cent). Political factors included the high levels of crime and violence (politically related) (48 per cent) and the fact that they saw no future in the country (48 per cent). The dominant professional factors cited were the general decline in health services in the country (44 per cent), poor management of health services (36 per cent) and the need to gain expe-rience abroad (24 per cent). Lastly, social factors which had significantly influenced these healthcare professionals' decision to emigrate were the need to find better living conditions (48 per cent) and family-related matters (12 per cent).

Table 3.7: Reasons for Leaving the Home Country	
Reason	Yes (%)
Economic factors	40
Political factors	36
Professional factors	25
Social factors	16
N = 25	
Note: Question is multiple response.	

5. Effects of Migration

The shortage of skilled healthcare professionals had a negative impact on the workloads of the staff who chose not to migrate (Republic of Zimbabwe, 1999). The shortage of doctors nationally in public healthcare institutions increased the workloads of medical practitioners. The MoHCW estimates the current doctor-to-patient ratio as one doctor to 6000 patients, but this study established that this is not common at all levels of healthcare. Data on doctors' workloads showed that those employed in district hospitals had heavier workloads than those in provincial and central hospitals (Table 3.8). While the outpatient attendance per doctor at Gweru Provincial Hospital was 1:20 858 in 1999, the attendance per doctor at Kadoma District Hospital was 1:30 015. Doctors posted in areas with lower levels of development clearly had a much heavier workload than those employed in more developed city areas.

Table 3.8: Patient Attendance at Selected Healthcare Institutions in Zimbabwe

		Variable	1998	1999	2000
Doctors	Gweru Provincial Hospital	No. of outpatients	145 220	149 221	51 001
		No. at post	7	8	8
		Outpatient attendance per doctor	20 746	18 653	8 650
	Kadoma District Hospital	No. of outpatients	171 372	168 522	155 462
		No. at post	7	6	6
		Outpatient attendance per doctor	24 482	28 087	2 5910
Nurses	Gweru Provincial Hospital	No. of outpatients	23 110	23 177	2 3428
		No. at post	238	232	235
		Outpatient attendance per nurse	97	100	100
	Kadoma District Hospital	No. of outpatients	171 372	168 522	155 462
		No. at post	105	113	112
		Outpatient attendance per nurse	1 632	1 491	1 388
	Epworth Polyclinic	No. of outpatients	22 440	38 000	42 000
		No. at post	5	5	4
		Outpatient attendance per nurse	4 488	7 600	10 500

In Zimbabwe, nurses form the backbone of the country's healthcare delivery system and they run most of the health centres in disadvantaged rural areas. Chasokela (2001) notes that nurses working in rural areas have, over the years, functioned in an increasingly expanded role, taking on the roles of pharmacist, doctor, physiotherapist and so forth. This has increased the workloads of nurses stationed in less attractive regions.

The MoHCW estimates that the current nurse-to-patient ratio is one nurse to 700 patients (Republic of Zimbabwe, 1999), but this study established that nurses employed at provincial health institutions have nurse-to-patient ratios lower than the national average. For example, in 2000 the nurse-to-patient ratio for Gweru Provincial Hospital was 1:100 (less than the national average), compared with the nurse-to-patient ratio of 1:1388 at Kadoma District Hospital (nearly twice the national average). The situation is worse for nurses employed at the health centres where doctor visits are rare. Thus, the nurse-to-patient attendance ratio in 2000 at Waverly Clinic (a health centre in Kadoma) stood at 1:7500 (more than ten times the national average) and at 1:10 500 for Epworth Polyclinic (an underdeveloped health centre situated at the outskirts of Harare). Nurses employed at healthcare centres endure very heavy workloads but the situation improves significantly as one moves to the district and provincial institutions. The study also established that less-qualified staff (nurse aides) were carrying out nursing duties at rural centres owing to the shortage of qualified healthcare professionals.

Poor job satisfaction and low morale are endemic among healthcare professionals in southern Africa (Bloom & Standing, 2001). This study established that healthcare professionals who remain in public employment increasingly seek ways to augment their salaries. These include moonlighting at private facilities and attending to non-medical businesses. While doctors have been able to establish private surgeries, nurses in Zimbabwe have been hampered from doing so by the current legal framework. Hence, for most nurses, migrating to the private sector remains the only viable option. However, some public sector nurses who choose not to migrate to the private sector are engaged in part-time work in the private sector to augment their salaries. This affects their performance in their public sector jobs. In the focus groups it was alleged that 'nurses in the public sector are engaging in a lot of part-time work in private clinics. By the time they come for their normal duties, they will be too tired to work. That is why we get poor service when we visit the clinic.'

The migration of skilled healthcare professionals from Zimbabwe has adversely affected the quality of care offered in the healthcare institutions. Consultation time available to patients has been reduced owing to the work pressure faced by the few remaining healthcare workers. One participant in the focus group pointed out that 'the shortage of nurses at the clinic means that patients have to wait for a long time before receiving medical treatment. When a patient eventually receives treatment, consultation is usually done hurriedly as the nurses work at a fast pace so as attend to a "multitude" of other patients waiting to receive the same service.'

The effects of the migration of healthcare professionals on the main users of public healthcare institutions have been many and varied. For instance, patients now have to wait for long periods before receiving medical attention. Some respondents noted that some patients spend practically the whole day waiting for medical attention. This time could have been spent on other income-generating activities and therefore has serious implications for the food security of poor households which are engaged in a daily struggle for survival. Consequently, they sink deeper into poverty.

Some focus group respondents complained that they had to walk long distances in search of healthcare institutions with adequate healthcare services. They noted that the local health centre was severely understaffed and patients did not get quality healthcare as they are sometimes attended to by the less qualified nurse aides. In addition, they also complained that they no longer received health education from healthcare professionals as they are too busy attending to patients.

Healthcare professionals' migration has severely compromised the quality of service provided to patients. Better trained and experienced professionals are lost from the public health sector as the economic crisis in the country continues to worsen. The burden of taking care of its users has fallen on the inexperienced junior doctors. While they have performed reasonably well in the prevailing circumstances, service delivery in major hospitals has sometimes ground to a halt when they engage in industrial action to press for better salaries and conditions of service. Private healthcare institutions have benefited from the disgruntlement of public sector healthcare professionals, many of whom they have recruited by offering attractive packages and better working conditions. Unfortunately, the poor are unable to access the health services these institutions offer as they charge exorbitant fees.

The role of traditional healers in contemporary society has diminished with the introduction of modern allopathic medicine. However, in recent years, traditional healers in Zimbabwe have begun to play an increasingly important role owing to the collapse of the formal health-care system. During the focus group discussions, it emerged that the shortage of healthcare professionals in public healthcare institutions has made it necessary for patients to seek alternative forms of healthcare. The poor, who cannot afford the high consultation fees charged in private health institutions, have resorted to visiting traditional and faith healers who charge affordable rates. Long queues can be observed at the residences of traditional and faith healers, which clearly attests to their popularity. Some traditional healers also claim to cure HIV/AIDS, a claim which has brought them considerable business in the face of the growing HIV/AIDS crisis in the country.

6. Conclusion

This chapter has provided an overview of the trends and effects of healthcare professionals' migration from Zimbabwe to 2002. On a national scale, healthcare professionals were moving to the private sector, which offered higher salaries and better working conditions. Some who chose not to migrate from the public sector were engaged in part-time work in private healthcare institutions, with negative effects on their public sector jobs. Nurses showed a higher likelihood of emigrating, suggesting that nurses in Zimbabwe were highly dissatisfied with their working conditions. The major push factors cited were economic, while political and professional factors also ranked high. The shortage of healthcare professionals resulted in increased workloads for those who remained. The migration had the greatest impact on the poor, who rely on the services offered by public healthcare institutions at subsidised rates. The remaining healthcare professionals were failing to cope and patients had to wait a long time before receiving medical attention.

Acknowledgements

I wish to thank the World Health Organisation (WHO) AFRO Region for funding the study through the Division of Health Systems and Services Development. I also gratefully acknowledge the technical assistance of Professor Jane Mutambirwa in conducting the study.

References

BLOOM, G & STANDING, H, 2001. Human resources and health personnel. *Africa Policy Development Review*, 1(1): 7–19.

BUCHAN, J & SOCHALSKI, J, 2004. The migration of nurses: trends and policy responses. *Bulletin of the World Health Organisation*, 82: 587–94.

CHASOKELA, C, 2001. Policy challenges for the nursing profession. *Africa Policy Development Review*, 1(1): 1–6.

COMMISSION FOR AFRICA, 2005. *Our Common Interest: Report of the Commission for Africa.* London: Commission for Africa.

GAIDZANWA, R, 1999. Voting with their feet: migrant Zimbabwean nurses and doctors in the era of structural adjustment. Uppsala: Nordiska Afrikainstitutet.

GRANT, H, 2004. From the Transvaal to the Prairies: the migration of South African physicians to Canada. Prairie Centre of Excellence for Research on Immigration and Integration Working Paper No. WP02-04.

JOHNSON, JM & REGETS, M, 1998. International mobility of scientists and engineers to the US: brain drain or brain circulation? *NSF Issue Brief*: 98–316.

MUTIZWA-MANGIZA, D, 1996. *The medical profession and the state in Zimbabwe: a sociological study of professional autonomy.* PhD Thesis, University of Warwick, Department of Sociology.

REPUBLIC OF ZIMBABWE, 1999. *Commission of review into the health sector, key messages report.* Government of Zimbabwe, Harare.

SARAVIA, NG & MIRANDA, JF, 2004. Plumbing the brain drain. *Bulletin of the World Health Organisation*, 82: 608–15.

WADDA, R, 2000. Brain drain and capacity building in Africa: the Gambian experience. Paper presented at the Joint ECA/IOM/IDRC Regional conference on *Brain Drain and Capacity Building in Africa*, 22–24 February 2000, Addis Ababa, Ethiopia.

WORLD BANK, 1995. *World Development Report: workers in an integrating world.* Washington DC: World Bank.

— 2000. Entering the 21st century. *World Development Report 1999/2000.* New York: Oxford University Press.

4 DISCRIMINATION AND DEVELOPMENT? IMMIGRATION, URBANISATION, AND SUSTAINABLE LIVELIHOODS IN JOHANNESBURG

LOREN B. LANDAU

1. Introduction

Many South African local governments feel they are facing a crisis of human mobility. Although they are formally empowered to create inclusive, secure and prosperous cities, urbanisation and international migration threaten to aggravate the HIV/AIDS crisis and raise the spectre of economic and political fragmentation and urban degeneration (see Beal et al., 2002). Although some expected elevated mobility rates were a temporary reaction to the lifting of apartheid era mobility controls, there is little evidence that movements into, through and out of South Africa's urban centres are slowing (South African Cities Network, 2004: 36; Balbo & Marconi, 2005). These dynamics bring with them both challenges and opportunities. However, if governments fail to develop empirically informed and proactive policy responses, international migration will threaten sustainable and equitable economic growth. Rather than replacing divisions with shared rules of economic and social engagement, discrimination against non-citizens threatens further fragmentation and social marginalisation. This chapter explores how exclusion based on nationality or community of origin affects initiatives 'to achieve a shared vision, amongst all sectors of our society, for the achievement of our goal of improving the quality of life for all citizens' (Gauteng Provincial Government, 2005: 3).

In investigating the potential effects of human mobility on sustainable urban development, this article draws on data collected over a three-year period through a combination of participant observation; secondary source analysis; interviews with migrants, service providers and advocates; and original survey research by the University of the Witwatersrand (Wits) and Tufts University (hereafter the Wits–Tufts survey). The survey was administered in early 2003 in seven central Johannesburg neighbourhoods with high densities of African immigrants: Berea, Bertrams, Bezuidenhout Valley, Fordsburg, Mayfair, Rosettenville and Yeoville. The sample also included South Africans, many of whom are new to the city. In total, 737 respondents were interviewed, 53 per cent South Africans and 47 per cent non-nationals. Fourteen per cent of the total sample came from the Democratic Republic of Congo, 12 per cent from Angola, 9 per cent from Ethiopia, 8 per cent from Somalia, 2 per cent from the Republic of Congo and 1 per cent from Burundi. (For more on the details of the survey, see Jacobsen & Landau 2003.)

Although these data represent some of the most comprehensive information on international and domestic migrants in central Johannesburg, they do not reveal the full extent of migrancy in the city. The sample does not, for example, include Mozambicans or Zimbabweans, two of Johannesburg's most numerous migrant populations. It also excludes wealthier migrants who move out of the inner city areas sampled. Moreover, owing to financial and logistical concerns it was not possible to construct a true sampling frame, so it is impossible to know whether respondents in the sample are typical of residents of those areas. The patterns of exclusion discussed here nevertheless illustrate many of the real and potential dangers of marginalising non-nationals. In addition to the survey discussed above, the author draws on four years of work in Johannesburg (2002–2006) during which he interacted extensively with migrants, service providers, advocates and government officials from throughout South Africa. As many of the findings reported here are drawn from participant observation, they can provide insights into the experiences of refugees in Johannesburg not available to the outside observer. That said, they are partially impressionistic and do not capture the full range of experiences, attitudes and policy deliberations.

2. The Prerequisites for Sustainable Urban Livelihoods[1]

Examining Gauteng Province's Growth and Development Strategy provides an entrée into current government thinking about urban governance and development in Johannesburg's home province. In this document, Gauteng emphasises the need to build institutions that facilitate interactions among, and service provision to, all city residents. That its first objective is the 'provision of social and economic infrastructure and services that will build sustainable communities and contribute to halving poverty' (Gauteng Provincial Government, 2005: 16) reflects their belief in the indivisibility of inclusivity and long-term planning. The means outlined to achieve this objective similarly echo an effort to shape a common destiny from cities characterised by fragmentation and exclusion. These include, inter alia:

• Building relationships and partnerships between all sectors of society
• Ensuring that the benefits of economic growth extend to all our people

- Strengthening cooperative and intergovernmental relations in a manner that reduces competition and reinforces combined efforts towards our national goal of creating a better life for all people
- Strengthening sub-continental and continental partnerships and relationships towards meeting the goals and objectives of the New Partnership for African Development (NEPAD) (Gauteng Provincial Government, 2005: 16–17).

Unfortunately, as elsewhere in the world, 'the desire to construct policies that will advantage cities in global markets [has led] those in power to ignore problems of liveability and sustainability' (Evans, 2002b: 141). This is evident in the language of urban regeneration within the city that often privileges improving property values in ways that make them inaccessible to their current residents (Winkler, 2006). It also appears in documents like Joburg 2030 (Johannesburg Corporate Planning Unit, 2002), a strategic plan that effectively ignores residents' heterogeneous backgrounds, aspirations and limitations. This has translated into concerted efforts to promote formal business and trade that, as President Mbeki (2003) and others argue, provide the poor with no guarantee of improved welfare (see also Sassen, 1997; Douglas, 1998; Castells, 1998: 162). Due to the legacy of apartheid, this means small numbers of relatively wealthy whites, together with a select few from other groups, are improving their economic standing while historically disadvantaged groups risk further marginalisation. Moreover, the models of urban regeneration used by provincial and city leaders often presume a population that wishes to stay permanently in the city. If liveability means creating a city that meets the needs of its residents, then the city must also provide the physical infrastructure and services for a population that does not see the city as its final destination.

Although the need to address issues of both domestic and international migration is evident in the large number of new arrivals to the city every year (see Section 2), local and provincial authorities have typically reacted to the presence of foreign migrants by implicitly denying their presence, excluding them from developmental plans, or allowing discrimination throughout the government bureaucracy and police (Vawda, 1999). This, of course, does nothing to alter migration dynamics that are rooted in regional socio-economic and political configurations (Kok & Collinson, 2006). In the words of one Johannesburg city councillor, 'as much as we might not want them here, we cannot simply wish these people away' (personal communication, 13 July 2005).[2] As these movements continue, discrimination based on nationality or community of origin threatens to create a new socially, economically and politically excluded 'underclass' with the potential to undermine the welfare of all urban residents (cf. Wilson, 2002 [1987]). The following sections outline the ways in which this is already taking place and attempt to chart future implications if current reactions to international migrants continue.

3. Migration and Xenophobia in South Africa

Since 1994, South Africa has entrenched its position as a regional focal point for trade and travel. Although there are few reliable statistics, the 1996 and 2001 censuses show the foreign-born population of the country steadily climbing (Crush & Williams, 2001). Accepting estimates at the high end of the spectrum – 850 000 to one million people, for example – means that about two per cent of the country's residents are foreign born. Although not as numerous as many South Africans suspect, foreigners are a highly visible and politicised group that is transforming many of the country's rural and urban areas.

Figure 4.1: Distribution of Non-Nationals in South Africa (2001)

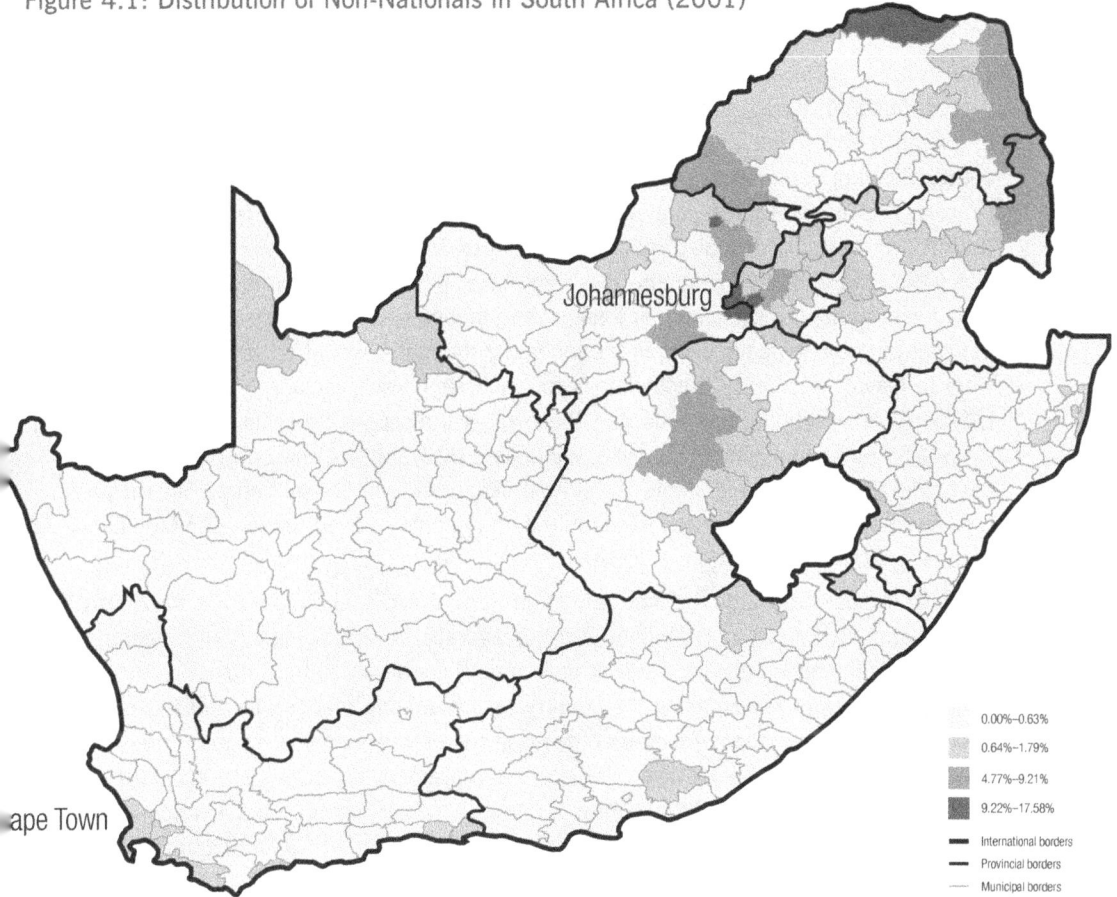

Although immigration and urbanisation affect all of South Africa, they are concentrated around nodes of regional trade and production (see Figure 4.1). As the State of the Cities report (South African Cities Network, 2004) suggests, many cities are effectively shrinking, while semi-rural settlements such as Nelspruit and White River are growing. In Gauteng Province, the primary destination for many international migrants, the foreign-born population has increased from 4.8 per cent to 5.4 per cent of the total, reflecting a jump from 66 205 to 102 326 people according to the 1996 and 2001 census. Statistics South Africa admits, however, that this is a severe undercount. A recent survey (n=1,100) in central Johannesburg, for example, revealed that close to a quarter of inner-city residents were born outside South Africa (Leggett, 2003).

As indicated above, foreigners are not the only ones moving to the cities. Leggett's (2003) study found that 68 per cent of inner-city Johannesburg residents reported moving to their present household in the last five years. Although shifts within the city partially explain this, at least 11 per cent of the city's South African residents counted in the 2001 census had been in Johannesburg for less than five years. This translates into an increase of about 300 000 people between 1996 and 2001, a figure far overshadowing the number of non-nationals. As black South Africans claim space in these previously 'forbidden cities', they are confronting non-nationals also seeking safety or livelihoods in the country's urban centres (see Landau, 2005).

Discrimination based on nationality starkly contrasts with the government's commitments to tolerance and social inclusion. West Africans (particularly Nigerians) are the archetypical antagonists, but South Africans include almost all poor blacks from elsewhere among the undesirables. A national 1998 survey conducted by the Southern African Migration Programme (SAMP), for example, revealed that 87 per cent of South Africans believed that the country was letting in too many foreigners. This figure may have declined somewhat as people have grown accustomed to living among foreigners, although the Wits–Tufts study found that 64.8 per cent of South Africans living in the inner city thought it would be good if most foreigners were to leave the country. Justifications for such sentiments include perceived connections between a non-national presence and the country's most visible social pathologies: crime, HIV/AIDS and unemployment (Crush & Williams, 2003). In Johannesburg, among the 85 per cent of South African respondents in a Wits–Tufts survey who thought crime had increased in recent years, almost three-quarters identified immigrants as a primary reason (see Landau & Jacobsen, 2004; also Leggett, 2003).

These exclusionary attitudes not only stem from street-level tensions but have also been shaped and legitimised by politicians and bureaucrats. In addressing a 1997 meeting about migration in the region, former Minister of Home Affairs Mangosuthu Buthelezi (1994–2004) outlined a series of crises facing the country before arguing that 'South Africa is faced with another threat, and that is the SADC ideology of free movement of people, free trade and freedom to choose where you live or work. Free movement of persons spells disaster for our country' (Buthelezi, 1997). More subtly, Johannesburg's Mayor reflected a widely held sentiment in his 'State of the City 2004' speech when reporting that 'while migrancy contributes to the rich tapestry of the cosmopolitan city, it also places a severe strain on employment levels, housing, and public services.' The availability of data limits the ability to measure the costs of international migration, although they are most likely dwarfed by those associated with movements within South Africa and other urban concerns.

4. Dividing the Urban Poor

The discriminatory sentiments outlined above, coupled with ignorance about migrants' rights, are promoting fragmentation in Johannesburg's inner city. This is evident in a range of areas critical to sustainable urban livelihoods, including access to identity documents, social services, markets and financial services, and interactions with the police and other regulatory bodies. The consequences – discussed in detail below – include economic losses, threats to security and health, and a less liveable city. Rather than ensuring that all city residents participate in planning processes and have access to markets, accommodation and critical social services, discriminatory practices are creating an underclass comprised of non-citizens from throughout the continent and domestic migrants who may be similarly excluded. 'For the most part, refugees and migrants are a silent group, never engaging with the authorities or drawing attention to themselves for fear of incurring official sanction or social wrath' (Beal et al., 2002: 125).

4.1   Documentation

Official identity papers cannot prevent discrimination or ensure social inclusion, but they are valuable for finding work, accessing social services and preventing arbitrary arrest, detention and deportation. Conversely, activities as innocuous as walking in the street or petty trading without the requisite documents are illegal in the state's eyes. Two key factors work against non-nationals acquiring the documents needed to help regularise their stay in South Africa. The first is job seekers' inability to apply for employment rights in the country. Instead, those coming to the country without an employment offer or study permit can only claim short-term tourist or study visas. Alternatively, they enter through irregular border crossings or apply for asylum. Indeed, tens of thousands of people, many from peaceful countries, have used the latter strategy to at least partially legalise their stay. The SADC Facilitation of Movement protocol may eventually ease entry for foreign nationals; although these benefits will only affect the small number who have passports.

The second obstacle to acquiring documentation is the Department of Home Affairs, the government branch responsible for registering residents and issuing documents to both citizens and non-nationals. One of the most corrupt departments during the apartheid period, administrative incompetence and irregularities flourished under Minister Buthelezi.[3] To overturn years of entrenched corruption and improve services, the new Minister launched a 'turnaround strategy.' There has, however, been little noticeable change in the levels of petty corruption that affect non-nationals. Even would-be refugees often must pay unofficial 'fees' simply to file an asylum claim (Segale, 2004). For many, the first of these payments goes to private security guards hired to keep order and regulate access to the Department of Home Affairs facilities. Inside the offices, applicants have had to pay 'translators' (even when they speak English) or offer fees to file their asylum claim, a process that is meant to be free. Those unable to cover the costs typically drop their claims and remain in the country without documents. Apart from their illegality and the threats to human dignity, these practices have generated economies within the Department of Home Affairs involving 'corruption strategists' and front-line staff who jockey for the most profitable posts.[4]

Those lucky enough to lodge an asylum claim and be given refugee status face further difficulties in acquiring suitable identity documents. The physical form of asylum seekers' documentation itself contributes to delays and irregular practices. Asylum-seekers, for instance, are issued with a single piece of paper (the 'Section 22' permit), often with handwritten amendments and conditions. Few employers or government agents, including the police and many healthcare workers, recognise these documents as legitimate. Moreover, after a few months in a coat or trouser pocket, the document is often worn, illegible, or simply lost. In such cases, asylum-seekers must re-enter the queues and seek a replacement. The document can also be easily destroyed, as it regularly is by corrupt police (Palmary et al., 2003: 113). Even those granted refugee status continue to face difficulties. A recent national study found that only 11 per cent of those granted asylum have been issued a 'refugee identity document' (Belvedere, 2003: 6). Those granted permanent residence status have also been subject to delays of months or years. Over the last two years there have been improvements – most newly recognised refugees now receive their documents within a month – but problems persist. The country is now slowly introducing a 'smart card' that should immediately be recognised by employers and service providers. At the time of writing, however, technical delays were preventing the widespread implementation of this system and it is unclear whether it will ever provide the intended protection.

4.2   Markets and financial services

Ready access to formal and informal markets for exchanging goods and services is critical to successful urban economies. Unfortunately, non-nationals are often systematically excluded from employment and income-generating opportunities through both formal and informal mechanisms. Many foreign citizens without the right to work – but with the skills and a willingness to do so – accept positions where they are paid below the minimum wage or work in inhumane conditions. Even those with employment rights report being turned away by employers who do not recognise their papers or their professional qualifications. Without money to have their qualifications recognised by the South African Qualifications Authority (SAQA), they have little choice but to seek other ways to generate income.

Patterns of exclusion are also evident in private sector industries where poor foreigners are typically unable to access even the most rudimentary banking services. Although current banking legislation technically prevents anyone other than permanent residents and citizens from opening bank accounts, this policy may be waived on a discretionary level (see Jacobsen & Bailey, 2004). Under pressure from lobbying groups, some banks have now begun extending services to refugees, but are still unwilling to open accounts for other African immigrants who do not have the requisite 13-digit identity number or foreign passport. Elsewhere in the world, banks have recognised the profits to be made from providing foreigners access to financial services; not only because they typically save at a higher rate than more secure local populations, but also because they frequently transfer money to and from other countries. At present, only wire transfer services and informal moneychangers are collecting the considerable profits from such transactions.

4.3.   Social services

A cocktail of inadequate documentation, ignorance and outright discrimination prevents many non-nationals who are legally in South Africa from accessing critical social services. Those in the country without documents face even greater obstacles. Section 5(1) of the South African Schools Act 84 of 1996, for example, declares that 'a public school must admit learners and serve their educational requirements without unfairly discriminating in any way.' Moreover, Article 27(g) of the Refugees Act (130 of 1998) states that: 'Refugees as well as refugee children are entitled to the same basic health services and basic primary education which the inhabitants of the republic receive from time to time' (cited in Stone & Winterstein, 2003). Despite these provisions, asylum seekers and refugees – to say nothing of other foreigners – face significant obstacles in accessing the educational services to which they are entitled. The de facto requirement that migrants pay school fees is the most obvious barrier to education and contradicts a prohibition on refusing admission to public schools on the basis of parents' inability to pay (DoE, 1988). Costs for transport, books and uniforms further exclude the often semi-destitute non-nationals who find their way to South Africa's cities. A 2000 study on the Somali refugee community in Johannesburg, for example, found that 70 per cent of Somali refugee children of school-going age were not in school (Peberdy & Majodina, 2000). Although few data exist on other groups, the Somalis are not unique and those without refugee papers face even greater problems.

A similar pattern of exclusion is reflected in access to health services. Section 27(1) of the Constitution states that everyone has the right to healthcare services, including reproductive healthcare. This clause is followed by Section 27(2) binding the state to take reasonable steps to realise these rights. Under law, refugees are entitled to have access to the same basic healthcare as South African citizens, although other migrants are required to pay additional fees.[5] Section 27(3) of the South African Constitution clearly states, however, that no one – regardless of nationality, documentation, or residency status – may be refused emergency medical treatment.

The inability or unwillingness of many hospital staff members to distinguish between different classes of migrants (coupled with xenophobia) often means that migrants, including refugees, are denied access to basic and emergency health services or are charged inappropriate fees. Non-nationals may not only be refused services outright: foreigners report being made to wait longer than South Africans before being seen and being subjected to other forms of discrimination. While waiting, one refugee overheard nurses talking about 'foreigners taking government money and having too many babies', and another reports a hospital staff member describing the hospital as 'infested' with foreigners. There are also accounts indicating that non-nationals are often denied full courses of prescribed medicines (see Nkosi, 2004; Pursell, 2005).

Failure to overcome these obstacles can have dire consequences. A recent national study of refugees and asylum-seekers found that 17 per cent of refugees and asylum seekers had been denied emergency medical care, often because of improper documentation or ignorance on the part of the admitting nurses (Belvedere, 2003). If one could calculate this as a percentage of those seeking such care, the figure would be much higher. In one particularly dramatic incident reported at a meeting of the Johannesburg Forced Migration Working Group, a pregnant Somali woman was refused service on the grounds that (a) delivery, unless problematic, did not constitute an emergency and (b) she could not pay the additional fee levied on foreigners (which as a refugee she was not required to pay). As a result, she ultimately delivered the child on the pavement outside the hospital, only to have it die a few weeks later. This is an extreme example, but speaks to broader patterns of exclusion from effective protection. Given their tenuous status in the country, often aggravated by a lack of proper identification and their relative ignorance of their rights, many foreigners simply accept these violations. Indeed, only 1 per cent of refugees who were refused health services lodged a complaint and 24 per cent report doing nothing, largely because they did not know what to do (Belvedere, 2003).

4.4   Investigations, detention and arrests

Throughout the country, lack of accountability, xenophobia, and immigrant vulnerability are resources that police exploit to supplement their income. In doing so, they can also address what many erroneously see as the root of crime in South Africa. Non-South Africans living or working in Johannesburg, for example, consequently report having been stopped by the police far more frequently than South Africans (71 per cent compared with 47 per cent in the Wit–Tufts University survey), despite having generally lived in the city for a shorter period. Although legally mandated to respect non-nationals' rights, police often refuse to recognise work permits or refugee identity cards. Some respondents even report having their identity papers confiscated or destroyed in order justify an arrest. Furthermore, there are numerous assertions (documented and undocumented) that police elicit bribes from apprehended persons in exchange for freedom (see Palmary et al., 2003: 113).

Beyond xenophobia, there are structural reasons why the police often target foreigners. Denied access to almost all formal banking services, poor immigrants must either stash cash in their homes or carry it on their bodies (Jacobsen & Bailey, 2004). Their tenuous legal status, (often) poor documentation, and tendency to trade on the streets (hawking or informal business) tempt some police officers to extract money from them as if, in the words of one officer, they were 'mobile ATMs.' As an Eritrean living in South Africa said, 'as foreign students we are not required to pay taxes to the government. But when we walk down these streets, we pay.' A study conducted in late 2000 indicates that the frustrations outlined above reflect systematic patterns of bias where asylum-seekers are arrested and detained for a variety of reasons: failure to carry identity documents, a particular physical appearance, the inability to speak any of the main national languages, or simply for fitting an undocumented migrant 'profile' (Algotsson, 2000). In practice, the burden of proof is on non-nationals to establish their legal status in the country or buy their way into freedom.

There are additional deviations from the law aimed at regulating or extracting resources from non-nationals. The 2002 Immigration Act, for example, effectively authorises the Department of Home Affairs to conduct searches, and make arrests and deportations outside of constitutional or other legal limitations.[6] Without muscle of their own, immigration officers rely on the South African Police Services (SAPS) and, occasionally, the National Defence Force (SANDF), to make arrests. More importantly, the SAPS has exploited this law to legalise what would otherwise be illegal raids on buildings inhabited by suspected criminals and, potentially, illegal immigrants. Often at night and away from supervision, police officers force entry, demand identity documents, and arrest both non-nationals and South Africans without respect for normal legal provisions. As unpalatable as these operations may seem, Yakoob Makda, the Director of Johannesburg's 'Region Eight' (i.e., the inner city) proudly (and without irony) reported their anti-crime-cum-anti-immigrant achievements to a public meeting convened to help combat social exclusion.[7] These efforts are, moreover, not limited to Johannesburg's city centre. Soon after South Africa's first democratic election, Alexandra township, north of the city centre, organised a campaign entitled 'Operation Buyelekhaya' (Operation Go Back Home) in an effort to rid the township of all foreigners (Palmary et al., 2003: 112). Nor are these efforts limited to Johannesburg. In 2002, Du Noon township outside Cape Town also passed a resolution expelling all foreigners and prohibiting them from returning (Southwell, 2002; Palmary et al., 2003: 112).

5. Implications for Sustainable Urban Livelihoods

The forms of exclusion outlined above are not only disturbing but also have the power to negatively affect Johannesburg's development trajectory. If we accept – as the city government says it does – that common, accountable institutions and fluid interactions among all groups are prerequisites for equitable and sustained growth, then any source of social fragmentation becomes a threat. In this regard, difficulty accessing housing, markets and financial and social services, together with continual targeting by criminals and the police, are immediately problematic. This section outlines a number of current and potential consequences of marginalising non-nationals and other migrants.

Economic exclusion: South Africa has a substantial skills gap that the government hopes to fill by spending millions of rands on skills training (DoL, 2005). However, few employers (including the government) capitalise on the economic potential of those already in their cities or who are likely to come in the near future, including international migrants. While South Africa faces an acute nursing shortage, for example, there are certified refugee nurses in South Africa who cannot find work. Instead of positively exploiting the presence of foreigners who are often well-educated and experienced, current policy criminalises them and drives processes of informalisation and illegality. In its efforts to protect citizens' rights and livelihoods, immigration policy has in fact promoted the illegal hiring of non-nationals in ways that continue to undermine the unions and depress the wages paid to all workers. Moreover, by encouraging non-nationals (and those who hire them) to work in the informal sector or shadow economy, the government deprives itself of an important source of revenue and helps create networks of corruption and illegality that will be difficult to eradicate.

Whatever the reasons, migrants' inability to access secure banking has manifold consequences that extend beyond those excluded from service. Perhaps most obviously, lack of access to financial services (particularly credit) discourages migrants from investing in the cities in which they live (see Leggett, 2003; Jacobsen & Bailey, 2004; Simone, 2004: 10). Such an obstacle can only aggravate infrastructural decay, limit job creation and prevent a kind of 'rooting' through investment that can help stabilise communities and promote long-term planning. Given the migrants' general entrepreneurialism, their exclusion from business will continue to have disproportionate effects.[8] Preventing migrants and those they hire from moving into the formal economy also denies the government a source of direct revenues (from taxes and licensing fees) and means that much of the business that takes place is, to a greater or lesser degree, illegal. This, in turn, weakens the law's (and the state's) legitimacy and regulatory power.

Access to social services: Education and healthcare are central to any population's economic and physical health (Annan, 1999: 4). In transforming urban settings, education serves a dual role. The first is to provide children and young people with the technical and analytical training they need to compete in and contribute to a specialised, skills-based economy. Obstacles to any group acquiring those skills will, consequently, project existing inequalities into future generations and limit the country's ability to adapt to new economic opportunities. Education serves a second, but no less critical, role: forging communities from strangers. Through the sustained interactions within the classroom, diverse groups learn common sets of rules, how to exercise civil rights and mutual respect. Thus, exclusion from education can create a subset of the population without the knowledge or skills to interact productively within the city.

While the inability to access education may have delayed effects, denying migrants access to health services has both immediate and long-term consequences. In the short term, it puts them at physical risk and endangers the welfare of those who depend on them. Where the denial of services contravenes published legislation, it also exposes public institutions to potentially costly legal action. Furthermore, denying basic health services raises the spectre of public health crises. While medical staff may discriminate between citizens and non-nationals, infectious agents are far less discerning. As long as migrants and South Africans continue to share urban space – often living in close proximity – those unable to access treatment become a danger to all those around them. A work force already weakened by the scourge of HIV/AIDS is in no position to face such an additional threat.

Crime and insecurity: Although many South Africans support the police's strategy of targeting foreigners on the assumption that they are behind most of the country's criminal activity, such actions are largely ineffective in establishing order or security. For one, there is no evidence that foreigners are disproportionately prone to criminal activity (Harris, 2001), and being obsessed with them distracts police from where they are needed (Palmary, 2002). Moreover, the general ineffectiveness of such policing strategies is leading citizens to accept criminal activity as part of their social landscape. Many South Africans interviewed as part of the Wits–Tufts study did not classify mugging as crime, for example, unless it involved the use of a firearm. In this context, people are seeking alternative means to manage crime. In some cases, this includes turning to groups like Mapogo a Mathamaga, a national investigation and 'goods recovery' company that works largely outside the law, but regularly draws on police information and backup (personal communication, Cecil van Schalkwyk, Director of Midrand office of Mapogo a Mathamaga, 25 July 2003). These irregular linkages between the police and private security 'de-legalise' the criminal justice system, robbing the state of one of its most basic functions and placing all city-dwellers at risk.

The arrest of people – whether South African or foreign – trading on the street or conducting other small business also affects the livelihoods of those arrested and their dependants. Cities must promote entry into trading markets rather than close this avenue to those who have few other options – a category of people well represented in inner city Johannesburg. Regularly targeting migrants who lack the documentation or capital to find work in the formal sector – despite many having skills to make contributions in this area – for by-law infractions only drives trade further underground and increases the likelihood that these migrants will turn to irregular, illegal or dangerous economic activities.

Community: Overcoming racialised fragmentation and avoiding new forms of exclusion means bringing together people from all sectors of the urban environment in ways that promote investment in a shared future. This was never going to be an easy task in South Africa's heterogeneous cities. Marginalising significant migrant communities, however, only creates an additional obstacle to achieving this objective. This is already visible in migrants' widespread sense of permanent dislocation, fostered by the violence, abuse and discrimination they experience in new residential communities. Rather than striving to integrate, foreigners instead cling to their outsider status, make conscious efforts to avoid close personal relationships with South Africans, and spend their time in South Africa planning their move elsewhere (Mang'ana, 2004; Araia, 2005; Amisi & Ballard, 2005). Indeed, more than three-quarters of the respondents in the Wits–Tufts survey (76 per cent) felt it important for migrants to retain their distinct character during their stay in the country and only 40 per cent of the non-South African respondents predicted they would be in South Africa in two years' time. Critically, journeys home or onwards often remain all but elusive for reasons of money, safety or social status. This leaves almost two-thirds of Johannesburg's non-national population effectively marooned in the city, but not wishing to take root there or invest in it. While it is impossible to force people to identify themselves with the communities in which they live, many undoubtedly would do so if the option were available.

This sense of isolation and transience is problematic, as it limits immigrants' investment in the cities in which they live. People preparing for onward journeys will not dedicate themselves to acquiring fixed assets and may maximise immediate profits at the expense of long-term planning. Such exclusion also limits cities' ability to capitalise on immigrants' valuable transnational connections. While Hunter & Skinner (2003) found that the immigrants' exotic products boosted overall sales in at least one Durban marketplace, the tendency to limit such sales represents lost opportunities. Similarly, studies have found that African tourists spend more in South Africa than their European and North American counterparts (Rogerson, undated). Nelspruit, for one, is prospering as a shopping centre for Mozambicans. Discouraging citizens from neighbouring countries from visiting may, consequently, result in considerable losses to the South African economy. Although domestic migrants may bring fewer skills and resources, their inclusion may similarly boost trade, investment and a sense of community.

Accountability and planning: Gauteng Province and the City of Johannesburg recognise that sustainable urban livelihoods can only be achieved when supported by accountable institutions that promote a set of overlapping goals among city residents. Discrimination based on national or community origins, like other arbitrary forms of exclusion, undermines this objective in two primary ways. First, for the reasons discussed above, people who do not feel welcome in South Africa's urban society are less likely to respect the rules and institutions dedicated to governing it. Migrants may attempt to dodge tax regulations, avoid census-takers, or actively subvert regulatory agencies they feel are more likely to prey on them than promote their interests. When people are not given the right to work, or the documents they need to secure housing, the result may be an increase in antisocial behaviour and criminal activity such as hijacking. Those who feel excluded are also unlikely to take part in participatory planning exercises such as the integrated development plan (IDP). Such self-exclusion makes government policies all the less likely to address city residents' priorities and needs and may, in time, diminish public institutions' efficacy and legitimacy (see Winkler, 2006).

Anti-foreigner sentiments and scapegoating have the second, more insidious, effect of making it more difficult to realise accountable and responsive public institutions. In the words of one immigrant, 'rumours … are continuously spread by everyone that foreigners are responsible for whatever is wrong. It is like, "Thank you, foreigners, that you are here, now we can blame you for everything." South Africans do not look at their own – they just ignore their own problems and pretend that foreigners cause all their problems' (in Beal et al., 2002: 124). Although such attitudes are not universal, the presence of a convenient scapegoat distracts South Africans from their public institutions' shortcomings and failed promises. The willingness to accept that foreigners are responsible for South African children not finding places in school, and for continued insecurity and unemployment, only distracts South Africans from the fundamental structural and institutional causes. Removing foreigners from South Africa's cities will not solve these acute social problems but so long as such expulsion remains a preferred solution, real progress is unlikely to be made.

6. Conclusions: Towards Sustainable Cities in an Era of Migration

Policy-makers and citizens in Gauteng and Johannesburg share a fundamental interest in overcoming fragmentation in pursuit of equity, accountability, wealth and security. Recognising that people born outside of South Africa are a permanent feature of Johannesburg means that initiatives towards these ends must include efforts to counter exclusion based on nationality. Failing to do so may condemn the city to a future of ghettos rather than ethnic enclaves (see Jurgens et al., 2002), social fragmentation and economic polarisation rather than creative tensions and dynamism, protection rackets and hijackings rather than investment and an expanding tax base. It will also threaten efforts to achieve NEPAD's goal of fostering political, social and economic integration in the region. There is more than one model of economic growth, but if growth and development are to be sustainable and meet standards of equity and human rights, international migrants cannot be ignored.

While one might ethically defend differentiating between foreigners and citizens within policy,[9] such distinctions are less viable in the context of a constitutional commitment to protecting the lives of all South African residents and upholding their rights. Not only is there a logical inconsistency in arguing that the government should improve the lives of city residents while implicitly promoting exclusion based on nationality; more pragmatically, there will be negative by-products if significant segments of a population are prevented from accessing safe accommodation, jobs and social services. These include poverty, social tensions, corruption, a higher crime rate and a greater risk of communicable disease – problems that affect all residents.

While citizenship and asylum laws must remain national, there is a heightened need for subnational actors to assert their influence on the country's immigration and asylum regime. Cities and provinces need to recognise that they can, and indeed must, actively advocate for an immigration regime that helps legalise – rather than marginalise – their residents. South Africa need not open its borders to all who wish to come, but its success depends on developing pragmatic, affordable and effective responses to those who find their way into the country and into its cities. If Gauteng Province wishes to foster intergovernmental collaboration, a dialogue among national, provincial and local government around migration policy could be a fruitful avenue.

Involving local government in these discussions is critical for a number of reasons. Not only is it charged with being developmental, but it is also empowered to make decisions that affect its communities (Gotz, 2004). Elsewhere in the world, local governments have begun issuing their own forms of documentation to all residents. Although this may not be viable in the South African context, local and provincial government could nevertheless develop programmes to foster inclusion by countering ignorance among police, civil servants, landlords and employers. This could include facilitating access to primary care clinics, life-saving medical care and legal services without regard to nationality or immigration status. Countering exclusion based on individuals' community of origin will not ensure secure and sustainable livelihoods, accountable institutions and unified communities. It can, however, make achieving these objectives a possibility.

References

ADEPOJU, A, 2003. Continuity and changing configurations of migration to and from the Republic of South Africa. *International Migration*, 41(1): 3-28.

ALGOTSSON, E, 2000. Lindela: at the crossroads for detention and repatriation. Johannesburg: South African Human Rights Commission.

AMISI, B & BALLARD, R, 2005. In the absence of citizenship: Congolese refugee struggle and organisation in South Africa. Forced Migration Working Paper No. 16 (April 2005).

ANNAN, KA, 1999, Foreword. In *UNICEF–Education: the state of the world's children*. New York: UNICEF.

ARAIA, TK, 2005. *Routes, motivations, and duration: explaining Eritrean forced migrants' journeys to Johannesburg*. MA thesis, University of the Witwatersrand.

BALBO, M & MARCONI, G, 2005. Governing international migration in the city of the south. Global Migration Perspectives No. 38. Geneva: Global Commission for International Migration.

BEAL, J, CRANKSHAW, O & PARNELL, S, 2002. *Uniting a divided city: governance and social exclusion in Johannesburg*. London: Earthscan.

BELVEDERE, F, 2003. National refugee baseline survey: final report. Johannesburg: Community Agency for Social Enquiry (CASE), Japan International Cooperation, and United Nations High Commissioner for Refugees.

BUTHELEZI, MG, 1997. Keynote address at the Southern African Migration Programme's conference: *After amnesty: The future of foreign migrants in South Africa*, 20 June 1997.

CARENS, J, 1992. Refugees and the limits of obligation, *Public Affairs Quarterly*, 6(1): 31-44.

CASTELLS, M, 1998. *The informational city: information, technology, economic restructuring and the urban–regional process*. Oxford: Blackwell.

CHESANG, G, 2005. *The law does not matter: corruption and the politics of refugee protection in post-1994 South Africa.* Paper presented to the 9th Conference of the International Association of Forced Migration, 9–11 January 2005, São Paolo, Brazil.

CRUSH, J & WILLIAMS, V, 2001. *Making up the numbers: measuring 'illegal immigration' to South Africa*, Migration Policy Brief No. 3. Cape Town: Southern Africa Migration Project.

— 2003. *Criminal tendencies: immigrants and illegality in South Africa*. Migration Policy Brief No. 10, Cape Town: Southern African Migration Project.

DAVIS, M, 1998. *Ecology of fear: Los Angeles and the imagination of disaster*. New York: Henry Holt and Co.

DEPARTMENT OF EDUCATION (DoE), 1998. Admission policy for ordinary public schools (October 1998). Pretoria: DoE.

DEPARTMENT OF HOME AFFAIRS (DoHA), 2005. Statement opening the National Counter-Corruption Workshop of the Department of Home Affairs, 12 October.

DEPARTMENT OF LABOUR (DoL), 2005. National skills development strategy 1 April 2005–31 March 2010. Pretoria: DoL.

DOUGLASS, M, 1998. World city formation on the Asia Pacific rim: poverty, 'everyday' forms of civil society, and environmental management. In Douglass, M & Friedmann, J (eds), *Cities for citizens: planning and the rise of civil society in a global age*. New York: John Wiley & Sons, pp. 107-38.

EVANS, P, 2002a. Introduction: looking for agents of urban change in a globalised political economy. In Evans, P (ed.), *Liveable cities? urban struggles for livelihood and sustainability*. Berkeley: University of California Press, pp. 222-47.

— 2002b. Political strategies for more liveable cities: lessons from six cases of development and political transition. In Evans, P (ed.), *Liveable cities? urban struggles for livelihood and sustainability*. Berkeley: University of California Press.

GAUTENG PROVINCIAL GOVERNMENT, 2005. *A growth and development strategy (GDS) for the Gauteng Province.*

GIBNEY, MJ, 1999. Liberal democratic states and responsibilities to refugees, *American Political Science Review*, 93(1): 169-81.

GOTZ, G, 2004. The role of local government towards forced migrants. In Landau, LB (ed.), *Forced migrants in the new Johannesburg: towards a local government response*. Johannesburg: Forced Migration Studies Programme.

HARRIS, B, 2001. *A foreign experience: violence, crime, and xenophobia during South Africa's transition*. Johannesburg: Centre for the Study of Violence and Reconciliation.

HUNTER, N & SKINNER, C, 2003. Foreigners working on the streets of Durban: local government policy challenges. *Urban Forum*, 14(4): 301-19.

KOK, P & COLLINSON, M, 2006. Migration and urbanisation in South Africa. Report No. 03-04-02 (2006). Pretoria: Statistics South Africa.

JACOBSEN, K & LANDAU, LB, 2003. The 'dual imperative' in refugee research: some methodological and ethical considerations in social science research on forced migration. *Disasters*, 27(3): 95–116.

JACOBSEN, K & BAILEY, S, 2004. Micro-credit and banking for refugees in Johannesburg. In Landau, LB (ed.), *Forced migrants in the new Johannesburg: towards a local government response.* Johannesburg: Forced Migration Studies Programme, pp. 99-102.

JOHANNESBURG CORPORATE PLANNING UNIT, 2002. *Joburg 2030.* Johannesburg: City of Johannesburg.

JURGENS, U, GNAD, M & BAHR, J, 2003. New forms of class and racial segregation: ghettos or ethnic enclaves? In Tomlinson, R, Beauregard, RA, Bremner, L & Mangcu, X (eds), *Emerging Johannesburg: perspectives on the postapartheid city.* New York: Routledge, pp. 56-70.

LANDAU, LB, 2005. Urbanisation, nativism and the rule of law in South Africa's 'forbidden' cities. *Third World Quarterly,* 26(7): 1115–34.

LANDAU, LB & JACOBSEN, K, 2004. Refugees in the new Johannesburg. *Forced Migration Review,* 19: 44–6.

LEGGETT, T, 2003. Rainbow tenement: crime and policing in inner Johannesburg. Pretoria: Institute for Security Studies.

LOGAN, J & MOLOTCH, J, 1987. *Urban fortunes: the political economy of place.* Berkeley: University of California Press.

LOGAN, J, WHALEY, RB & COWDER, K, 1998. The character and consequences of growth regimes: an assessment of twenty years of research. *Urban Affairs Review,* 32: 603–30.

MANG'ANA, JM, 2004. *The effects of migration on human rights consciousness among Congolese refugees in Johannesburg.* MA thesis, University of the Witwatersrand.

MBEKI, T, 2003. The second economy, what it is and what is needed to meet the growth and development challenges it presents. Address to the National Council of Provinces, 11 November 2003.

NKOSI, NG, 2004. *Influences of xenophobia on accessing health care for refugees and asylum seekers in Johannesburg.* MA thesis, University of the Witwatersrand.

PALMARY, I, 2002. *Refugees, safety and xenophobia in South African cities: the role of local government.* Johannesburg: Centre for the Study of Violence and Reconciliation.

PALMARY, I, RAUCH, J & SIMPSON, G, 2003. Violent crime in Johannesburg. In Tomlinson, R, Beauregard, RA, Bremner, L & Mangcu, X (eds), *Emerging Johannesburg: perspectives on the postapartheid city.* New York: Routledge, pp. 101-22.

PEBERDY, S & MAJODINA, Z, 2000. Just a roof over my head? Housing and the Somali refugee community in Johannesburg. *Urban Forum,* 11(2): 273–88.

PURSELL, R, 2005. *Access to health care among Somali forced migrants in Johannesburg.* MA thesis, University of the Witwatersrand.

REPUBLIC OF SOUTH AFRICA (RSA), 1998. Refugees' Act. Office of the President. Government Gazette, 402(19544).

ROGERSON, C, n.d. *The rise of African tourism to South Africa.* SAMP Policy Brief No. 13, Cape Town.

SASSEN, S, 1997. Cities in the global economy. *International Journal of Urban Sciences,* 1: 11–31.

SEGALE, T, 2004. Forced migrants and social exclusion in Johannesburg. In Landau, LB (ed.), *Forced migrants in the new Johannesburg: towards a local government response.* Johannesburg: Forced Migration Studies Programme.

SIMONE, A, 2004. *For the city yet to come: changing African life in four cities.* Durham: Duke University Press.

SOUTH AFRICAN CITIES NETWORK, 2004. *State of the cities report.* Johannesburg: South African Cities Network.

SOUTHWELL, V, 2002. Protecting human rights: recent cases – Du Noon expulsion of foreign nationals. Johannesburg: South African Human Rights Commission.

STATISTICS SOUTH AFRICA (STATSSA), 2001. Census 2001.

STONE, L & WINTERSTEIN, S, 2003. *A right or a privilege? Access to basic education for refugee and asylum seeker children in South Africa.* Pretoria: National Consortium of Refugee Affairs.

THE PRESIDENCY, REPUBLIC OF SOUTH AFRICA, 2002. Immigration Act, 2002. *Government Gazette,* Vol. 443 (31 May 2002). No. 13.

VAWDA, S, 1999. Foreign migrants, governance and local development strategies: a case study of international African migrants in Durban. Paper presented at the 4th International Congress of Ales Hrdlicka World Anthropology at the Turn of the Centuries 31 August–4 September, Prague.

WILSON, WJ, 2002 [1987]. The truly disadvantaged: the inner city, the underclass, and public policy. In Bridge, G & Watson, S, *The Blackwell City Reader.* Oxford: Blackwell.

WINKLER, TA, 2006. *Kwere Kwere journeys into strangeness: reimagining inner-city regeneration in Hillbrow, Johannesburg.* PhD Thesis, University of British Columbia, Vancouver.

Notes

1   The author's definition of sustainable livelihoods is drawn from Logan & Molotch, 1987; Logan et al., 1997; Davis, 1998; and Evans, 2002a.

2   Johannesburg's metropolitan government has slowly begun to consider migrants as a vulnerable group, although it is unclear whether it is making efforts to include them in local decision-making priorities.

3   When opening the National Counter-Corruption Workshop of the Department of Home Affairs in 2005, a representative for the Minister openly admitted, 'On the corruption cards, our Department scores very high …' (DoHA, 2005). See also Adepoju (2003) for a discussion of the corruption surrounding the pass law system managed by the DoHA.

4   A senior internal investigator within the DoHA described these networks to the author in great detail during an informal meeting on 30 June 2005. His wish to remain anonymous has been respected. See also Chesang, 2005.

5   Section 27 (g) of the Refugees Act 130 of 1998 (see also s 27 (b)) (RSA, 1998). For more on refugee access to health care, see Pursell, 2005.

6   See Section 3 (Powers of Department) in the Immigration Act (The Presidency, RSA, 2002).

7   The report was delivered at a poverty alleviation workshop organised by the Johannesburg Development Agency (JDA), 'Poverty and Exclusion in the Inner City', Johannesburg, 14 May 2003.

8   Despite numerous obstacles, the Wits–Tufts survey found international migrants still create jobs faster than South Africans. Only 20 per cent of South Africans reported having paid someone to do work for them in the past year, compared to 34 per cent of international migrants. Even more significantly, 67 per cent of the people hired by the migrants were South Africans. See also Hunter & Skinner (2003).

9   For more on the ethics of asylum and immigration, see Carens, 1992, and Gibney, 1999.

5 LODGING AS A MIGRANT ECONOMIC STRATEGY IN URBAN ZIMBABWE

MIRIAM GRANT

1. Introduction

Sub-Saharan Africa has the highest urbanisation rates in the world, with major acceleration occurring during the last two decades. In 1982, the overall urban population was a mere 21,8 per cent, but this increased rapidly to 36 per cent by 2003, and is expected to reach 50 per cent by 2030 (Kessides, 2005; UN-HABITAT, 2004–2005). Between 1990 and 2003, sub-Saharan Africa's urban growth rate of 4,6 per cent was almost double the population growth rate of 2,5 per cent (Kessides, 2005, based on World Development Indicators, 2005). Migration plays a central role in this rapid urbanisation, with circular migration dominant in most African countries (Grant et al., 2007).

When migrants arrive in urban areas, they have few affordable shelter choices. This situation is worsened by the phenomenal growth of African urban slums. From 1990 to 2001, the population of these slums increased by approximately 65 million people, with an average annual growth rate of 4,49 per cent. By 2001, almost three in every four urban dwellers (72 per cent), or a total of 166,2 million people, were living in slums (UN-HABITAT, 2004–2005).

In sub-Saharan Africa, the 1990s was thus a pivotal period of urban transformation. National and local governments, whose plans and policies were geared towards an ideal of home ownership even for the urban poor, were overwhelmed by sheer numbers – urban growth driven by migration streams and natural increase rates – which defied fiscal abilities to meet even minimal basic human needs. Most migrants who entered urban areas had to rely on extended family members, friends and their own resourcefulness to secure shelter – with affordability and availability often limited to some type of rental accommodation. Whether in squatter settlements, peri-urban abandoned farms, or established homes in every type of density, rental shelter emerged as the dominant supplier in African cities, mirroring the situation in most cities of the developing world.

Across the globe, the urban poor are severely constrained by lack of affordable shelter options, inflexible financial institutions, local governments that cannot keep pace with the housing and service needs of burgeoning cities, and national housing policies that largely ignore the prevalence and significance of rental shelter. In many cities in developing countries, two-thirds or more of the housing stock is rental (Malpezzi, 1990). The types of rental shelter vary widely by location, culture and built form. In Latin American cities, many families rent rooms in consolidated self-help settlements (Gilbert, 1983) and most households make space for other families in order to supplement their income (Gilbert & Varley, 1991; Gilbert et al., 1993). In cities such as Bangkok (Yap & de Wandeler, 1990), Calcutta (Roy, 1983) and Cairo (Abu-Lughod, 1971), households often rent land on which to build their own shelters. Rakodi (1997) asserts that wherever access to land and home ownership is limited the majority of people become tenants. In South African cities, it was estimated that by 1996 more than a million households lived in backyard shacks or formal rooms in the backyards of other households (Crankshaw et al., 2000). Watson & McCarthy (1998) emphasise the pivotal role of the household sector, or small private landlord, in providing rental shelter for the urban poor.

As African cities continue to expand at rates often double the national norm, their coping mechanisms are being strained to capacity. One area of extreme pressure is the provision of housing and basic services. Limitations such as prohibitions on squatting, high costs of new housing and acute shortages of formal rental shelter force many African urban dwellers to turn to lodging, or the informal rental of rooms and part-rooms, as the only available, affordable option. In some cities, such as Nairobi, lodging includes renting rooms in squatter settlements where illegality of tenure has not precluded commercial development (Amis, 1996).

With the exception of informal shelters erected for the sole purpose of renting, 'lodging' involves the creation of living quarters by the process of involution (the division of existing space). Often, low-income households either add a room to their houses (usually self-built over a long period of time as resources become available) or increase the density of their existing space in order to rent to lodgers and ensure a steady, modest source of monthly income. Schlyter & Tipple (1998) have coined the term 'multi-habitation' for the situation where people – who do not define themselves as one household – share a living space that is not designed for multi-family purposes.

Space for lodgers may be created by dividing houses, rooms or part-rooms or renting out available servants' quarters, cottages or shanties. Space may be altered quickly to conform to immediate needs. For example, lodging space may be expanded to include a room, two rooms or a house, or decreased when an owner decides that more space is needed for their household or extended family members, thus taking precedence over lodging income. With flexible terms and the absence of a written contract, lodging is the rental shelter type that is most sensitive to demand.

In some situations, though, this is a two-edged sword, since the absence of regulation may cause hardship to vulnerable low-income households. Owners can arbitrarily raise rents, levy extra charges for female household heads with children, or demand that lodgers leave at short notice. In particular, lodgers with children have to worry about the possible 'annoyance' factor of their children's activities and noise, and many may feel they have to send their children to live with rural relatives in order to retain their urban lodging space. Divided families also result from the limitations of living in one room, particularly when children become teenagers. In addition, where ordinary houses have been expanded into patchworks of ten or more lodging rooms, the basic water and sewage provision is woefully substandard and inadequate. These lodging houses increase immediate urban density and exert tremendous strain on urban services. They are also characterised by a complete lack of privacy and other stresses that result from severe overcrowding. Auret (1995) identifies lodgers as the most stressed urban group.

Despite these drawbacks, 'lodging is the one adaptation that successfully circumvents, however precariously, a system characterised by bottlenecks, high and inflexible standards, bureaucracy, and prices that ensure that the most modest homes remain but pipedreams for the majority of urban poor' (Grant, 1996: 254–5). Lodging is one of the most popular choices in rapidly expanding African cities with acute housing shortages. For recent migrants, it offers an affordable urban locale while they seek employment. Since many urban residents maintain strong rural ties, lodging provides the flexibility to accommodate this mobility. Although many lodgers have extended periods of urban residence, long-term plans do not usually include either home ownership or retirement in urban areas. Tacoli (1998) describes households where some members have migrated but maintain strong links with extended family in rural home areas and regularly exchange resources as 'multi-spatial.'

In a context where new low-income houses are unaffordable for the vast majority of poor urban residents and where formal rental shelter is scarce, lodging is one of the few viable housing options other than squatting. Without the restrictions of formal leases, migrants seek out lodging that meets their particular situation, needs and aspirations. This chapter reveals the interface between lodging and the needs of urban migrants as they seek to negotiate an urban existence that will provide resources for both urban- and rural-based family members during a period of accelerated urbanisation and economic turbulence. It discusses the role of lodging as a critical component in urban migrants' priorities and long-term strategies.

2. Zimbabwe and Gweru

The 1990s were characterised by considerable growth in Zimbabwe. The 1992 census reported a population of 10,4 million, with 31 per cent in urban areas, while the 1998 estimate was 11,9 million with an urbanisation rate of 40 per cent by the year 2000. The intercensual (1982–1992) household formation rate of 3,04 per cent indicated that households were being formed nationwide at a level close to that of the population growth. This indicator, combined with the accelerated urbanisation rate, had serious implications for shelter provision in Zimbabwean cities (Grant, 1996: 248).

Zimbabwe's economic woes began even before Independence in 1980 when President Mugabe inherited slightly more than US$697 million in private, bilateral and multilateral debt. This debt, and economic advice from Washington, were among the main causes of the current economic plunge that started in late 1997 (Bond & Manyanya, 2003). The IMF/ World Bank-sponsored Economic Structural Adjustment Program (ESAP) in 1991/92 laid the groundwork for extreme economic hardships. These included massive formal sector retrenchments, an official unemployment rate of 40 per cent and sudden and frequent increases in the cost of basic food and services. Average real wages fell by 33 per cent between 1990 and 1997. By 1997, inflation had reached 45 per cent, some 46 per cent of all households had incomes below the food poverty line and 42 per cent of urban households were poor. Given widespread retrenchments and food and basic commodity shortages, increasing numbers of households could not meet minimal basic needs (Raftopoulos et al., 1998: 11). The situation has deteriorated drastically since then, with the result that Zimbabwe has been in a spiral of 'nearly uninterrupted economic chaos' since 1998 (Bond & Manyanya, 2003).

The other key event was the rapid spread of the HIV/AIDS pandemic. By 1997, between 20 and 50 per cent of pregnant women were HIV-positive at 23 surveillance sites (UNAIDS, 1998). World Health Organisation data indicated an HIV prevalence of 25,84 per cent of the population in the same year (WHO, 1998). This pandemic has had a devastating social, economic and demographic impact. Breadwinners have died, households have used scarce resources for medicine and funerals, widows have had to reconfigure households, and grandparents and other extended family members have had to take responsibility for AIDS orphans (Grant & Palmiere, 2003).

This chapter investigates how the flexible and relatively inexpensive nature of lodging affects the economic coping strategies of the urban poor. It also explores the fluidity of household composition and the extent to which workers and dependants shift between rural–urban locales as the cost of urban services and staples escalates.

It is based on a longitudinal study of 100 lodging households between 1993 and 1995, when economic and social circumstances worsened considerably. The medium-sized city (1992 population 128 000) of Gweru was the site of the study. Located halfway between Harare, the capital, and the secondary city of Bulawayo, Gweru is the capital of Midlands Province, an industrial city, a key centre of a large agricultural hinterland and an important destination for rural–urban migrants and intra-urban migrants (Grant, 1995). Gweru is a typical medium-sized Zimbabwean city in that strict pre-Independence legislation was enforced, resulting in influx controls, chronic shortage of housing and prohibition of squatting. After 1980, the government legislated that most rental housing be converted to home ownership, and promoted building campaigns for low-income urban homes. Despite these efforts, municipalities could not build or convert quickly enough to meet the insatiable demand fuelled by high growth levels and in-migration, with the result that Gweru's official waiting list was 14 468 by 1990 (Grant, 1996).

This study entailed purposive, stratified sampling to capture lodgers in all density areas: peri-urban, low, medium and high density. While the sample is far from representative, the study was intended to reveal the vulnerability, household fluidity and coping strategies of a diverse group of lodgers over a three-year period characterised by rapid economic and social change. Types of lodging ranged from primitive rooms in peri-urban cottages (formerly used to house farm labourers), to rooms or part-rooms in private homes (where owners were supplementing their incomes), to lodging houses in low/medium- and high-density areas. In high-density areas there was a booming business in overcrowded, poorly serviced conglomerate houses that filled most of the lot and housed nine to 12 families. In low/medium-density areas, former white-owned houses had been converted to lodgings and every room on the premises was rented out, including former servants' quarters. In some areas a few blocks from the CBD, almost all these spacious houses had been converted to lodgings. The properties were usually characterised by poor upkeep and general deterioration (Grant, 1996).

3. Migration and Demographic Profile of Lodgers

The lodgers in the study were almost evenly divided between male (45 per cent) and female (55 per cent) respondents, although at this time male household heads were still predominant (83 per cent). Almost three-quarters (74 per cent) of respondents had been born in a rural area and the majority of these lodgers originated from rural areas other than rural Gweru. Only one-quarter of lodgers were born in an urban area and most of these were born in smaller towns in Midlands Province, followed by Gweru and Harare. The small proportion of urban-born lodgers largely reflects pre-Independence residential restrictions on African families.

The study revealed that these lodgers had made an average of four lifetime moves, with an average of five moves for males and three for females. Almost half of the lodgers had moved to Gweru seeking employment and altogether 63 per cent had moved either in search of work or because of a transfer. After employment and transfers, the next most important reasons for migrating were family (often wives coming to Gweru to join their husbands) and education. Slightly more than half of the lodgers had moved to Gweru directly from a rural area, underlining the town's importance as a target destination for rural dwellers. Just over a third had migrated from different cities and towns, and this group was almost evenly divided between migrants from the two dominant cities of Harare and Bulawayo and those who had generally originated in smaller towns. Exclusive of transfers, Gweru is an important choice for migrants who are moving up or down the urban hierarchy in search of employment. As a medium-sized city, it is still perceived as an accessible locale for rural migrants and yet is large enough to hold the possibility of employment for both rural and urban migrants.

The predominant household type was nuclear (40 per cent), 22 per cent of households included extended family members, and only 10 per cent comprised couples only. Almost one-fifth (17 per cent) were single male or female households, a reflection of the growing trend of lone females migrating to the city to look for work. Altogether, 57 per cent of lodging households included children, household size ranged from one to nine persons, and the average was 3,4 persons.

Most lodgers (88 per cent) rented just one room, with the rest able to afford two rooms. In many cases this constituted a small house. Table 5.1 shows that most lodgers had been in Gweru for more than a year, with more than half having been there for more than five. The table also shows, however, that lodgers had moved frequently, with the vast majority having been in their present lodging for less than five years and a substantial 42% for less than one. This illustrates the constant search by lodgers for better conditions, price, location, space or overall circumstances. Since they generally find lodging by walking around neighbourhoods or by word of mouth, search behaviour is itself quite informal and precarious.

Table 5.1: Length of Time in Gweru and in Present Lodging

Time	Time in Gweru (%)	Time at present lodging (%)
Less than 1 year	5	42
1 to 5 years	42	46
6 to 10 years	14	8
More than 10 years	39	4

4. Economic Characteristics of Lodgers

In 1993, the majority of lodging households were heavily tied to formal sector employment, with 56 per cent participating in the formal sector only, 22 per cent just in the informal, and 17 per cent in both formal and informal. This reflects not only the industrial nature of Gweru but also the legacy of the colonial labour migration system, with the vast majority of formal work targeted at males.

Almost three-quarters of lodging households relied on just one mode of livelihood and for the majority (75 per cent) this was formal sector employment. This would render these households particularly vulnerable as the ESAP took hold and factories began massive retrenchments. One-quarter of households relied on two modes of livelihood and 2 per cent on three modes in 1993. Although the average wages were 31 per cent higher in formal sector employment than in informal, there was a considerable range in both sectors, with some formal employment paying as little as Z$90 per month while vegetable sellers were earning Z$300–500 or more per month. In some cases, perks available from formal employment, such as housing, were far more valuable than the wage itself. The data reveals a major gender gap. Comparing average incomes for men and women, women's average incomes were significantly lower, at 55 per cent and 82 per cent of men's average incomes in the formal and informal sectors respectively.

Rents increased by approximately 21 per cent over the three-year period (Table 5.2). During this time, rents of less than Z$100 per month became scarcer, and by 1995 almost three-quarters of lodgers paid between Z$100 and Z$199 per month. A key determinant of increased rents was the cost of utilities, which were usually included in the rent. For example, the Central Statistical Office Consumer Price Index for 1993–1998 shows that, using 1990 as a base of 100, rents, rates and utilities had increased nationwide by 219 per cent by 1995. Lodgers were committing a higher proportion of their monthly incomes to rent, averaging 27 per cent by 1995. However, the percentage of lodging households that had to pay 30 per cent or more of their earnings for rent declined to 20 per cent in 1995. Some lodgers thus took advantage of the flexibility within the system to move to cheaper accommodation and reduce their expenditure.

Table 5.2: Increases in Rent 1993–1995			
	1993	1994	1995
Average monthly rent (Z$)	103	119	125
% lodgers paying <Z$100 for rent	48	33	16
% lodgers paying Z$100-199 for rent	48	55	72
Average % monthly income spent on rent	22	21	27

Food prices also escalated but expenditures rose only slightly from Z$159 in 1993 to Z$185 in 1995. Also during this time, the total percentage of monthly income spent on food declined from 37 per cent to 23 per cent. Although most lodgers admitted that they cut back on food if they were short of funds at the end of the month, this is still a significant decrease in the proportion of income spent on food. Indeed, the CSO's Consumer Price Index (1993–1998) showed that food prices increased by 389 per cent between 1990 and 1995.

Total household expenses for lodgers increased by 35 per cent over the three-year period, from Z$324 to Z$437. In 1995, the CSO calculated the Total Consumption Poverty Line (TPL) (which includes food as well as non-food minimum need requirements such as housing and transport) for the urban Midlands as Z$235,95 per person per month. For lodgers, total household expenses absorbed 78 per cent of incomes in 1993, but this dropped to 67 per cent in 1995. However, by 1995, one-fifth of households had expenditures that exceeded income. Some households were awaiting a pension payout after the death of the wage earner, while others were hoping to receive help from extended family members. Whether they were scraping by on savings, short-term high interest loans, or the goodwill of neighbours and relatives, these particular households were extremely vulnerable. Unless they could secure funds right away, they would most likely be forced to leave their lodgings and possibly return to the rural areas.

The CSO's Consumer Price Index indicates that by 1995 the entire consumer package had increased by almost 370 per cent (based on a 1990 level of 100). Structural adjustment programme conditions included the removal of state subsidies on food, medical care and education. Food and medical expenses increased by 389 per cent and 411 per cent respectively. There were also sharp increases in medical care costs, coinciding with the escalation of the HIV/AIDS pandemic.

The next section examines how lodging households attempted to deal with retrenchments and sharp and sudden increases in basic commodities. It explores strategies of joining informal sector activities, encouraging more household members to work, increasing the number of modes of livelihood and reinforcing the safety network role of rural homes and extended family members.

5. Lodging Household Incomes, Earners and Modes

Faced with galloping inflation and frequent increases in everyday expenses, the economic strategies of these lodger households became critical to their survival and many coped by increasing their household incomes. Average household income increased from Z$464 (US$69) in 1993 to Z$954 (US$110) in 1995, as shown in Figure 5.1.

Figure 5.1: Average Monthly Household Income

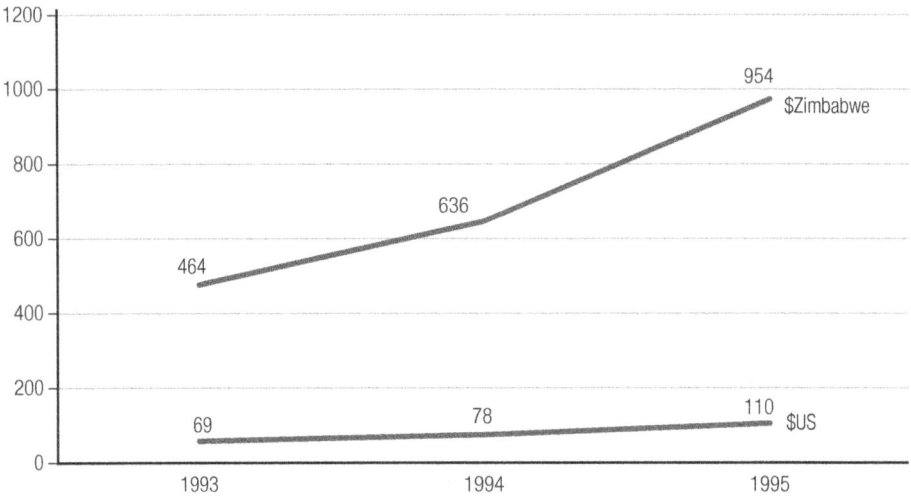

Households increased their monthly incomes in two ways (see Figures 5.2 and 5.3). One way was to increase the number of earners. In 1993, almost four-fifths of households had just one earner, but this decreased to just over half by 1995. The proportion of households with two earners doubled, from 20 per cent to 40 per cent over the three-year period, and the proportion with three earners increased from one to eight per cent. Another way was to increase the number of modes of livelihood. In 1993, 73 per cent of households relied on just one mode of livelihood and 25 per cent relied on two modes (Figure 5.3). This distribution changed significantly over the next two years. By 1995, only 40 per cent of households relied on one mode and 40 per cent on two modes. In addition, the proportion of households engaged in three modes grew from 2 per cent to 20 per cent. Quite a few households (37 per cent) added self-employment activities. Some retrenched husbands joined their wives in tailoring, or selling vegetables at small stands. Almost one-fifth (17 per cent) of households added more wage earners, which in many cases included wives, young people or extended family members. A small number of households sublet their limited space and rented out to other lodgers for added monthly income. These changes are clear indicators that households quickly realised that they had to expand their economic base to provide some insulation against the shocks of retrenchments and high inflation.

Opportunities for self-employment were more limited for lodgers than for home owners. Lodgers usually did not have access to yards for gardening or for establishing workshops, nor did they have the option of subletting their lodging space. In addition, as Schlyter (2003) notes in her study of lodgers in Chitungwiza, lodgers are constrained by lack of security and lack of neighbourhood networks for small businesses, since they tend to be highly mobile.

Figure 5.2: Lodging Households by Number of Earners

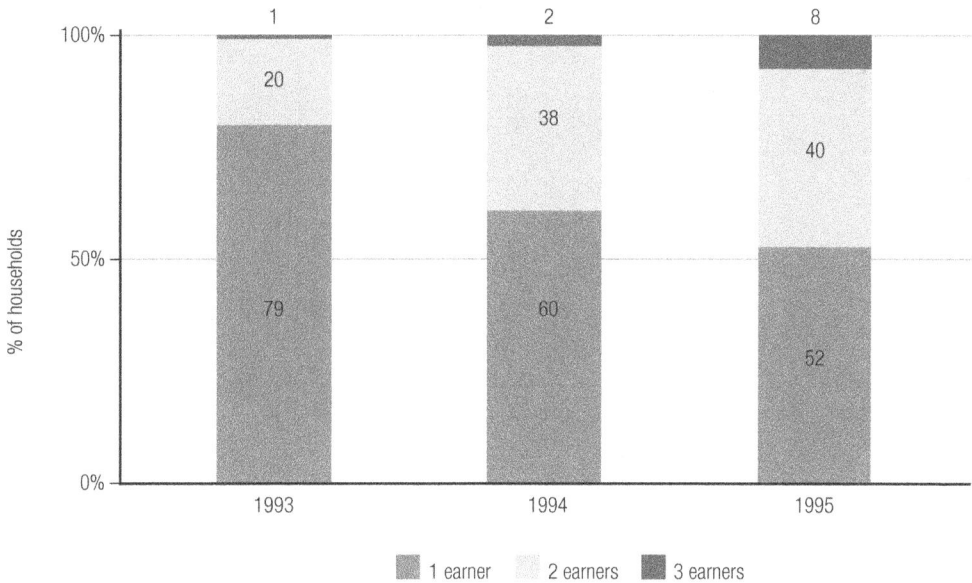

Short-term strategies were varied and included the following:

- Sending wives to rural areas to farm. This would provide households with food and extra income. Young children often accompanied their mothers, and school fees were less expensive in rural areas
- Taking in lodgers (i.e., subletting) for extra income
- Borrowing from friends (50 per cent) and family members (26 per cent)
- Making handicrafts to sell in Botswana and buying goods there for resale back in Zimbabwe
- Engaging more household members in waged and self-employment activities
- After a male wage earner was retrenched, expanding the wife's self-employment micro-enterprise.

Figure 5.3: Lodging Households by Number of Modes of Livelihood

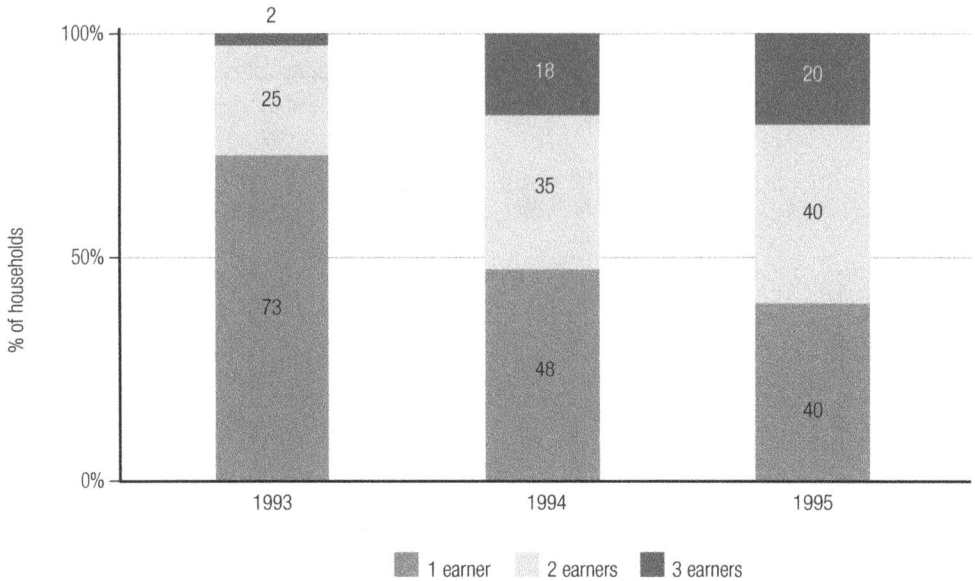

Long-term strategies also covered a wide range, but the two most prevalent included getting a better job or waged employment (34 per cent) and building their own house (34 per cent). Obviously, lodgers who were hoping to secure better paying jobs did not think retrenchments would continue, or believed that they would still obtain decently paid work. Building one's own home is an important goal, but most lodgers were not aware of the cost of even the cheapest new houses. Other long-term strategies included doing more in the informal sector (11 per cent), moving to rural areas to farm (9 per cent), forming a cooperative (3 per cent), taking courses (3 per cent) and relying on savings (2 per cent).

Another key immediate economic strategy was to reduce expenses. Almost two-thirds of households admitted to cutting back on food. Many would substitute tea for a meal and would cut back on the number of cooked meals to conserve both food and fuel. For the majority, meat became a luxury item. As transport costs increased (by 1995 they were more than 200 per cent higher than in 1990), workers started to walk into the city to go to work, rather than taking buses or combis (informal mini-bus taxis). This was no small sacrifice, since it entailed rising very early in the morning and walking for 60 to 90 minutes to get to work. Not only did this add two to three hours to the working day, it further exhausted workers and left them with much less time for their family. It also wore out shoes, another expense many could ill afford. Workers made do by stuffing their shoes with rags or newspapers where holes had been worn in them.

Some lodgers moved closer to work and others moved to rooms that did not have the extra expense of electricity. In the winter months, wives were sent out to the bush around the city to bring back firewood for household use and for sale. Household composition was often altered (see below). Later on in the 1990s, children were kept out of school to save on school fees. This did not appear to be the practice for this group of lodgers at the time of this study, although some households were using the option of cheaper rural schools.

6. Household Composition

Despite the fact that the majority of lodging households were limited to one room, household sizes increased over the three-year period (Figure 5.4). Smaller one-to two-person households decreased from 34 per cent to 24 per cent and three- to five-person households decreased slightly from 51 per cent to 44 per cent. Disturbingly, households of six to ten persons more than doubled, from 15 per cent to 32 per cent.

Figure 5.4: Changing Household Size

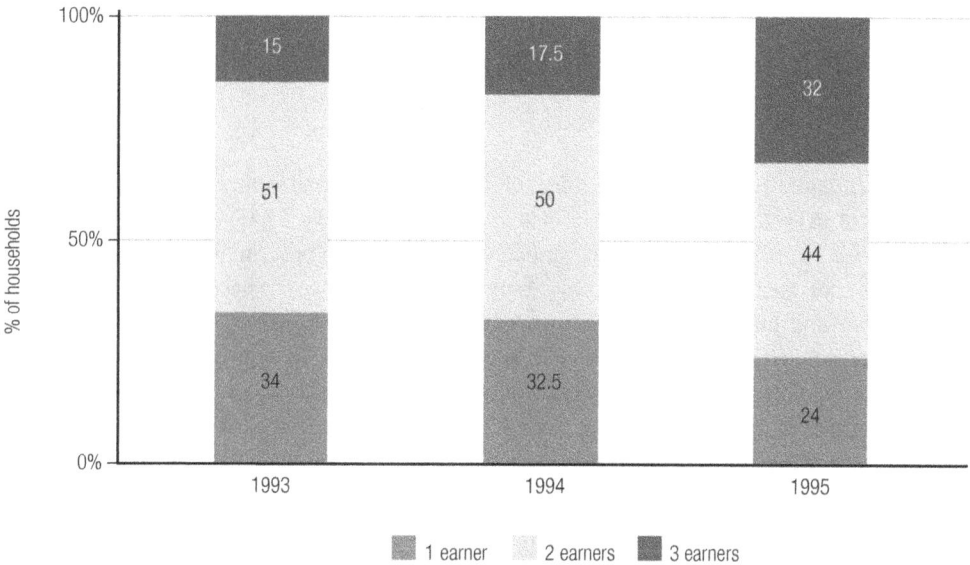

In 1993, just over half of the households were split between their rural homes and Gweru. With wives and children away for months at a time, extended family members could come to Gweru and look for work. The lodging household can expand and contract more easily than others to meet priorities. For example, it can easily move to a larger or smaller living space as required. The presence of extended family members who could contribute to the household was also important for vulnerable female household heads who had only one mode of livelihood and many dependents to support. Some female household heads lost access to rural homes through divorce or abandonment by their husbands. This diminished their support networks and access to food and a different locale, especially for their children. By 1995, one-fifth of households had at least some family members in the rural areas, including children in rural schools.

Just over three-quarters of lodging households had children or young people present. Young people who had finished school were encouraged to try to find work or to help out with microenterprises. Extended family children, including orphans, added to the dependency ratio of households and increased the burden on income earners to meet the basic needs of all household members. The presence of orphans indicates the heightened impact of the HIV/AIDS pandemic. Lodging households were almost evenly divided between those whose dependency ratio worsened (34 per cent) and those for whom it improved (32 per cent). One household increased in size from one to ten members, only one of whom was from the extended family. This indicates that the entire family moved to Gweru to join the male wage earner once he had become established, although the wife continued to commute back and forth in order to farm. In some cases, original lodgers had shifted back to their rural homes and had let adult sons or daughters and their families take over their lodgings. The rural areas were important default locales for those lodging households that needed a place to send children for school or whose retrenched members decided to farm and to use that food and income to supplement the family's urban existence.

7. Conclusion

This chapter has analysed the range of strategies of a small group of migrant lodgers during a critical period in Zimbabwe. The first major effects of the ESAP were felt in the everyday lives of the urban poor through retrenchments and unemployment; increased health and school user fees; increased housing, service, transport and basic commodities costs; high inflation; and the overall stress of everyday struggles. In addition, the social and economic costs of the rising HIV/AIDS pandemic were felt in the loss of wage earners and thus savings and the reconfiguration of households, often in the form of taking in orphans. By 1995, many in the group of lodging households (one-fifth) whose expenses exceeded income had endured the shock of the death of wage earners and found themselves in an extremely vulnerable position. The urban poor are particularly vulnerable to any calamity, whether retrenchment and unemployment, abandonment through death or divorce, unforeseen major expenses related to illness and death, or incomes that cannot match accelerated costs and inflation.

In response, some households moved elsewhere in Gweru or to other cities, while others moved back to rural areas to escape the cash-intensive existence of city life. However, those who remained (which most likely included only the more successful adaptors) provide some indication of strategies under difficult and precarious economic conditions.

Gweru remains an important destination for migrants from rural areas and smaller towns as well as from the larger cities of Bulawayo and Harare. Many migrants were attracted by Gweru's accessibility and its reputation as an industrial centre with jobs. This group of lodgers was almost evenly divided between relative newcomers (who had been there five years or less) and long-term residents, and almost all lodgers moved frequently between lodgings.

Among this group of lodgers there was originally a heavy reliance on one wage earner and one mode of livelihood. When retrenchments and unemployment took hold, households were forced to act quickly and strategically to ensure their continued urban existence. Strategies included engaging extended family members as extra agents to earn cash or to help in the household while others went out to earn. Many households had divided families, with the return of wives and children to rural areas to farm and attend cheaper schools. This was the result of crowded lodgings, lack of access to yards and water for gardening, and the high costs of urban food and school fees. The separation of families would have serious long-term consequences, particularly as prices of transport rose and families were less able to move easily back and forth between urban and rural locales. One could argue that the colonial migrant labour system as a cause of separation of families was replaced by the economic stringency driven by the ESAP. A longitudinal study of migrants based in Harare found that by 1994 only half as many migrants as in 1988 felt that their future lay in Harare, indicating that in-migrants felt less secure about urban life, employment and earning potential (Potts, 2000).

Lodging households in Gweru also encouraged more household members to earn cash, whether in wage labour or self-employment. The strong evidence for an increase in both the number of earners and the number of modes of livelihood indicates successful strategies. More subtle strategies were reducing food consumption, taking children out of school or sending them to cheaper – and lower quality – schools, and cutting back on transport and other consumer goods. This is a slippery slope that will have serious effects on health, quality of life and future prospects (especially for children) over the long term.

Finally, household composition was transformed, most likely as a result both of calamities and longer-term strategies such as separation of families and inclusion of extended family members' earning efforts. Immediate and longer-term strategies were working for many households and lodging played a key role in their ability to adapt quickly.

The present situation in Zimbabwe – slightly more than a decade later – is dire in the extreme. Three-quarters of the population are unemployed; the economy shrank by almost 50 per cent between 1999 and 2005; most people rely on remittances from the three to four million Zimbabweans living abroad; and at 1200 per cent the inflation rates are the highest in the world (*The Economist*, 23 September 2006). In 2002, the WHO reported HIV infections at 33,7 per cent and also recently reported that Zimbabwean women now have the lowest global life expectancy at 34 years, compared with males at 37 years (*The Telegraph*, April 2006).

The current situation was worsened considerably by the government-instituted Operation Restore Order (Operation Murambatsvina), a major national urban demolition and eviction programme begun in May 2005 to 'clean up' its cities. Tibaijuka (2005) estimates that 700 000 people lost either their homes or their livelihoods – or both – and indirectly another 2,4 million people were affected. Homeowners were forced to demolish rooms or entire houses that were declared illegal, forcing massive displacement, family separation and increased vulnerability. Most of those affected lost most or all of their assets, plunging lodgers and homeowners into further destitution. At the time of her report, Tibaijuka (2005) witnessed thousands of people sleeping in the open, either in the rubble of their destroyed homes, in rural areas or in official transit camps. Within this context and with the ensuing state of fear of soldiers, police and officials, only lodgers who are lucky enough to have 'legal' shelter will have a chance of remaining in urban areas in Zimbabwe.

Acknowledgements

I wish to acknowledge the generous support of the University of Calgary's URGC (University Research Grants Committee) for this research.

References

ABU-LUGHOD, J, 1971. Cairo: 1001 years of the 'City Victorious.' Princeton, NJ: Princeton University Press.

AMIS, P, 1996. Long-run trends in Nairobi's informal housing market. *Third World Planning Review*, 18(3): 271–85.

AURET, D, 1995. Urban housing: A national crisis? Gweru: Mambo Press, in association with The Catholic Commission for Justice and Peace in Zimbabwe.

BOND, P & MANYANYA, M, 2003. *Zimbabwe's plunge: Exhausted Nationalism, Neoliberalism and the Search for Social Justice*, Harare: Weaver Press.

CRANKSHAW, O, GILBERT, A & MORRIS, A, 2000. Backyard Soweto. *International Journal of Urban and Regional Research*, 24(4): 841–57.

GILBERT, A, 1983. The tenants of self-help housing: choice and constraint in the housing markets of less developed countries. *Development and Change*, 14: 449–77.

GILBERT, A & VARLEY, A, 1991. *Landlord and tenant: housing the poor in urban Mexico*. London: Routledge.

GILBERT, A, CAMACHO, O, COULOMB, R & NECOCHEA, A, 1993. *In search of a home: rental and shared housing in Latin America*. London: UCL Press.

GRANT, M, 1995. Movement patterns and the medium-sized city: Tenants on the move in Gweru, Zimbabwe. *Habitat International*, 19(3): 357–369.

— 1996. Vulnerability and privilege: Transitions in the supply pattern of rental shelter in a mid-sized Zimbabwean city. *Geoforum*, 27(2): 247–260.

GRANT, M & PALMIERE, A, 2003. When tea is a luxury: the economic impact of HIV/AIDS in Bulawayo, Zimbabwe. *African Studies*, 62(2): 213–40.

GRANT, M, CRUSH, J & FRAYNE, B, 2007. Migration, HIV/AIDS and urban food security in southern and eastern Africa. SAMP African and Migration Development Series No. 3, Cape Town.

KESSIDES, C, 2005. The urban transition in sub-Saharan Africa: implications for economic growth and poverty reduction. The World Bank, Washington, DC.

MALPEZZI, S, 1990. Rental housing in developing countries: issues and constraints. Rental housing: proceedings of the expert group meeting. Nairobi: UNCHS (United Nations Centre for Human Settlements).

POTTS, D, 2000. Urban unemployment and migrants in Africa: evidence from Harare 1985–1994. *Development and Change*, 31: 879–910.

RAFTOPOULOS, B, HAWKINS, T & AMANOR-WILKS, D, 1998. UNDP (United Nations Development Project) Human Development Report: Zimbabwe. Harare: UNDP.

RAKODI, C, 1997. Residential property markets in African cities. In Rakodi, C (ed.), *The urban challenge in Africa. Growth and management of its large cities*. New York: United Nations University, pp. 371–410.

ROY, D, 1983. The supply of land for the slums in Calcutta. In Angel, S, Archer R, Tanphiphat, S & Wegelin, E (eds), *Land for housing the poor*. Singapore: Select Books, pp. 98-109.

SCHLYTER, A, 2003. Multi-habitation. Urban housing and everyday life in Chitungwiza, Zimbabwe. Uppsala : Nordiska Afrikainstitutet.

SCHLYTER, A & TIPPLE, G, 1998. Multihabitation. Proposal for a research program. Newcastle and Uppsala.

TACOLI, C, 1998. Rural–urban interactions: a guide to the literature. *Environment and Urbanisation*, 10: 147–166.

TIBAIJUKA, A, 2005. Report of the fact-finding mission to Zimbabwe to assess the scope and impact of Operation Murambatsvina. New York: United Nations.

UNAIDS, 1998. Epidemiology: AIDS in Africa. UNAIDS, Johannesburg. Available at http://www.unaids.org/publications/documents/epidemiology/determinants/aepap98.html.

UN-HABITAT, 2004–2005. *State of the world's cities: trends in sub-Saharan Africa.*

WATSON, V & McCARTHY, M, 1998. Mental housing policy and the role of the household rental sector: evidence from South Africa. *Habitat International*, 22(1): 49–56.

WORLD HEALTH ORGANISATION, 1998. Report on the global HIV/AIDS epidemic: The evolving picture region by region. Geneva: WHO.

YAP, K & DE WANDELER, K, 1990. Low-income rental land and housing in Bangkok: an overview. UNCHS (Habitat). Rental housing: proceedings of an expert group meeting. 13–17 November, 1989. Nairobi: United Nations Centre for Human Settlements.

6 MIGRATION AND THE CHANGING SOCIAL ECONOMY OF WINDHOEK, NAMIBIA

BRUCE FRAYNE

1. Introduction

The population of Namibia's capital city, Windhoek, has been growing at an annual rate of 5.4 per cent in recent years, the largest annual growth rate in its history. The 2001 population of Windhoek was about 224 000, which represents almost half of all urban residents in the country (Municipality of Windhoek, 2001). While not unique to Namibia, rapid urbanisation in the context of slow economic growth makes it difficult for urban managers to cater adequately for a growing population's economic and infrastructure needs. It is within this context that this research considers the welfare of relatively poor migrants to Windhoek and how they survive under difficult conditions.

Most of the population growth is taking place in Katutura, a large area to the northwest of the city, previously designated an African township, where about 60 per cent of the city's population live on about 20 per cent of its land (Pendleton, 1998). It is estimated that the population of Windhoek will double between 2000 and 2015 as a result of both natural population growth and rural–urban migration (Municipality of Windhoek, 1996b: Vol. 1: 20; Frayne & Pendleton, 2001, 2003). Of total migration to the city between 1990 and 2000, more than two-thirds has been to Katutura (Municipality of Windhoek, 2001, Vol. 1: 62). Moreover, some 67 per cent of migrants in the sample in this study had moved to Windhoek since Independence in 1990, with 42 per cent having arrived in the period 1996–2000. The majority were born in the rural north of Namibia, with 79 per cent of the first-generation migrants in the sample coming from the central rural north (Oshiwambo-speaking regions), which is more than double the percentage of non-migrants with the same mother tongue.

Windhoek is by no means an exception, as urbanisation and increasingly complex forms of mobility are on the rise throughout southern and eastern Africa. This chapter is based on a study conducted by the author in Katutura and rural districts of Namibia in 2000 (Frayne, 2001). The study is important for understanding the changing social economy of Namibia, and the findings resonate with the challenges urban managers face within the region.

It has been argued elsewhere that prior to Namibian independence in 1990 both stabilised residents and contract migrants faced enormous economic pressures (Frayne, 2001). Recent studies show that the contemporary situation for urban residents is not much improved (Simon, 1991; Pendleton, 1991, 1996, 1998; Pomuti & Tvedten, 1998; Peyroux & Graefe, 1995; Frayne & Pendleton, 2001). Although employment opportunities have broadened with independence, the sheer volume of urban growth appears to negate the potential benefits for the urban poor (Pendleton, 1998: 72; Hansohm, 2000). A survey undertaken in the informal areas of the city reported an unemployment rate of 46 per cent amongst household heads (Peyroux & Graefe, 1995). The growth in the informal economy is largely in response to the real constraints on employment in the formal sector (Norval & Namoya, 1992; Pendleton, 1996).

This tension between migration, urbanisation and urban poverty has been variously described as an 'urban crisis' and conceptualised as a transfer of rural poverty to the urban context (Pile, et al., 1999: 1; Pomuti & Tvedten, 1998; Tvedten & Nangulah, 1999). Moreover, vulnerability and deprivation are increasingly viewed as an urban problem, which is more severe than the situation in the rural areas (Pomuti & Tvedten, 1998: 122). Devereux et al. (1995: 41) make the following observations with regard to urban poverty:

> Competition for employment is fierce, wages are low, and many [unskilled shanty dwellers] are forced to eke out a subsistence in the urban informal sector. The informal sector itself is underdeveloped, with an overemphasis on petty-commodity trading, which, in many quarters, has reached saturation point. Urban poverty is thus a growing phenomenon in Namibia and the situation is likely to deteriorate further if employment opportunities are not created in both rural and urban areas.

At face value, this line of argument appears to be supported generally by the data. For example, in 1991, some 67 per cent of migrants reported the lack of employment as a 'serious problem' they faced in Windhoek (Pendleton, 1991). In the same survey, 70 per cent of the sample reported food shortages as a 'serious problem.' However, although consistently high unemployment rates are reported amongst households in Katutura, and migrants face the highest levels of unemployment in the city (Municipality of Windhoek, 1996a, 2001; Pendleton, 1996; Pomuti & Tvedten, 1998), data also show that, on aggregate, poor urban residents are not as vulnerable as they were prior to Independence. In a comparison of household data collected from Katutura between 1991 and 1996, Pendleton (1998) reports a decrease in the proportion of households that consider food to be a 'serious problem' from 70 per cent to 30 per cent. In addition, similar decreases have been reported in the problems associated with debt and health. Using the same indicators and sample population, this study found a further decrease, with only 11 per cent of respondents reporting food as a 'serious problem.'

How is this apparent contradiction to be explained? Unemployment is high, rural–urban migration continues, and yet respondents themselves report lower levels of hunger than was the case only ten years ago. The stated improvement in the food situation from 1991 to 2000 leads one to the hypothesis that this hidden 'income' is most likely in the form of food. In addition, the primary source of migrants is the rural north, Owamboland in particular, where land continues to be used productively. Food transfers from rural households to migrants during the colonial era were not documented, but this study and Pendleton's (1991, 1996) recent work confirm that this is a new factor amongst both migrant and non-migrant house-holds. In addition, migrants have, since Independence, become a highly mobile group, making frequent visits to the rural areas each year (Pendleton, 1996; Frayne & Pendleton, 2001, 2003). Social linkages between the rural and urban areas thus appear to make for greater mobility and potential for transporting goods between households. Therefore, the apparent contradiction might be best explained by the increasing fluidity of rural–urban linkages in Namibia. This, in turn, has been made possible by the deregulation of the labour market, and the freedom of movement now possible under a new and independent government.

Section 2 situates the research within its scholarly context and discusses the issues in the context of the literature on migration and urban livelihoods in Namibia. Section 3 describes the methodology of the research, Section 4 examines the transfers of food between rural and urban households, Section 5 discusses urban agriculture in Windhoek, Section 6 focuses on household level demographic coping strategies, and Section 7 looks at circular and reciprocal migration trends. The concluding section summarises key research findings and reflects on their implications for development in Namibia and the region, and for future research.

2. Literature and Conceptual Framework

Previous scholarship has emphasised the importance of urban wages for the survival of rural households in Namibia, and more broadly within southern Africa (Wilson, 1972; Beinart, 1980; Murray, 1981; Moorsom, 1995; Potts, 2000; Crush et al., 2006). Linked to this concept of rural dependency on urban incomes is the conventional wisdom that unilinear rural–urban migration and urbanisation, as part of the development process, are increasingly replacing cyclical labour migration (Ferguson, 1996; Pomuti & Tvedten, 1998; Smit, 1998; Crush & Soutter, 1999). However, cities in Southern Africa have recently been described as being 'in crisis' (Baker & Aina, 1995; Potts, 1995, 2000; Moser, 1996, 1998; Todaro, 1997; Pomuti & Tvedten, 1998; Koc et al., 1999; Pile et al., 1999). Limited industrial growth, rising unemployment and urban poverty demonstrate the inconsistencies of development practice, which aims to relieve rural and urban poverty through urbanisation and economic growth strategies (Lipton, 1977, 1982; Todaro, 1969, 1995, 1997). Yet despite high rates of unemployment, rural–urban migration persists, as does urbanisation (Ellis & Harris, 2004).

Although still largely rural, more than 50 per cent of southern Africa's population is expected to be living in urban areas by 2030 (UN-HABITAT, 2004–2005). At present, at least one-third or more of the urban population in much of southern and eastern Africa live below the poverty line (Kessides, 2005; Drimie et al., 2006). The combination of rapid urbanisation and poor economic performance has led to the proliferation of slums throughout the region. Nearly three-quarters of all urban residents in sub-Saharan Africa live in slums (UN-HABITAT, 2004–2005).

As a result of these deteriorating conditions – and within the constraints of economies limited by declining per capita agricultural yields, structural adjustment and trade liberalisation (including export-oriented agricultural policies, reductions in wage employment and reductions in welfare policies), environmental stress, war and natural disasters – the challenge for national and municipal governments to meet even basic needs is immense (IDRC, 1997; Potter & Lloyd-Evans, 1998; Crush et al., 2006). Equally, the pressure on the poor to fill this resource gap themselves is extreme within the context of growing urban poverty. Yet migration continues apace. How then, do urban residents, and in particular migrants, survive in increasingly hostile urban environments?

In contrast to the household level studies that have been done in rural areas on economic entitlements, urban food security measures and strategies have generally been considered at the city level (Dando, 1980; Sen, 1981; Rotberg & Rabb, 1983; Watts, 1983, 1987, 1991; Currey & Hugo, 1984; Bowbrick, 1986; Glantz, 1987; De Waal, 1990; Devereux, 1993, 1999; Devereux & Næraa, 1996; Young, 1996; Potts, 2000). However, it is well documented that urban poverty is often most acutely felt at the household level (Moser, 1996, 1998; UNICEF, 1998, 2000; Devereux, 1999; Tvedten & Nangulah, 1999; Barrett & Carter 2000; Mougeot, 2005). Moreover, the most direct and possibly most threatening consequence of poverty is limited or threatened food security and consequent hunger, despite adequate levels of food security being reported at the city scale. Urban poverty reduction strategies generally aim at increasing productivity within the manufacturing and retail sectors (i.e., increasing employment opportunities). Yet, with persistently high levels of urbanisation and limited economic opportunity, vulnerability to hunger and its associated problems is not adequately addressed in the majority of the urban centres of the developing world (Drakakis-Smith, 1990, 1991, 1995, 1997; Moser, 1996, 1998; Todaro, 1997; UNICEF 1998; Potts & Mutambirwa, 1998; Koc et al., 1999; Mougeot, 2005). Recognising the failure of the formal economic and urban sectors to provide the levels of service and employment required to address increasing poverty in much of the developing world, the international and local development and research communities have drawn into their ambit the question of how urban populations feed themselves under constrained and difficult conditions (Mougeot, 2005).

The conceptual framework for this research is the centrality of mobility as the mechanism underpinning urban livelihoods. In this framework, both urban and rural households share in the livelihood process, with resource flows moving from urban to rural and from rural to urban contexts. This study examines the pathways used by individuals and households to navigate the increasingly complex social and economic terrain that is contemporary Namibia and, more broadly, southern Africa. The interactions between rural and urban systems are continuous within this framework, suggesting the evolution of a more integrated rural–urban social and economic system that moves beyond the traditional bounds of the rural–urban dichotomy. This is what the author has termed urban–rural reciprocity, a process which increasingly underwrites the new social economy of migration (Frayne, 2001, 2005; Crush et al., 2006).

In the analysis of urban livelihoods, therefore, this research is situated at the intersection of three different bodies of scholarship: urbanisation and survival; migration; and economic entitlement. It contributes to an emerging theory of urban entitlement and connects with the growing body of theoretical and empirical work on migration and survival (Watts & Bohle, 1993; IDRC, 1997; Drakasis-Smith, 1997; Moser, 1998; Devereux, 1999; Potts, 2000; Crush et al., 2006).

Figure 6.1: Conceptual Framework – Reciprocal Migration and Livelihoods

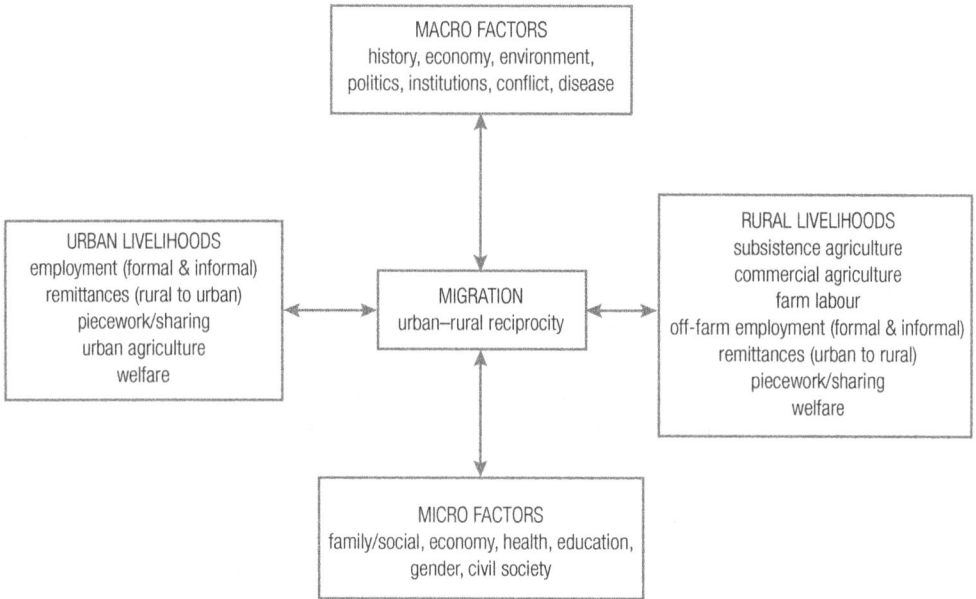

As described by Frayne and Pendleton (2001), the migration process – which is funda-mental to the livelihoods of rural and urban households – occurs through a complex interplay between the macro and micro contexts of any given migrant's geography. Although individual and/or household agency usually prevails in decisions to migrate (except in cases of forced migration due to disaster, including conflict), historical, economic and political/institutional contexts all contribute to the decision-making process. Similarly, micro factors such as fam-ily dynamics and needs, household welfare, health and education influence the migration process. This process is dynamic and iterative, and increasingly dramatic in southern Africa. Indeed, studies of both internal and cross-border migration show clearly that all forms of mobility are on the rise in southern Africa and that migration is an increasingly important dimension of households' livelihoods in the region.

3. Methodology

The methodology of this study used two data collection techniques, the standardised questionnaire survey and in-depth, semi-structured case study interviews. These two methods complement each other by providing generalised information through the survey and more fine-grained information through the in-depth interviews. Given the importance of the sending areas in the research, the methodology was extended beyond the original proposal to include in-depth interviews in the rural areas. Using this approach to track rural–urban migrants between sending and destination points made it possible to answer the research questions posed by this study:

1. How does rural–urban migration contribute to the household's ability to diversify economic risk and opportunity?

2. Do social relations between the rural and urban areas promote urban food security and, if so, in what ways and by what mechanisms (economic entitlement)?

3. Are rural–urban links part of an established cyclical migration pattern, or do they represent a demographic and social transition from rural to urban?

This methodology was innovative in two ways. First, by combining quantitative and qualitative approaches to the question of migration, it created the methodological synergy needed to uncover the multidimensional nature of 'the household' as a unit of analysis (an important consideration where households are fluid and may extend across time and space). Secondly, the rural homes (places of origin) of migrants interviewed in the urban centres were identified and rural household members were selected for in-depth interviews in the rural areas. This helped to provide data and information on the migration and reciprocity process from both the urban and rural perspectives. In order to evaluate possible changes over time, use was made of secondary survey data from a variety of sources available in Windhoek.

Given that Windhoek is almost ten times the size of any other urban area in Namibia, and that as the capital city it provides a destination for all sectors of Namibian society, it was selected as the research locale for the quantitative survey and urban household case studies. Because most of the growth in the city occurs within the former African township of Katutura, the urban component of the research was undertaken there. Katutura is the primary destination of migrants to the city and appears to have the strongest urban–rural linkages in Windhoek. Furthermore, it is home to more than half of the city's entire population and represents the poorest (and most vulnerable) sectors of society. It should be noted that the name 'Katutura' is used to refer to both the formal area of the township and the informal areas to the northwest of the city.

Within each of the various residential areas of Katutura selected for the survey, the number of housing sites was counted. The number of surveys allocated to a particular area was then divided into the number of dwelling sites in order to arrive at a sample interval. An arbitrary point within each residential section was selected as the starting point. While the head of the household is considered to be the primary decision-maker, to gain insights into intricate dynamics within and between urban households and their rural components it was necessary to interview other members of the household as well. For example, migration in recent years has achieved closer gender parity than was the case under the male-dominated contract labour system (Frayne, 2001). This change, together with the fact that social, political and economic conditions vary according to gender in Namibia, made it crucial that the methodology was designed to make a gender analysis of the data possible (Lipinge & LeBeau, 1997). Therefore, it was decided to select adult respondents (those aged eighteen and above) within each household systematically.

There were 305 interviews conducted through a standardised survey which included 95 mostly closed-ended questions. A systematic random sampling technique was used for sample selection. Questions were designed to collect information at the household and the individual levels and were divided into five parts to collect information on demography and socio-economic characteristics, migration and household arrangements, food/commodity transfers and remittances between rural and urban households, social linkages and urban agriculture. Data was collected through local interviewers fluent in local languages.

In addition, semi-structured in-depth interviews were also conducted with 31 urban and ten rural respondents. Convenience sampling, derived from introductions through the survey and community connections, was used to select the interviewees. Local interviewers and languages were used to facilitate communication. Questions were grouped into five sections, covering socio-economic and demographic information, migration history, rural and urban assets, food security and commodity transfers.

The research resulted in three major findings that help to explain the urban food security conundrum described in the introduction to this chapter and also help answer the research questions. Despite the conclusion that urban poverty is increasing in Windhoek, the evidence from this research suggests that urban households are increasingly reliant on transfers of food from the rural areas to supplement their urban food budgets. The results also demonstrated that it is impossible to understand this household-level coping mechanism in the urban areas without also understanding the complexity of rural–urban linkages and the high degree of social reciprocity that makes them possible.

4. Rural–Urban Food Transfer and Survival

The primary argument of this study is that migrants survive in the urban areas in part because of food they receive from the rural areas. Some 62 per cent of the Windhoek households sampled had received food from relatives in the rural areas, and a further 4 per cent from friends, over the previous year (Table 6.1). This represents two-thirds of all the households surveyed, including those that did not have first-generation migrants living in them (i.e., all members born in Windhoek, which is 14 per cent of the sample).

Table 6.1: Incidence of Household Receiving Food from Relatives and Friends in the Rural Areas over the Past Year (2000)

	Receive food from relatives		Receive food from friends	
	N	%	N	%
Yes	190	62	11	4
No	115	38	294	96
Total	305	100	305	100

Even more significant is the fact that about 58 per cent of the households reported being sent food between twice and six times per year. Respondents also said they had received a wide range of products, some of which are seasonal, including cultivated and wild foods, and some meat, poultry and fish (Table 6.2).

Pearl millet (mahangu) is the staple cereal crop in Namibia, and when asked what quantity of particular food items were sent to the household the last time they received food, the amount of millet reported was significant. Forty-eight per cent of the respondents claimed that they received between five and 19 kilograms of millet the last time it was sent to them, with about one-quarter of the sample receiving between 20 and 50 kilograms (Table 6.3).

Table 6.2: Type of Food People Report Receiving from the Rural Areas (2000)

Food Type	N	%
Pearl millet (mahangu)	150	42
Other cereals	13	4
Meat and fish	31	9
Commercial foods	14	4
Wild foods	147	41
Total	355*	100

*Note that multiple respondents were possible, hence N=355.

Table 6.3: Amount of Millet Received the Last Time by People in Household (2000)

Amount	N	%
1–4kg	51	27
5–9kg	26	14
10–19kg	64	34
20–50kg	48	26
Total	189	100

Besides millet, fish is important, as are wild foods. Commercial foods, which would be purchased in a store, are of very little significance (N values range from 0–4). Given the generally low levels of rural cash income, and widespread poverty, it is not surprising that the food the rural household has access to is available through farming or collection from the bush. The most common wild food sent to urban households is spinach, which provides micronutrients and is also culturally important. Seasonal fruit is also sent, both fresh and dried. The following testimony illustrates this reliance on the productive capacity of the land for the type and volume of food sent to urban relatives:

> We send mahangu flour, beans and dried spinach, when someone is visiting them from here [Owamboland], or if they visit us. We don't send money, and the food is only sent a few times per year, perhaps five or six. This is partly because we have to rely on visitors to transport the goods to Windhoek, which is not a regular thing, and also because food is not as abundant here as we would like.

These rural–urban transfers of food further indicate the central role of migration and urban–rural links in levels of urban food security at the household level. The survey shows that the latest amount of millet received lasted nearly half of all households about one month, and a further 16 per cent of households between two to six months. Moreover, 81 per cent of respondents rated the food they receive from the rural areas as 'important' or 'very important' to the household, with a further 11 per cent reporting that the food they received was 'critical to their survival' (Table 6.4).

Table 6.4: Importance of Food Sent from the Rural Areas to Urban Households (2000)		
How important is this food to the household?	N	%
Not important at all	1	1
Somewhat important	15	8
Important	50	26
Very important	104	55
Critical to our survival	20	11
Total	190	100

The importance of the food to survival is further validated by the responses given when asked why food was sent to the household from the rural areas. Of the rural respondents, 79 per cent said it is to help the members of the urban households feed themselves. Approximately 91 per cent of the urban respondents reported consuming the food they receive exclusively, with only 6 per cent using some of it for business purposes (the remaining 3 per cent was given away to family and friends). Without these food transfers, food insecurity and malnutrition among migrant households would undoubtedly be significantly higher than current levels.

5. Urban Agriculture in Windhoek

It is well established that households in many cities in the world engage in urban agriculture as a means of improving food security (Koc et al., 1999; Mougeot, 2005). Mass urbanisation and a rise in urban poverty are factors central to the development of urban agriculture. It is therefore important to quantify the extent to which urban agriculture is used by households in Windhoek to contribute to their level of food security.

Urban agriculture does occur in Windhoek, despite the climatic constraints. Five per cent of the sample were involved in some form of urban agriculture, and a further 4 per cent knew of someone else in the city growing some food themselves (total of 9 per cent). General observation in the area confirms that, although it is limited in incidence and scale, urban agriculture exists in Windhoek. On average, urban agricultural produce saves households approximately NA$60 per month in groceries that they would otherwise have to purchase from a retail outlet. In Namibia, this is a significant amount of money, and indicates the potential importance of improved conditions for urban agriculture in cutting the cost of food for poorer households.

Although less than one per cent of respondents reported keeping urban livestock (within a ten kilometre radius of the city), it is possible that this activity is under-reported. When asked whether or not they knew of any neighbours or friends who kept livestock in the city, little more than 3 per cent said that they did. Also, goats were observed on numerous occasions within the city limits. However, the fact that the municipal and health bylaws are strict about this might explain people's reluctance to admit that they have urban livestock. Nonetheless, the numbers are small and these figures appear to correctly indicate the very limited extent to which people are engaged in livestock production within the urban area of Windhoek. Even with more proactive policies, the strained water supply of the city and the limited biomass available suggest that keeping livestock in the city and its environs has limited potential in the future under current systems of land use and water allocation.

Despite the potential that might exist for the expansion of this sector, the current low levels of production again point to the importance of food sources beyond the urban boundary in feeding poorer urban households. The quantity of food being produced in the city suggests that urban agriculture does not play a significant role in ameliorating urban food insecurity at the household level in Windhoek.

6. Demographic Coping Strategies and Survival

Sen (1981) argued that when entitlement to food is threatened as a result of economic shock or stress, rural households employ various coping strategies to ameliorate those entitlement failures. One such strategy is to increase sharing between households. Sen's conclusions are supported by this study, which recorded limited intra-household reciprocity within the boundaries of the Windhoek urban area (less than five per cent of the sample reported borrowing food with any regularity), in contrast to the rural situation.

The findings demonstrate that there are strong links between rural and urban households, and that coping strategies are based on these. Thus, while it is not possible to transpose Sen's (1981) analysis of intra-household sharing onto the urban context in Windhoek, it is plausible to argue that urban households reduce their food gap by invoking rural entitlements that are theirs by virtue of their social links. This is an unexpected application of the entitlement approach with regard to household sharing, but is valid nonetheless and emphasises the dominance of urban–rural links in the urban survival equation.

Limited intra-household reciprocity in urban areas is therefore closely related to the substantial connection and flow of food between urban and rural households. These very networks provide the 'social infrastructure' that promotes links between urban migrants and their places of origin. This social infrastructure (capital) is also responsible for a number of demographic activities that help promote food security in urban areas (and vice versa, in that rural areas also benefit from the transfer of money and other commodities from the urban areas).

In cases where urban households, both migrant and non-migrant, experience economic stress and strained food availability, sending children and adults to live with rural relatives is a common practice. This strategy is referred to as 'distress migration' in the entitlement and coping literature (Devereux, 1999: 11), in describing the process of migration by rural households to urban areas in search of employment as a result of failing sources of entitlement in the rural context. However, in this study it is equally valid to talk about distress migration of both children and adults in the urban area. Seventy per cent of the sample indicated that they sent their children to stay with relatives elsewhere. The primary reason given by respondents (35 per cent) was that the children are sent away because there is not enough money to support them in Windhoek (Table 6.5). Of those children sent away, at least 90 per cent live with relatives in the rural areas of Namibia, and about 70 per cent stay away from their home in Windhoek for more than a year at a time.

Table 6.5: Reasons Why Children are Sent to Live with Relatives (2000)		
Reasons	N	%*
Not enough money to provide for them	81	35
No schools in Windhoek for them	29	12
Not enough time to look after them properly	44	19
* Column percentage not equal to 100 as multiple responses possible.		

Another demographic adjustment (distress migration) strategy of struggling urban migrants and/or households is to send adult members to the rural areas, either as returnees or, in some instances, as new migrants to the rural homestead. The burden of providing the daily food requirements for an extended household where few are employed in any significant fashion is immense. This strategy of returning adults to the rural areas therefore helps to minimise the need to ration food, sell off assets, borrow food or money, or engage in crime as a means of survival (all of which are coping and survival strategies invoked in response to failing entitlements).

Vulnerability to hunger in the rural context is determined in part by the variability and reliability of food sources (Sen, 1981; Devereux, 1993, 1999). The results of this research show that a loss of entitlement sources increases vulnerability and hunger in Windhoek. The most marginal and vulnerable urban households were those that had poor or non-existent relationships with kin in the rural areas and few social or economic urban resources. In other words, the limitation of their social infrastructure directly curtailed their entitlement to both urban and rural resources. Typically, these households comprised young, single males and were often involved in piecework and crime, or female-headed households that relied on the informal sector for their income (see Frayne, 2004, for a detailed discussion of the gender aspects of vulnerability and urban food security). Although these cases represent a small proportion of the sample, they are significant because they illustrate the importance of urban–rural links in the survival equation, while also helping to identify the most vulnerable members of society. In most cases, however, returning to the rural areas permanently was not perceived as a solution to the household's current circumstances of deprivation, and the urban area remains the destination of first choice.

7. Circular and Reciprocal Urbanisation

Social networks have been described as important in understanding the demographic strategies employed by rural and urban households to ameliorate economic stress and improve food security. In this regard, the survey found that 85 per cent of the respondents are migrants to Windhoek, and only five (1.6 per cent) of the households sampled reported having no relatives in the rural areas of Namibia. The fact that more than 98 per cent of the sample have relatives in the rural areas, and 86 per cent of respondents say they visit their relatives and friends in the rural areas at least once a year, confirms the strength of social ties between urban and rural households in the country. These strong and dynamic social connections underpin the reciprocal characteristics of the Namibian social economy.

Remittances by migrants living in urban centres back to their rural households are a well-established tradition in Namibia (Pendleton, 1994; Moorsom, 1995; Frayne & Pendleton, 1998, 2003; Pomuti & Tvedten, 1998). The historical pattern of forced migration to meet the colonial labour needs of Namibia has given way to voluntary migration, precipitated by the increasing reliance of rural households on non-farm incomes (UNICEF/NISER, 1991; Pendleton, 1994). The recent decline in the formal urban economy in Namibia has reduced urban migrants' income-earning opportunities, thereby diminishing their potential to send money back to rural households. Yet studies show the importance of urban earnings to the survival of rural households, especially during times of economic hardship (Devereux et al., 1995; Moorsom, 1995; Pendleton, 1994).

Given this tension between rising need and falling earning potential, it is not surprising that the percentage of households remitting money to rural households has not increased over the past ten years. Sixty-three per cent of respondents in this study said they sent no money to family elsewhere, which is the same proportion that responded to a similar question in a household survey carried out in Katutura in 1991 (Pendleton, 1991). However, the actual number of people remitting money from urban to rural areas has increased substantially, given that the absolute number of migrants to Windhoek has doubled over the same period. This suggests that the number of rural households that receive urban remittances continues to rise, and that this source of income is therefore increasingly important. A rural respondent described the role of remittances as follows:

Hunger is not generally a problem. Even in years when there is not enough rain, we are able to get enough money to buy what we need. This comes from our relatives in town, who work and get money. Without them, there could be a serious food shortage here, especially when there is drought.

The amount of money sent to rural relatives varies, although the median category is NA$101–150 (sent 'every few months'). Compared to the average household remittance of NA$156 reported in 1991, average amounts sent have not increased over the past decade (Pendleton, 1991). It is also significant that about 50 per cent of households remit money to rural relatives every month, or at least every two or three months. The amounts of money and the frequency of remittances support the argument that rural households continue to depend on their urban counterparts for income, although the actual value of the remittances has remained static.

Placing a monetary value on food transfers from the rural areas to urban households is difficult, not least because of seasonal variation. However, it is noteworthy that during the year of the survey (2000), half of all households sampled reported that they used millet that came as food transfers from the rural areas. This food item alone is estimated to cost about NA$60 per month for a household of four, if substituted with commercial maize meal. This value compares favourably with the value of money remitted to rural households every few months. However, a greater percentage of urban households receive food regularly than remit cash to rural relatives. The economic balance appears to have shifted in favour of urban households over the past decade.

The economic values associated with demographic reciprocity are complex, but the research did record the importance of urban incomes for supporting parents and children based in the rural areas. The largest proportion of remittances (85 per cent) is sent to parents and/or children living in the rural areas. This figure highlights the importance of the social and economic ties between extended families that straddle the rural and urban sectors. These very networks are key for our understanding of the persistence of cyclical migration in Namibia. The increase in urban poverty and the limitations of economic opportunities available to migrants make rural–urban interdependence an integral characteristic of the Namibian social economy.

In the past, migration to urban areas was largely temporary in both legal status and practicality and served the labour needs of the colonial system. A cyclical pattern of movement was typical (although more permanent migration with families to urban areas did occur simultaneously). Today, this form of cyclical migration of labour is much less significant, and is being replaced by the equally mobile but more complex phenomenon of 'reciprocal migration.'

Conventional wisdom assumes that urbanisation is both sustained and unilinear. However, this process is seen as slower in southern Africa than elsewhere, and to have been hindered by the economic slowdown of the past decade because of slow industrial growth and limited employment opportunities. While permanent urbanisation certainly continues in the region, the persistence of non-commercial agricultural production and a rise in urban poverty have set in motion a complex system of cyclical or reciprocal migration between rural and urban areas. Pressures on rural systems of production are increasing as per capita economic opportunities in urban areas are decreasing, and it appears to be this interplay of factors that is increasing the interdependency of urban and rural systems, spawning a new form of urbanisation within Namibia. This form of multi-layered and complex 'disorderly urbanisation' is described in this research as 'reciprocal urbanisation' in the Namibian context. This new form of urbanisation appears to be enhanced by modern communications and transport technologies, which make the flow of information and people across geographic space easier than ever before in the country's history.

This finding challenges current theory that relies on the unilinear model of migration and urbanisation, and suggests that the urban futures of countries like Namibia are likely to be intimately tied to rural systems, and that the two will operate in a very direct symbiosis. This symbiosis will have political, social, economic and environmental dimensions.

8. Conclusions

The findings of this research are sufficiently provocative to suggest a number of important research directions. Within Namibia, a range of future research is indicated, which includes both the rural and urban sectors. At the rural end of the spectrum, the importance of rural agriculture suggests that protecting rural productivity at the household level is crucial, and this includes addressing issues of land tenure, technology and the environment.

The environmental impact of urbanisation is typically researched within the urban context, with rural environmental inquiry being carried out as an unrelated endeavour. However, migration and urbanisation might well have significant impacts on the rural environment in Namibia, with important consequences and policy implications for both rural and urban livelihoods that cut across rural and urban sectors. This research raises a potentially important question about the extent to which rural–urban migration promotes the degradation of the rural environment and at the same time contributes to the social and economic development of the rural population.

The logic behind this question is that access to money by rural migrants in the urban areas results in return-spending in the rural areas. This spending makes a range of modern goods and services affordable for rural households, which might well promote local development objectives. A good example of this is the recent rise in the number of brick houses built in the rural areas, which then reduces the reliance on local forest resources for construction. Conversely, the number of vehicles is rising in the rural areas, with significant negative effects on the environment (people drive on tracks in the bush between homesteads, and from the homesteads to town). Also, an important focus of investment for urban dwellers is rural livestock herds. Numbers of livestock rose between 1990 and 2000 and may have significant negative environmental consequences that would in turn affect urban livelihoods.

At the urban end of the spectrum, it is likely that urban agriculture will provide a significant source of urban food in the future. There is therefore a need to undertake research in Namibia into intensive, small-scale agricultural irrigation systems that are water-conserving and that can be applied at the household level in the city. In addition, ways to manage urban livestock are likely to become increasingly relevant, and proactive research in this direction is important. This work may have application to other countries in the region.

Moving to the regional scale, it seems probable that the form of reciprocal urbanisation described in this paper is not unique to Namibia. Similar conditions and processes are at work elsewhere in the region, and beyond. In her most recent work on Zimbabwe, Potts (2000) suggests that migrants in the urban areas are directly dependent on their rural land, and that recent urban difficulties may have resulted in increased rural productivity. The migration and urbanisation phenomenon is sufficiently complex in Namibia to challenge modernist views of unilinear urbanisation. Potts (2000: 831) concurs for Zimbabwe: 'Indeed, the nexus between rural production, migration and urbanisation is too complex to comprehensively address through neoliberal assumptions about economic growth and private ownership of land.'

In addition to Zimbabwe, it is likely that similar dynamics are at work in other countries in the region with similar social and economic histories. These would include Malawi, South Africa and Zambia. While South Africa is often regarded as 'unique' in the region, it is possible that a similar situation might be observed in certain parts of the country. Smit (1998) argues that rural ties are important in the urbanisation process for rural migrants who move to Durban. Rural–urban linkages warrant further investigation in Namibia, given the failure of industrial growth in creating employment. If 'reciprocal urbanisation' is the emerging reality in the region, research is urgently needed to further uncover the dynamics at work, as these have direct implications for the way development practitioners might shape policy and practice, with poverty alleviation as a central objective.

The general issue of coping (demographic and food transfers) raises another important question in relation to these findings: What happens when sources of rural food supply are interrupted? Because of their long histories of civil war, it is likely that Angola and Mozambique offer pertinent case studies of the consequences of disrupting rural productive systems and limiting rural–urban mobility. In both Angola and Mozambique the urban boundary has been largely impermeable as a result of the sustained conflict, limiting the flow of people and food between rural and urban centres. These case studies help us understand urban households' coping strategies when access to rural food supplies is disrupted. Urban agriculture, for example, might well play a significant role in promoting urban food security, but further investigation is required. In the case of Mozambique, now that the war is over, are people reclaiming rights to rural land and growing food there? If so, will the direction of urbanisation conform to the emerging pattern of reciprocity evident in Namibia?

The research questions posed here aim to address the degree to which the Namibian food security situation is illustrative of other countries in the region. If the findings in Namibia indicate a new form of social and economic organisation in southern Africa, as suggested by the conceptual framework in the earlier discussion in this chapter, development policy and planning will need to reshape its agenda accordingly. Certainly migration, and in particular the new form of reciprocal migration – the reciprocity between urban and rural households described in this study – will be central to that agenda.

Acknowledgements

This research was funded by the International Development Research Centre (IDRC) of Canada under the Cities Feeding People Program and the Social Sciences and Humanities Research Council (SSHRC) of Canada. The author gratefully acknowledges the additional financial and in-kind contributions made by the Regional Network on AIDS, Livelihoods and Food Security (RENEWAL); the International Food Policy Research Institute (IFPRI); Queen's University (Southern African Migration Programme and the Southern African Research Centre); the Social Sciences Division of the Multi-Disciplinary Research and Consultancy Centre at the University of Namibia; and the international NGO Ibis (WUS-Denmark), Windhoek.

References

BAKER, J & AINA, T, 1995. *The migration experience in Africa.* Uppsala: Nordiska Afrikainstitutet.

BARRETT, C & CARTER, M, 2000. Directions for development policy to escape poverty and relief traps. In *Africa notes.* Institute for African Development, Cornell University. Ithaca, NY, pp: 1–5.

BEINART, W, 1980. Labour migrancy and rural production: Pondoland c. 1900–1950. In Meyer, P (ed.), *Black villagers in an industrial society: anthropological perspectives on labour migration in South Africa.* Cape Town: Oxford University Press.

BOWBRICK, P, 1986. The causes of famine: a refutation of Professor Sen's theory. *Food Policy,* 11(2): 105–24.

CRUSH, J & SOUTTER, C, 1999. Natural family conditions: narratives of stabilisation and the South African coal mines, 1910–1970. *South African Geographical Journal,* 81(1): 5–14.

CRUSH, J, FRAYNE, B. & GRANT, M, 2006. Linking migration, HIV/AIDS and urban food security in southern and eastern Africa. RENEWAL Research Paper. Washington DC: International Development Research Institute.

CURREY, B & HUGO, G (eds), 1984. *Famine as a geographical phenomenon.* Dordrecht: Reidel.

DANDO, W, 1980. *The geography of famine.* London: Edward Arnold.

DE WAAL, A, 1990. A reassessment of entitlement theory in the light of the recent famines in Africa. *Development and Change,* 21: 469–90.

DEVEREUX, S, 1993. *Theories of famine.* New York: Harvester Wheatsheaf.

— 1999. Making less last longer: informal safety nets in Malawi. IDS Discussion Paper No. 373, University of Sussex, Institute of Development Studies.

DEVEREUX, S & NAERAA, T, 1996. Drought and survival in rural Namibia. *Journal of Southern African Studies,* 22(3): 421–40.

DEVEREUX, S, FULLER, B, MOORSOM, R, SOLOMON, C & TAPSCOTT, C, 1995. Namibia poverty profile. SSD Research Report No. 21. Social Sciences Division of the Multi-Disciplinary Research Centre. University of Namibia, Windhoek.

DRAKAKIS-SMITH, D, 1990. Food for thought or thought about food: urban food distribution systems in the Third World. In Potter, R & Salau, A (eds), *Cities and development in the Third World,* London: Mansell, pp. 100–20.

— 1991. Urban food distributions systems in Asia and Africa. *Geographical Journal*, 157: 51–61.

— 1995. Third World cities: sustainable urban development I. *Urban Studies*, 23(4–5): 659–77.

— 1997. Third World cities: sustainable urban development III – basic needs and human rights. *Urban Studies*, 34(5–6): 797–823.

DRIMIE, S, FRAYNE, B & TEFASSE, G, 2006. RENEWAL Ethiopia background paper: HIV/AIDS, food and nutrition security. Commissioned by CIDA and Irish Aid. Addis Ababa: International Food Policy Research Institute.

ELLIS, F & HARRIS, N, 2004. New thinking about urban and rural development. Keynote Paper for DFID Sustainable Development Retreat, University of Surrey, Guildford, 2004.

FERGUSON, J, 1996. Urban trends on the Zambian Copperbelt: a short bibliographic note. *Journal of Southern African Studies*, 22: 313–4.

FRAYNE, B, 2001. *Survival of the poorest: migration and food security in Namibia.* PhD Thesis, Queen's University.

— 2004. Migration and urban survival strategies in Windhoek, Namibia. *Geoforum*, 35: 489–505.

— 2005. Eating away from home: rural productivity and urban survival in Namibia. *Journal of Contemporary African Studies*, 23(1): 51–76.

FRAYNE, B & PENDLETON, W, 2001. Migration in Namibia: combining macro and micro approaches to research design and analysis. *International Migration Review*, 35(4): 1054–85.

— 2003. *Mobile Namibia: Trends in National and International Migration.* SAMP Migration Policy Series No. 27. Cape Town: Institute for a Democratic Alternative in South Africa (IDASA).

GLANTZ, M (ed.), 1987. *Drought and hunger in Africa: denying famine a future.* Cambridge: Cambridge University Press.

IIPINGE, E & LEBEAU, D, 1997. Beyond inequalities: women in Namibia. *Southern African Resource and Documentation Centre (SARDC)*, Harare, Zimbabwe.

HANSOHM, D, 2000. Alternative paths of economic development in Namibia. In Fuller, B & Prommer, I (eds), *Population-development-environment in Namibia: background readings.* Laxenburg: International Institute for Applied Systems Analysis (IIASA), pp. 165–84.

INTERNATIONAL DEVELOPMENT RESEARCH CENTRE (IDRC), 1997. *Development research in urban agriculture: an international awards program.* International Development Research Centre (IDRC), Ottawa, Canada.

KESSIDES, C, 2005. The urban transition in sub-Saharan Africa: implications for economic growth and poverty reduction. Washington: The World Bank.

KOC, M, MAC RAE, R, MOUGEOT, L & WELSH, J (eds), 1999. For hunger-proof cities: sustainable urban food systems. International Development Research Centre (IDRC). Ottawa: IDRC.

LIPTON, M, 1977. *Why poor people stay poor: urban bias in world development.* London: Temple Smith.

— 1982. Why poor people stay poor. In Harris, J (ed.), *Rural development: theories of peasant economy and agrarian change.* London: Hutchinson, pp. 66-81.

MOORSOM, R, 1995. *Underdevelopment and labour migration: the contract labour system in Namibia.* Windhoek: Dept. of History, University of Namibia.

MOSER, C, 1996. Confronting crisis: a comparative study of household responses to poverty and vulnerability on four poor urban communities. Environmentally Sustainable Development Studies and Monograph Series, 8. World Bank, Washington, DC.

— 1998. The asset vulnerability framework: reassessing urban poverty reduction strategies. *World Development*, 26(1): 1–19.

MOUGEOT, L (ed.), 2005. *AGROPOLIS: The social, political, and environmental dimensions of urban agriculture.* Earthscan, London, UK/International Development Research Centre, Ottawa: Canada.

MUNICIPALITY OF WINDHOEK, 1996a. The Windhoek structure plan. City of Windhoek, Windhoek, Namibia.

— 1996b. 1995 residents survey report. Volume 1, Volume 2, Volume 3. City of Windhoek, Windhoek, Namibia.

— 2001. Windhoek urbanisation report. City of Windhoek, Windhoek: Namibia.

MURRAY, C, 1981. *Families divided: the impact of migrant labour in Lesotho.* New York: Cambridge University Press.

NORVAL, D & NAMOYA, R, 1992. The informal sector within Greater Windhoek. Windhoek: First National Development Corporation.

PENDLETON, W, 1991. The 1991 Katutura survey report. Namibian Institute for Social and Economic Research. Windhoek: University of Namibia.

— 1994. *Katutura: a place where we stay: life in a post-apartheid township in Namibia.* Windhoek: Gamsberg Macmillan.

— 1996. *Katutura: a place where we stay.* Ohio University Centre for International Studies. Ohio University Center for International Studies Athens.

— 1998. Katutura in the 1990s. SSD Research Report No. 28, Social Sciences Division of the Multi-Disciplinary Research Centre. University of Namibia, Windhoek.

PENDLETON, W & FRAYNE, B, 1998. Report of the findings of the Namibian migration project. Windhoek: Social Sciences Division Research Report No. 35, Multi-Disciplinary Research Centre, University of Namibia.

PEYROUX, E & GRAEFE, O, 1995. *Precarious settlements at Windhoek's periphery: investigation into the emergence of a new urban phenomenon.* Windhoek: CRIAA.

PILE, S, BROOK, C & MOONEY, G (eds), 1999. *Unruly cities?* London: Routledge.

POMUTI, A & TVEDTEN, I, 1998. Namibia: urbanisation in the 1990s. In *In search of research*, Namibian Economic Policy Research Unit (NEPRU) Publication No. 6, Windhoek: NEPRU.

POTTER, R & LLOYD-EVANS, S, 1998. *The city in the developing world.* Essex, UK: Longman.

POTTS, D, 1995. Shall we go home? Increasing urban poverty in African cities and migration processes. *Geographical Journal*, 161(3): 245–64.

— 2000. Worker-peasants and farmer-housewives in Africa: the debate about 'committed' farmers, access to land and agricultural production. *Journal of Southern African Studies*, 26(4): 807–32.

POTTS, D & MUTAMBIRWA, C, 1998. Basics are now a luxury: perceptions of the impact of structural adjustment on rural and urban areas in Zimbabwe. *Environment and Urbanisation*, 10(1): 55–66.

ROTBERG, R & RABB, T (eds), 1983. *Hunger and history.* Cambridge: Cambridge University Press.

SEN, A, 1981. *Poverty and famines. An essay on entitlement and deprivation.* Oxford: Clarendon Press.

SIMON, D, 1991. Windhoek: Desegregation and change in the capital of South Africa's erstwhile colony. In Lemon, A (ed.), *Homes apart: South Africa's segregated cities.* London: Chapman, pp. 174-90.

SMIT, W, 1998. The rural linkages of urban households in Durban. *Environment and Urbanisation*, 10(1): 77–88.

TODARO, M, 1969. A model of labour migration and urban unemployment in developing countries. *American Economic Review*, 69: 138–48.

— 1995. *Economic development in the Third World.* Harlow: Longman.

— 1997. Urbanisation, unemployment, and migration in Africa: theory and policy. Policy Research Division, Population Council, Working Paper No. 104. New York: Population Council.

TVEDTEN, I & NANGULAH, S, 1999. Social relations of poverty: a case study from Owambo, Namibia. Draft Research Report. Chr. Michelsen Institute, Bergen, Norway.

UN-HABITAT, 2004–2005. State of the world's cities: trends in sub-Saharan Africa. Nairobi: UN-HABITAT.

UNICEF, 1998. *The state of the world's children, 1998.* Oxford: Oxford University Press.

— 2000. *The state of the world's children, 2000.* Oxford: Oxford University Press.

UNICEF/NISER, 1991. A situation analysis of children and women in Namibia. NISER, University of Namibia, Windhoek.

WATTS, M, 1983. *Silent violence: food, famine and peasantry in northern Nigeria.* Berkeley: University of California Press.

— 1987. Drought, environment and food security: some reflections on peasants, pastoralists and commoditi-sation in dryland West Africa. In Glantz, M (ed.), *Drought and hunger in Africa: denying famine a future.* Cambridge: Cambridge University Press, pp. 171-211.

— 1991. Entitlements or empowerment? famine and starvation in Africa. *Review of African Political Economy,* 51: 9–26.

WATTS, M & BOHLE, H, 1993. Hunger, famine and the space of vulnerability. *GeoJournal,* 30(2): 117–25.

WILSON, F, 1972. *Labour in the South African gold mines, 1911–1969.* Cambridge: Cambridge University Press.

YOUNG, L, 1996. World hunger: a framework for analysis. *Geography,* 81(351) Part 2: 97–110.

7 MIGRANTS, URBAN POVERTY AND THE CHANGING NATURE OF URBAN–RURAL LINKAGES IN KENYA

SAMUEL O. OWUOR

1. Introduction

One response to increased urban poverty in Africa involves the strengthening and adaptation of the urban–rural linkages that have always been such an important part of urbanisation processes on the continent (Potts & Mutambirwa, 1990). Many urban households have rural components to their livelihoods and retain strong links with rural areas, while some keep part of their asset base in rural areas (Foeken & Owuor 2001; Owuor, 2003). These combined urban and rural residences and livelihoods have been called 'multi-spatial livelihoods' by Foeken and Owuor (2001). Rural livelihood sources accessed by urban households are embedded in the linkages, interaction and reciprocity that are evident between them and their rural household members, homes or areas.

It is common for urban Kenyans to identify themselves with an 'urban house' and a 'rural home', which partly explains why the majority are never permanent residents in towns. A rural home is normally the ancestral land that is passed on from father to son. Traditionally, the daughter does not qualify to inherit her father's ancestral land because she is expected to get married and make her 'home' with her husband's family. The urban migrant who identifies him/herself with a rural home is a well-established phenomenon of African migration (Oucho,

1996; Francis, 2000). In Kenya, as elsewhere in sub-Saharan Africa, the urban bias of development is symbiotic with the migrants' rural bias toward home – a place to visit periodically, to which they will retire and where eventually they will be buried (Owuor, 2004, 2005).

According to Tacoli (2002) rural–urban interactions include spatial linkages – flows of people, of goods, of money and other social transactions between towns and countryside – and sectoral interactions between 'urban' sectors in rural areas (e.g., rural non-farm employment) and 'rural' sectors in urban areas (e.g., urban agriculture). Through these interactions or linkages, households increasingly rely on both rural- and urban-based resources for their livelihoods – that is, many households straddle the city and village for their livelihoods (Satterthwaite & Tacoli, 2002).

Although urban dwellers have always maintained links with the rural areas, economic crisis and structural adjustment in the last two decades seem to have produced fundamental and interrelated changes in urban–rural linkages:

> African urban residents have long maintained strong social and economic links with their rural 'home' areas, although the nature of those links has varied over time, as the nature of migration streams has adapted to changing economic and political circumstances, and from country to country with variations in factors such as colonial policy, urban history, and land tenure and land availability. The recent era of severe economic decline and structural adjustment has seen such linkages assume a new and vital significance (Potts, 1997: 449).

First, new forms of migration have emerged or old ones have intensified and others have slowed (Tacoli, 1997). Research in the 1990s indicated that the rate of rural–urban migration was decreasing, while return migration from the city to the rural 'home' was emerging (Tripp, 1996; Potts, 1997; Baker, 1997; Tacoli, 1998; Okali et al., 2001). Circular migration between urban and rural areas was also increasing (Smit, 1998). A review of recent empirical evidence on migration and urbanisation in francophone West Africa suggests that economic crisis may increase circular migration between towns and villages (Beauchemin & Bocquier, 2003). While acknowledging that urban out-migration is not a new phenomenon, Beauchemin and Bocquier (2003: 10) argue that:

> It seems to be increasing in importance. In addition to the traditional return flows of migrants, a new kind of urban-to-rural migration, linked to economic crisis, has appeared … since the early 1980s. The job market degradation and the deterioration of the standard of living created new relationships between migration, employment and education. In the past, people moved to town to attend school or to find a job. Today, the opposite is quite frequent. A large number of people who have been fired from formal sector jobs return to the villages. In addition, some urban residents with jobs, confronting their incomes to the urban cost of living, choose to return to rural areas where incomes are lower but where food and housing are almost free.

Secondly, rural links have become vital safety valves and welfare options for urban people who are very vulnerable to economic fluctuations (Gugler, 1991; Potts, 1997; Smit, 1998; Frayne, 2004). There is evidence of a significant shift in the nature of transfers of goods and cash between urban and rural households, in the sense that remittances from urban to rural areas are declining (Bah et al., 2003) and transfers of food from rural to urban areas are increasing, not only in amount and frequency but also in importance:

It appears that far more food is now being brought in from rural areas, which of course greatly enhances urban residents' vested interests in maintaining their social and economic rural links. These transfers can rely on surpluses generated by existing rural kin or on urban residents returning in the rainy season to culti- vate, which they would probably not choose to do if they could afford urban food prices or could gain access to sufficient land in town to grow food (Potts, 1997: 466).

Urban households with limited social connections to rural areas are the most vulnerable to hunger. In contrast, those with active rural–urban linkages enjoy significant transfers of food from rural areas that offset hunger and vulnerability in the urban context (Frayne, 2004). For the large majority of urban dwellers, food from rural areas is important for the household's food security situation (Mulinge & Jayne, 1994; Mwangi, 1995; Tripp, 1996; Krüger, 1998; Muzvidziwa, 2001; Frayne, 2004). For others, rural produce (when sold) is an additional source of household income (Potts & Mutambirwa, 1990; Rakodi, 1995; Fall, 1998).

While migrants continue to rely on food from their rural homes, there is some evidence that remittances to rural areas are declining as urban dwellers find it harder to spare any money (Potts, 1997: 466). The decline in remittances in amount and real terms is a consequence of the increasing employment insecurity and the cost of living in town. Greater economic hardship and other important aspects such as the increasing cost of education, healthcare, housing and food have led to migrants sending less in remittances than before. Despite the decline in urban to rural remittances, social links between migrants and their rural home areas remain as strong as ever (Tacoli, 2002). For many migrants, this is not only a part of their social identity but also a way of spreading their assets (and risk) across space and maintaining a safety net which helps in times of economic and social insecurity in cities (Bah et al., 2003: 20).

Thirdly, to reduce household expenses, a husband may return his wife and all or some of the children to the village while he remains in town (Rakodi, 1995; Potts, 1997; Frayne, 2004). Also observed is a pattern where the wife goes to the rural areas for a substantial period during the main agricultural season and visits at other times of the year for shorter periods (Rakodi, 1995). With the wife returning to the rural home to engage in farming and children returning to attend school in the village, the family can face economic hardships better (Beauchemin & Bocquier, 2003) and at the same time the rural base is kept as a 'safe haven' (Bigsten, 1996).

Similarly, young people unable to find jobs in town may return to the rural home out of choice or be sent there by their parents. Fostering urban children at the rural home is also common among female-headed households. For example, Muzvidziwa (2001) and Nelson (2001) found that female-headed households in Zimbabwe and Kenya sent their children to stay at the rural home as a cost-cutting measure. The high costs of education in urban schools may push parents to return children to rural areas where schools and other related expenses are relatively cheap (Potts, 1997). Another reason for leaving family members behind in rural areas is a lack of housing in town (Potts & Mutambirwa, 1990). For Beall (2002), such arrangements support the argument that urban households' livelihood strategies cannot be seen in isolation from their wider context. In that case, the practice illustrates the role played by rural families in helping to reduce vulnerability for urban households (Frayne, 2004). Access to rural assets is therefore, according to Krüger (1998), at least a supplementary – if not essential – element for securing and stabilising the livelihood systems of many vulnerable urban households.

This chapter explores the hypothesis that with the present trends of economic hardships, increased cost of living and urban poverty, 'falling back' on rural areas and specifically reliance on rural food and income sources is, or has become, increasingly important in the livelihood of many migrants in sub-Saharan African cities. The chapter examines the nature, extent and direction of urban–rural linkages, including (1) social reciprocity between urban and rural areas; (2) flows of money and goods between urban and rural areas; and (3) return migration from urban to rural areas.

2. Social Reciprocity Between Urban and Rural Areas

This chapter uses survey results and in-depth case studies carried out in Nakuru town, Kenya, between 2001 and 2003. The first phase (in 2001) was a general survey of 344 households, using a standardised pre-coded questionnaire. The second phase (in 2002) consisted of in-depth interviews or case studies with 16 households drawn from the initial sample. Of these 16 households, five were further selected for the third phase – the rural visits (in 2002/2003) – a continuation of the in-depth studies, but at the respondents' rural homes.

Social reciprocity (or interactions) between urban and rural areas can be analysed within the context of regular visits that occur between urban-based and rural-based members. In the last quarter of 2001, during the general survey, all respondents were asked if the household head and/or spouse had visited their rural areas; 80 per cent had done so. Table 1 presents a summary of the characteristics of visits to the rural areas by Nakuru town households.

There were various reasons for visiting the rural homes or plots. Typically due to kinship and family ties, urban dwellers are obliged to occasionally visit their family members and relatives who live in the rural areas. Essentially, these visits are meant to maintain and foster kinship and family relations. It is for these reasons that about three-quarters of the plots were visited by the Nakuru town households 'to see or visit' the rural household or family members and relatives (Table 7.1). For both migrants and non-migrants, and especially the urban poor, this is not only part of their social identity but also an important safety net during periods of economic and social insecurity in the cities. So strong is this bond that urban households continue to visit the rural areas regardless of the distance from Nakuru and in spite of high transport costs.

Table 7.1: Visits to the Rural Home or Plot in the Last Quarter of 2001 (%)		
Purpose of visit*	See/visit rural-based family or relatives	71.1
	Attend to rural farming activities	55.9
	Attend to cultural ceremonies	29.5
	'Holiday' from town life	24.9
Number of visits	Less than 5 visits	54.7
	5 to 9 visits	16.0
	10+ visits	29.2
Frequency of visit	More often than monthly	17.5
	Monthly	21.2
	Every two to four months	37.8
	Once/twice a year	23.5

Source: 2001 Survey (N=349 plots).
*Total > 100% due to combined answers.

For more than half the respondents, the second reason for visiting rural areas is to attend to farming activities. From time to time, the household head and/or spouse visited the rural plot to supervise or participate in these activities. The third reason is to attend family functions and events such as weddings and funerals. Lastly, it is a practice for some townspeople to visit the rural areas for their annual leave, school holidays, or at long weekends and on public holidays just to get out of the town environment.

The frequency of visits to the rural areas differs from household to household and is likely to be influenced by factors such as the distance to the rural area, the purpose of visit and the relationship of the household head to the rural-based household and family members. On average, half of the plots had been visited fewer than five times, while another quarter had experienced at least ten regular visits (Table 7.1). About two-fifths of the plots were visited on a monthly basis or more and another two-fifths every two to four months, while the rest were visited only once or twice a year.

The nearer the rural home or plot is, the higher the interaction. Those who farm in a rural area also visit the rural plots more frequently than those who do not. Urban households practising rural farming are likely to frequent their rural plots to oversee, and sometimes participate in, farming activities. The frequency of visiting rural plots is also higher when the wife is living at the rural home (or at the plot). This is logical because the family bond between the urban and the rural parts of the household is maintained through such frequent visits. For example, one respondent explained that: 'Since my wife and children went to live at home, I visit them any time I get an opportunity and there is no question about it. I cannot live in Nakuru town for more than two or three months without seeing them.'

The number of days spent in the rural areas per visit varied from one to seven days and, in a couple of cases, a month. Owing to 'commitments in town', the preferred length of stay in the rural areas for any given visit was between one and seven days. Even then, many spent only one or two days, preferably at weekends and on public holidays. Longer visits are made during annual leave, school holidays or at the Christmas and New Year breaks. The Christmas holidays are traditionally the time when people living in town return to the rural home to celebrate with their relatives. One middle-aged male respondent maintains his parents' tradition of going to the rural home in December:

> Even though my father lived and worked in Nakuru town, it was tradition for us to go home once a year in December. My parents liked celebrating Christmas at home. I do the same even now. I prefer going home with my family in December.

That does not, however, prevent his wife from going to their rural home more than once in a year:

> I go home more often than my husband. I prefer going home in April, August and obviously in December, all during school holidays. In many instances, my husband sends me to supervise and help in farming and to find out how the people at home are doing. I do not have a definite number of days I stay at home. It can be one day or two weeks, depending on what has taken me there.

Even though Nakuru townspeople wish to visit their rural areas as often as possible, they are limited by the high travel costs, especially for those whose rural plots are far from Nakuru. For half of the households, the frequency of visiting rural areas has decreased with time; for about a quarter there has been no change, and for another sixth the frequency has increased. People can no longer comfortably afford to make as many trips to their rural homes or plots as they did before. To reduce transport costs, some households no longer travel to the rural home with the entire family, except for once every one or two years. However, it is still common for both the husband and wife to attend a close relative's funeral.

Others are simply unable to afford the high transport costs to their rural home, like the respondent quoted below, who nevertheless continues to maintain links with his wife at home whenever an opportunity arises:

> Until the 1990s, I visited my family at home regularly, thrice or four times a year. I can no longer afford that because transport costs have become unbearable and life is more expensive nowadays than it was. As much as I would have liked to go home more often than I do now, I am restrained by the high transport costs. However, I rely on relatives who often go home while my wife relies on relatives who are coming back to Nakuru from home. Through that, she is able to send me some food and I am also able to send her some money.

However, there are circumstances when the rural plot may be visited more frequently for a certain period of time during the year. This could be because of the illness of a family member or a close relative at home or when one is building a house at home.

The flow of visits is not only from Nakuru to the rural areas but also the other way round. Eighty-six per cent of the respondents confirmed that their rural-based family members or relatives do visit them in Nakuru for various reasons. The reasons for the reverse flow are quite similar to urban dwellers' reasons for visiting the rural areas. Again, the main reason is the normal 'to-see-them' visits between close relations. Besides these, rural family members and relatives may come to Nakuru to get medical attention, to collect farm inputs, for family ceremonies, or 'when in a problem' that needs the urban household's attention. Some bring money from the sale of farm produce while others come to obtain money for purposes such as farming activities or school fees. Generally, they bring food from the farm with them and in return they go back with purchased (food) items from Nakuru.

Even so, the rural-to-urban visits are nowadays not common because urban households can no longer afford to accommodate their relatives in town for a long time:

> These days we do not just entertain those unplanned visits from any relative like long ago. We cannot afford to accommodate them for long even if they should come. Life in town is expensive. We prefer planned visits with a specific purpose.

This is not the case with multi-spatial households where the wife and children live at home. In such cases, rural-to-urban visits are quite similar to the urban-to-rural visits described above. The rural part of the household, i.e., wife and children, are bound to visit the urban household, i.e., the husband/father, on a regular basis.

3. Flows of Goods and Money between Urban and Rural Areas

3.1 Urban-to-rural flows

Generally, the flow of goods between urban and rural areas was not easy to capture because of its complexity, involving as it does a wide range of goods and varied quantities in space and time. What came out generally from the survey results is that when urban household members visit their rural homes or plots, they bring purchased food items, non-food items or money with them. Similarly, when the rural household members or rural-based relatives visit Nakuru townspeople, they go back with similar items. Other goods find their way to the rural areas for specific purposes; for example, presents (e.g., clothes), building materials, farm inputs, or items for funerals.

Besides the flow of goods, further questions were asked about the urban-to-rural flow of money. The results presented in Table 7.2 show that about three-quarters of Nakuru town households contributed financially to their rural household or family members. The frequency of sending money and the amount vary. For example, the frequency is likely to be higher for multi-spatial households and for rural farmers. Exchange of money also occurs when urban household members visit their rural plots: 77 per cent of respondents reported that they normally give money to their rural household members, parents or other close relatives on most of their visits to the rural areas.

The reasons for sending money to the rural areas were basically for general upkeep, i.e., to support the family at the rural home; what respondents called 'money to buy sugar.' Money is also sent for farming purposes or for paying school fees (Table 7.2). On specific requests, money may be sent for a festivity, a funeral or for medical purposes.

Table 7.2: Urban-to-Rural Flow of Money (%)		
Remitting money to rural areas (N=327 households)	Yes	73.1
	No	26.9
Frequency of sending money (N=239 households)	More often than monthly	5.0
	Monthly	35.1
	Every two to four months	41.4
	Once or twice a year	18.4
Reasons for sending money (N=239 households)*	General upkeep	90.4
	Farming purposes	57.3
	Payment of school fees	23.8
Change in frequency of sending money (N=239 households)	Decreased	54.8
	Increased	19.7
	No significant change	25.5
Source: 2001 Survey. *Total > 100% due to combined answers.		

Given the tension between rising need and falling wages, it is not surprising that over half of the households in Nakuru send money back home less frequently. A quarter have not experienced any change, while for a fifth the frequency has somehow increased (Table 7.2). Though they still continue to send money back home, the decline in remitting money to the rural areas is being felt slightly more by low- and very-low-income households.

Nevertheless, as part of the household, the husband in town will always endeavour to support the rural household members. According to an elderly grandmother in the rural area, the exchange of money and goods between parents at home and their children in town and/or between a husband in town and his wife at home is mutual. For that matter, according to her, nothing is changing: "My son has always been very good to us. Although life is expensive in town, he can still manage to send us something small every now and then."

3.2 Rural-to-urban flows

Besides the urban-to-rural flow of money and goods, both food and non-food items flow from rural to urban areas as well, through the urban household members, rural household members or other relatives. First, even though urban households send money back home or to the rural plots, there are indications that the reverse is also true, albeit sporadically. In other words, some urban households also receive money from the rural plots: 5 per cent of the household heads (and/or spouses) who visited the rural plots brought money back with them, while 3 per cent of the rural-based household members who visited their urban households brought some money with them from the rural home or plot.

Secondly, as part of the complex socio-economic ties, it is common to observe exchanges of food items occurring between the urban and the rural parts of the household or rural-based family members. More often than not, when urban household members visit their rural counterparts, they take with them purchased items such as salt, sugar, milk, bread, tea, cooking fat, and so on. In return, they are given food from the shamba (plot or farm) to bring back to town for consumption. The most common items are green maize, local vegetables, sweet potatoes, cassava, maize or millet flour, groundnuts, fruit and chickens. These are ideally regarded as not being commonly available to the town dweller. Exchange is common between parents living at the rural home and children who have migrated to towns. Similarly, when the rural-based members visited the urban household, they took food from the shamba with them and went back with purchased food and non-food items from town.

However, to increase their food security in town, a large majority of households nowadays rely on their own rural production. Through regular visits to their rural homes or plots, urban dwellers are able to practise rural farming, directly or indirectly, through the cooperation of rural household members, rural-based family members or through hired farmhands. For the large majority, rural farming is an additional food and income source for the households concerned (Table 7.3). Rural crop cultivation and livestock-keeping constitute an additional source of food for about two-thirds of the urban households practising it and an additional income source for more than half of them.

Table 7.3: Importance of Rural Farming Activities (%)		
	Crop cultivation (N=173)	Livestock-keeping (N=111)
Could not survive without it	74.6	39.6
Major income source	16.2	2.7
Additional income source	57.2	54.1
Major food source	23.7	0.9
Additional food source	66.5	67.6
Source: 2001 Survey. Total > 100% due to combined answers.		

The importance of rural farming is stressed further by the fact that three-quarters of the crop cultivators indicated that they 'could not survive without it', with it being a 'major food source' to a quarter of them. Livestock is an important source of food and income only in situations where need arises and therefore acts as a form of social security. The following four respondents explained the importance of rural farming for their households:

On average, we used to spend about 150 shillings on food, almost on a daily basis. Since we started cultivating our own food, the food budget has been reduced to about half that amount. In addition, we get a little money when some of the produce is sold.

The maize and beans in this house come from the shamba at home. With a good harvest, I rarely buy maize and beans in this house. I can therefore use that money for other things. I could not have survived without this. Life has become so difficult.

Our plot has been of great importance to us. The money we got when we sold our produce helped us to pay for our children's school fees.

> When I have a financial problem, I sell one or two of my cows at home. For example, I have sold a number of my cows to pay our children's school fees. To me, having cows at home is an asset and a form of security because you can sell one whenever you are in trouble.

Food from own rural production reaches the urban household through rural–urban linkages. Urban households are progressively more involved in rural farming as a source of food rather than relying on food gifts and are intertwined within the social reciprocity between the migrant and his or her relatives at the rural home. Though reciprocity still exists in various forms, this particular kind is shifting from merely receiving food gifts to procuring own food from rural areas. In addition, there are signs that people are buying food items cheaply from rural markets for consumption in town or sometimes even for business.

4. Return Migration

In addition to the reciprocity and economic flows, there is emerging evidence of new forms of urban–rural linkages, namely where part of the urban household – especially the wife of the male head and/or children – is sent to the rural areas. Data from the general survey reveals that in about one-third of the married households the wife and children had stayed for some period of time in the rural areas. Moreover, at the time of the survey, 39 households could be considered multi-spatial, i.e., where the wives of the male heads were actually living at the rural home, mostly together with their children. Some had lived at the rural home from almost immediately after their marriage, while others went to live at their rural homes at various stages of their marriage.

The primary reason for sending some of the urban household members to the rural areas is economic (Table 7.4). Some of the urban household members were sent there because there was not enough money to support them in town and because education for the children was cheaper in the rural area. Living in the rural area, the wife could concentrate on farming as a way of producing food for the family.

Table 7.4: Reasons for Sending Wife and Children to Live at Home (%)*		
	Wife (N=89)	Children (N=73)
Not enough money in town	29.2	38.4
To concentrate on farming	73.0	-
Problem of housing	15.7	15.1
Education is cheaper at home	-	43.8

Source: 2001 Survey.
* Only for those whose wife or children had ever stayed at home. The reasons in each case reflect combined answers.

After 12 years of town life, the following respondent was forced to go and live at home because life in town had become harder and harder:

> My husband does not have enough income to support us in town. His carpentry business has not been doing well for the past few years. This has been his main income source since 1989 when he married me. Since we had access to the rural plot and given that life is relatively cheaper at home, we decided to go and live there. My husband is now living in Nakuru alone.

For another wife, when her husband retired from the civil service, it was the loss of a regular source of income that induced her to move to the rural home. Instead of living in town during her husband's retirement, she decided to go and live at their rural home in 1991 and to concentrate on farming. For the same economic reasons, another respondent, who earns a monthly income of KSh4500, was unable to take care of his wife and five children in Nakuru, let alone fit everyone into his one-room house:

> A few years after our marriage, I suggested that my wife live at home because my salary was, and still is, too small to live with them here. I had a house at home and there was land for her to cultivate. She normally visits me at least once a year and I also visit them whenever I can. Without her agreement about living at home, I could not have survived with all of them in Nakuru. She gets most of their food requirements from the shamba. I am therefore left to concentrate on looking for school fees and once in a while sending them something small for sugar and salt.

In a few cases, the reasons were basically socio-cultural: to build a homestead, to get to know the rural home and the parents-in-law, to take care of sick parents, or to fulfil traditional rites. Even when the children are not accompanied by their mother, it is common for them to be sent to the rural area to stay with their grandparents when the household experiences economic stress and limited food availability. Being unable to provide for their unemployed son, this respondent decided to send him to the rural area, albeit temporarily:

> At the moment, our youngest son is living at home with his grandmother. He recently did a course in Nakuru but was not lucky enough to get a job. Being unemployed, there is not enough money to take care of him here in Nakuru. He is better off at home helping there with farming for the time being, as we look for something for him to do here in Nakuru.

Through this split-migration practice, ties between urban and rural areas are enhanced, while at the same time reducing the food demand of urban households. The burden of providing the daily food requirements for a large household where few are in gainful employment is immense. This strategy of ruralising the urban household therefore helps to minimise the measures of meeting the household's food shortages.

5. Poverty and Interaction

Social and economic interaction occurs between urban and rural areas regardless of income category, the only differences being in their frequency and intensity. Irrespective of income, more than half of the household heads and/or their wives had visited the rural plot or home during the last quarter of 2001. However, owing to financial constraints, the poor (defined as those with a monthly income of KSh5000 or less) were not able to visit their rural plots as regularly as the non-poor. For example, almost all (91 per cent) the household heads and/or spouses in the non-poor group (those with incomes over KSh10 000 per month) had visited at least one of their rural plots, compared to two-thirds of the poor category. Moreover, the frequency of visits to the rural plot or home was much higher among the non-poor.

There is also some difference between the poor and the non-poor in terms of the purpose of visits. Farming-related visits are comparatively more important for the non-poor, while meeting the rural relatives is more often the reason for undertaking the trip among the poor. It is through such 'just-to-see-them' visits that the poor are able to maintain strong links with the rural areas and kin, and therefore ensure a place to fall back on 'in case of anything in town.'

The same trend can be seen with remittances. Although town dwellers send money back home regardless of income, a larger proportion of the non-poor did so and also somewhat more frequently than the poor. Even then, the poor and non-poor showed no clear differences as far as the change in sending money to the rural home was concerned. About 60 per cent of respondents in both groups held the opinion that the frequency of sending money had decreased over time. The same holds for the perceived decrease in frequency of visits to the rural home or plot. However, because these interactions are complex, it is not easy to draw conclusions about the changes that may be taking place between 'town' and 'home.' For example, it may very well be that it is not the frequency of sending money that matters but how much is sent.

Finally, there is some difference between the two income groups as to whether the wife had ever lived in the rural home. For the poor, this was the case with 50 per cent of the households, against 31 per cent of the non-poor. Poor households do this as a coping strategy, i.e. because of lack of income to support them in town.

6. Conclusion

The impossibility of living on typical urban wages in Africa has been dubbed the 'wages puzzle' by Jamal & Weeks (1993). That people do survive is testimony to their ingenuity, determination and sheer hard work. A host of coping strategies have been developed. One of these is falling back on rural resources. Although the types of interaction examined here, as well as their effects, should not be over-generalised, a pattern can be discerned which may be used to gain an understanding of the emerging relationship between urban households and their rural homes or plots. Household-level food transfers from rural to urban areas have become more important with increased urban poverty, while the transfer of money and goods from town to the rural areas has decreased in real value. The flow of food resources from the rural kin to urban households therefore contradicts the common assumption that rural areas or kin act only as recipients of goods and services originating from town.

Returning one's wife and children to live temporarily or permanently in the village seems to be a survival strategy with two benefits: (a) it makes living in town less expensive; and

(b) more food can be obtained from the rural home. Consequently, the economic balance of urban–rural linkages appears to have shifted in favour of the urban households. Although it is difficult to ascertain trends because of the complex nature of the interactions, there are indications that urban–rural ties, which have always been a vital part of African migration processes, have become more important for urban households. Urban residents are looking to rural areas as a subsistence fallback. Maintaining both an urban and rural base provides a safety net, especially for the urban poor in times of economic hardships.

However, rising transport costs in recent years have reduced the frequency of home visits for many people, particularly when long distances are involved. In addition, the quantities of remittances and goods (or gifts) have declined, as the cost of living in urban centres has soared. This does not necessarily imply weakening bonds. For many people who move to the city, the countryside and their native village still remain reference points, both culturally and in terms of family life. The linkages that persist between urban and rural households are central to urban households' ability to survive.

Many development theorists and practitioners have, until recently, viewed rural and urban areas as two mutually exclusive entities with their own unique populations, activities, problems and concerns. However, this does not reflect the realities of multi-spatial livelihoods, which include both urban and rural elements. Interactions between urban and rural areas play an important role in the processes of rural and urban change. It is essential that policies and programmes reflect the importance of the 'urban' part of rural development and the 'rural' part of urban development. In other words, urban development strategies must take account of the rural links and context. The answer to urban poverty cannot be found in the urban areas alone. Policies which neglect this may increase poverty and vulnerability for those groups.

Acknowledgements

I wish to thank the Netherlands Foundation for the Advancement of Tropical Research (WOTRO) for financial support, and the African Studies Centre, Leiden, for granting me visiting fellow status during this study.

References

BAH, M, CISSE, S, DIYAMETT, B, DIALLO, G, LERISE, F, OKALI, D, OKPARA, E, OLAWOYE, J & TACOLI, C, 2003. Changing rural–urban linkages in Mali, Niger and Tanzania. *Environment and Urbanisation*, 15(1): 13–23.

BAKER, J, 1997. Introduction. In Baker, J (ed.), *Rural–urban dynamics in francophone Africa*. Uppsala: Scandinavian Institute of African Studies, pp. 11–25.

BEALL, J, 2002. Living in the present, investing in the future: household security among the urban poor. In Rakodi, C & Lloyd-Jones, T (eds), *Urban livelihoods: a people-centred approach to reducing poverty*. London: Earthscan, pp. 71–87.

BEAUCHEMIN, C & BOCQUIER, P, 2003. *Migration and urbanisation in francophone West Africa: A review of the recent empirical evidence*. Paris: DIAL, Document de Travail.

BIGSTEN, A, 1996. The circular migration of smallholders in Kenya. *Journal of African Economies*, 5(1): 1–20.

FALL, A S, 1998. Migrants' long-distance relationships and social networks in Dakar. *Environment and Urbanisation*, 10(1): 135–45.

FOEKEN, D & OWUOR, SO, 2001. Multi-spatial livelihoods in sub-Saharan Africa: rural farming by urban house-holds – The case of Nakuru Town, Kenya. In de Bruijn, M, van Dijk, R & Foeken, D (eds), *Mobile Africa: changing patterns of movement in Africa and beyond*. Leiden: Brill, pp. 125–40.

FRANCIS, E, 2000. *Making a living: changing livelihoods in rural Africa*. London: Routledge.

FRAYNE, B, 2004. Migration and urban survival strategies in Windhoek, Namibia. *Geoforum*, 35: 489–505.

GUGLER, J, 1991. Life in a dual system revisited: Urban–rural ties in Enugu, Nigeria, 1961–87. *World Development*, 19(5): 399–409.

JAMAL, V & WEEKS, J, 1993. *Africa misunderstood, or whatever happened to the rural–urban gap?* London: Macmillan.

KRÜGER, F, 1998. Taking advantage of rural assets as a coping strategy for the urban poor: the case of rural–urban interrelations in Botswana. *Environment and Urbanisation*, 10(1): 119–34.

MULINGE, M & JAYNE, TS, 1994. Urban maize meal consumption patterns: strategies for improving food access for vulnerable urban households in Kenya. A paper presented at the symposium 'Agricultural Policies and Food Security in Eastern Africa', Nairobi, Kenya, 19–20 May.

MUZVIDZIWA, VN, 2001. Keeping a foot in the village: Masvingo urban women. *Journal of Social Development in Africa*, 16(1): 85–99.

MWANGI, AM, 1995. *The role of urban agriculture for food security in low income areas in Nairobi*. Nairobi and Leiden: Ministry of Planning and National Development and African Studies Centre, Food and Nutrition Studies Programme, Report No. 54.

NELSON, N, 2001. Gikuyu families in Nairobi at the end of the millennium: the impacts of changing livelihoods and residential patterns on parenting, sibling responsibility and the care of ageing parents. A paper presented at the workshop 'African Urban Economies', Leiden, Netherlands, 9–11 November.

OKALI, D, OKPARA, E & OLAWOYE, J, 2001. *Rural–urban interactions and livelihood strategies: the case of Abba and its region, southern Nigeria*. London: International Institute for Environment and Development (IIED), Working Paper No. 4 on Rural–Urban Interactions and Livelihood Strategies.

OUCHO, J, 1996. *Urban migrants and rural development in Kenya*. Nairobi: Nairobi University Press.

OWUOR, SO, 2003. *Rural livelihood sources for urban households: a study of Nakuru town, Kenya*. Leiden: African Studies Centre, ASC Working Paper No. 51.

— 2004. Urban households ruralizing their livelihoods: The changing nature of urban–rural linkages in an East African town. A paper presented at the 'African Studies Centre Seminar Series', Leiden, Netherlands, 16 December.

— 2005. Coping with urban poverty: a study of farming within Nakuru town, Kenya. *Hekima – Journal of the Humanities and Social Sciences*, 3(1): 84–101.

POTTS, D, 1997. Urban lives: adopting new strategies and adapting rural links. In Rakodi, C (ed.), *The urban challenge in Africa: growth and management of the large cities*. Tokyo and New York: United Nations University Press, pp. 447–94.

POTTS, D & MUTAMBIRWA, C, 1990. Rural–urban linkages in contemporary Harare: why migrants need their land. *Journal of Southern African Studies*, 16(4): 677–98.

RAKODI, C, 1995. The household strategies of the urban poor: coping with poverty and recession in Gweru, Zimbabwe. *Habitat International*, 19(4): 447–71.

SATTERTHWAITE, D & TACOLI, C, 2002. Seeking an understanding of poverty that recognizes rural–urban differences and rural–urban linkages. In Rakodi, C & Lloyd-Jones, T (eds), *Urban livelihoods: a people-centred approach to reducing poverty*. London: Earthscan, pp. 52–70.

SMIT, W, 1998. The rural linkages of urban households in Durban, South Africa. *Environment and Urbanisation*, 10(1): 77–87.

TACOLI, C, 1997. The changing scale and nature of rural–urban interactions: recent developments and new agendas. In UNCHS/HABITAT, *Regional development planning and management of urbanisation: experiences from developing countries*. Nairobi: UNCHS/HABITAT, pp. 150–61.

— 1998. Rural–urban interactions: a guide to the literature. *Environment and Urbanisation*, 10(1): 147–66.

— 2002. *Changing rural–urban interactions in sub-Saharan Africa and their impact on livelihoods: a summary*. London: International Institute for Environment and Development (IIED), Working Paper No. 7 on Rural–Urban Interactions and Livelihood Strategies.

TRIPP, AM, 1996. Urban farming and changing rural–urban interactions in Tanzania. In Swantz, M L & Tripp, AM (eds), *What went right in Tanzania: people's response to directed development*. Dar es Salaam: Dar es Salaam University Press, pp. 98–116.

8 REMITTANCES AND DEVELOPMENT: THE IMPACT OF MIGRATION TO SOUTH AFRICA ON RURAL LIVELIHOODS IN SOUTHERN ZIMBABWE

FRANCE MAPHOSA

1. Introduction

The volume of remittances to developing countries has grown significantly in recent years: the total value flowing through official channels worldwide more than doubled between 1998 and 1999 (Gammeltoft, 2002; Ratha, 2003; McKinley, 2003). Developing countries receive an estimated US$80 billion annually in remittances (Ratha, 2003). However, the total amount remitted is much higher than these figures because a large number of transactions are carried through informal channels. Remittances have become the second largest source of external funding in Africa after direct foreign investment (DFI) and ahead of official development aid (ODA). They are therefore an important source of finance and foreign exchange for many

African households and nations; in fact, a number of developing countries rely more on remittances than on official aid (Gammeltoft, 2002).

As van Doorn (2002a) states, remittances have the potential to create positive outcomes for migrant source areas. Unlike other forms of aid, remittances usually do not carry any obligations, constraints or preconditions and they do reach the intended beneficiaries (who are often low-income families) because of the absence of government interference (Stein, 2003).

Although the focus on remittances is not a new phenomenon in migration studies (Black, 2003), they have not received much attention from policy-makers in the countries of origin (McKinley, 2003). As Taylor and Fletcher (2001) note, the complex dynamics of migration, remittances and development are among the least researched and understood topics. As a result, the development potential of remittances has generally not been fully exploited. Countries that have recognised this potential have developed strategies to encourage the flow and effective use of remittances (Lopez et al., 2001; Orozco, 2003; McKinley, 2003; Stein, 2003).

While several studies on international migration from Zimbabwe to South Africa have been carried out (Paton, 1995; Sachikonye, 1998; ILO/SAMAT, 1998; Zinyama, 1990, 2000; Crush & Williams, 2002; Kanyenze, 2004) the role of remittances, especially from undocumented migrants, remains unexplored both as a research and a policy issue. Zimbabwean migrants working in South Africa, including undocumented migrants, transfer significant value to their communities of origin in the form of remittances. This is the most important source of income for many households in the southern districts of Zimbabwe. It is therefore important to recognise both the current and potential benefit of remittances to the migrants' households and communities of origin, and to create a regulatory and policy framework and set up institutional arrangements to enhance the potential contribution to poverty reduction and sustainable development. Careful study, investigation and debate are needed to inform the development of appropriate and effective policies (McKinley, 2003, Stein, 2003). This chapter makes a contribution of this kind, intended to inform policies and help create an environment conducive to the flow and effective use of remittances sent home by Zimbabwean migrants in South Africa.

2. Defining Remittances

There is no consensus on the definition of 'remittances.' This makes it difficult to estimate the total value of remittances transferred to a particular country or region (Taylor & Fletcher, 2001). Many definitions confine remittances to cash or financial transfers. While the term 'remittances' usually refers to cash transfers only, remittances can also be in kind (van Doorn, 2002b). Adams (1991) adopts this inclusive definition and defines remittances as 'money and goods' that are transmitted to the households back home by people working away from their communities of origin. Taylor and Fletcher's (2001) definition is even broader, as it includes monetary or cash transfers and other transfers such as consumer goods, capital goods and skills and technological knowledge. In this chapter, the term 'remittances' is used in this broad sense and includes both cash and non-cash remittances. This definition makes it possible to fully appreciate the migrants' contribution to the welfare of their non-migrant relatives and their communities of origin.

Remittances can be formal or informal depending on the channel through which they are transferred. Formal remittances are those sent through official channels such as bank transfers and money transfer organisations, and informal ones are those sent through unofficial channels such as private money couriers, friends and relatives, or taken home by the migrants themselves (Meyers, 1998; McKinley, 2003; Orozco, 2003). The official channel for sending remittances depends on a number of factors, such as the existence of banking and other financial institutions, the speed, efficiency and security of the system, and the educational status of the sender and the recipient. Undocumented migrants are less likely than documented ones to send their remittances through official channels.

Remittances can be sent individually or collectively. Collective remittances are sent by groups of migrants, usually as members of arrangements commonly referred to as hometown associations (HTAs). These are groups of migrants from particular communities who come together to pool resources to help develop their home communities. There is a substantial volume of literature focusing on the development role of HTAs, particularly in Latin and Central America (Lopez et al., 2001; Taylor & Fletcher, 2001; Orozco, 2003).

3.   Explaining Remitting Behaviour

Chimhowu et al. (2003) classify the theoretical explanations for remitting behaviour into three schools of thought: (a) risk-sharing; (b) altruism; and (c) a combination of risk-sharing and altruism. According to the risk sharing school, remittances are instalments for individual risk management. As premium payments for future risk, remittances allow the remitter and the remaining household members to secure their livelihoods in the event of external shocks such as loss of employment by the remitter, or drought in the case of the recipient. Remittances are part of a mutually beneficial and enforceable contract between the remitter and the recipients. The main problem with this approach is that it views remitting behaviour as motivated purely by rational economic considerations, thus overlooking altruism as a possible factor in remitting behaviour.

The altruism perspective views remitting as motivated by an obligation to the household. Remittances are sent out of affection and responsibility towards the family. The migrant is simply part of a spatially extended household that is reducing the risk of impoverishment by diversifying across a number of activities. In this school of thought, migration is considered to be a family decision and remitting is part of fulfilling family obligations. According to this view, poorer households would receive more remittances than richer ones. The third school of thought combines altruism and self-interest to explain remitting behaviour. Here, various factors determine who remits and how much is remitted. These include the economic situation in the host country, the socio-demographic characteristics of the migrants, their length of stay in the host country, the efficiency of the transfer facilities, the exchange rates and risk factors.

According to Taylor and Fletcher (2001), the discourse on the development impact of remittances is influenced by two broad views: pessimistic and optimistic. The pessimistic or 'migrant syndrome' perspective views remittances as payment for the labour exported from source regions through migration. Migration negatively affects productivity in the migrant-sending areas by removing labour from the sending communities. Remittances only partly compensate for this loss of labour. If labour-sending communities or households are the poorest, the loss of production due to labour migration increases their poverty. The benefits of migration may not be to the poor if the cost of migration is costly and risky. This means that migrants would then come from the middle or upper segments of the migrant-sending communities, not from the poorest households. This means that the gap between the poor and the richer households is increased.

The optimistic perspective views migration as part of an overall family strategy to raise income, obtain funds for investment and insure against risks. Remittances, or even the potential for remittances, can loosen production and investment constraints, setting in motion a development dynamic in poor rural environments. Migration increases household income by shifting people from the low income rural sector to the relatively high income urban and foreign economy. The loss of population to migration increases the average incomes of those left behind and remittances may increase them even further.

The existing literature on remittances suggests that most remittances are used for consumption. Such 'unproductive' uses include satisfying basic consumption needs, buying medicines, building houses, and spending on conspicuous consumption (Black, 2003). Generally, a small proportion of remittances is used for savings and 'productive investment' such as income- and employment-generating activities. Ballard (2003) points out that this failure to invest remittances 'productively' should not be seen as indicating a lack of entrepreneurial skills on the part of migrants and their kinsfolk but rather as the consequence of structural obstacles at the local, national and international levels.

4.   A Case Study of Southern Zimbabwe

The fieldwork for this chapter was carried out in Ward 7 of Mangwe District in the Matabeleland South Province of Zimbabwe (Figure 8.1). The Ward is located about 100 kilometres south of Plumtree, the administrative town for Mangwe District, and about 200 kilometres from Bulawayo, Zimbabwe's second largest city. It is in an agro-ecological region characterised by low rainfall patterns, poor soils and persistent droughts. Owing to the harsh economic conditions, harvests are generally very low and income from crops is insignificant. Crops are grown mainly for domestic consumption. Cattle stocks have been drastically reduced by recurrent droughts. Wage employment is low, with most people in wage employment employed as migrant workers outside the District, within or outside the country.

A variety of research tools were used, including a questionnaire administered to a sample of 150 households. Group discussions and individual unstructured interviews were also conducted with community leaders. Focus group discussions were held with school-leavers, school-going youths and current and returned migrants.

Figure 8.1: Map of Study Area

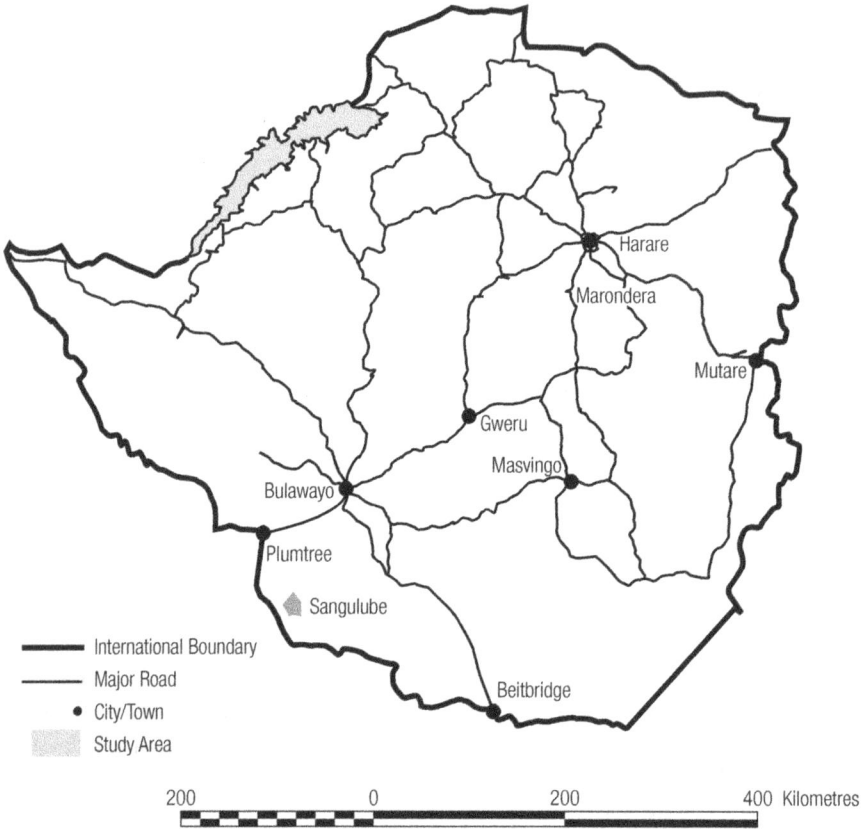

Of the 150 households in the sample, 103 (68,7 per cent) had at least one member who had migrated to South Africa. Hobane (1999) earlier found that 62 per cent of the working population in the same community were working either in South Africa or Botswana. Despite an intensified crackdown on undocumented migrants in the two countries, the rate of migration has been increasing over the last few years. This trend is attributable to the worsening economic situation in Zimbabwe, which is characterised by, among other things, rising unemployment and the continued decline of the Zimbabwean dollar against currencies such as the South African rand and the Botswana pula.

The main reasons given by respondents for migrating to South Africa were economic (Figure 8.2). More than half of them (52 per cent) cited unemployment as the reason why people migrate to South Africa. With limited employment opportunities and lack of income from agriculture, migration to South Africa to seek employment seems to be the only available option for most of the people in this part of the country. Agricultural production, especially crop production, is not an economically viable option because of drought. Cattle, which used to be the mainstay of the economy, have been decimated by drought and are no longer a sustainable option for increasing household income.

Figure 8.2: Reasons for Emigration

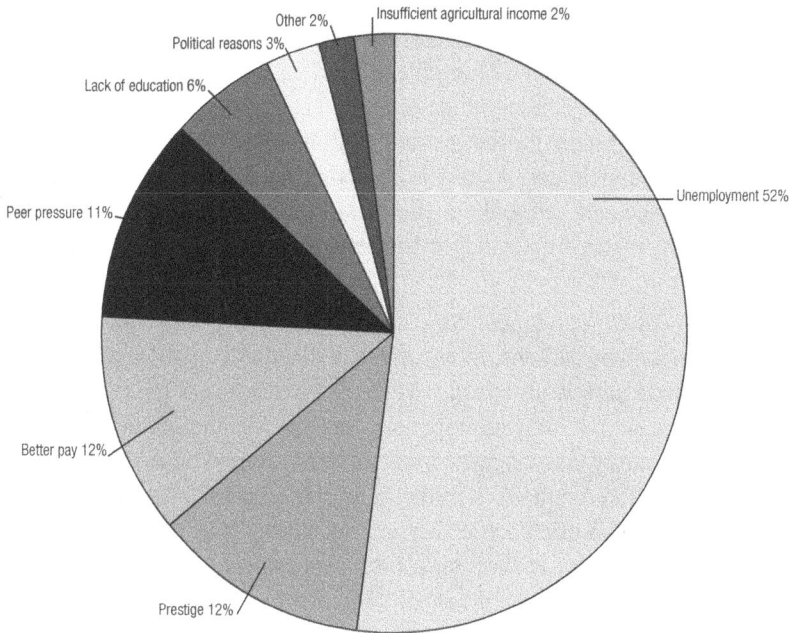

Other factors such as peer pressure (12 per cent), better pay (12 per cent) and prestige (11 per cent) also play roles in the decision to migrate. To many Zimbabweans in this part of the country, migrating to South Africa is a 'rite of passage', a signal of a man's maturity. Among the youths, particularly male youths, those who have not been to South Africa are often despised because they are perceived as *ibhare* (unsophisticated).

5. Remittance Behaviour

Of the 103 households with at least one member working in South Africa, 77 per cent reported receiving remittances. The main reason given for non-remitting was unemployment of the migrant. Various derogatory terms used for those who do not send remittances indicate that remittances are generally expected. A migrant who does not send remittances back home is referred to as *umadliwa*, deriving from the noun *ukudliwa*, meaning to be eaten up or devoured. The connotation is of a person who has been devoured by the pleasures of South Africa, especially one who spends all his money on women and beer, forgetting relatives left behind. Alternatively, such a migrant is referred to as *umgewu*. Although this carries the same connotations as *ukudliwa* and *ukugewuka*, from which the noun *umgewu* is derived, it was not possible to establish the origins of the word. It could be slang or a derivative of one of the languages spoken in South Africa.

Cash was received either as South African rand or Zimbabwean dollars. Sending money in foreign currency depends on two considerations. One is the recipient's literacy level, especially numerical literacy: the recipient must be able to understand the transactions that take place on the black market, where the probability of being swindled is high if one does not appreciate the mathematics involved. The other consideration is the urgency with which the money is needed. When there is a pressing need, such as outstanding school fees or medical expenses, it becomes convenient for the remitter to change the money into Zimbabwean dollars before it reaches the recipient. If there is no urgent need, money can be sent in foreign currency so that the recipient can look for the most favourable rate on the parallel market. Trust is very important in these transactions because, as an illegal activity, dealing in foreign currency is risky.

Non-cash remittances include foodstuffs such as maize meal, sugar, salt and cooking oil, and consumer goods such as bicycles, radios, sofas, agricultural inputs and building material. Most of the remittances sent were in kind. There are two reasons for this preference. The first is that most non-cash remittances respond to the specific and immediate needs of their recipients. When the country was facing shortages of basic commodities, particularly between 2002 and 2003, non-cash remittances in the form of food provided relief to the recipients. The other reason is the non-existence of banking facilities. Cash remittances are therefore sent for specific purposes such as school fees, medical expenses, debts and funeral expenses, and for buying building materials and livestock. The proportion of the cash remittances that goes to savings is very low.

Figure 8.3: Channels for Cash Remittances

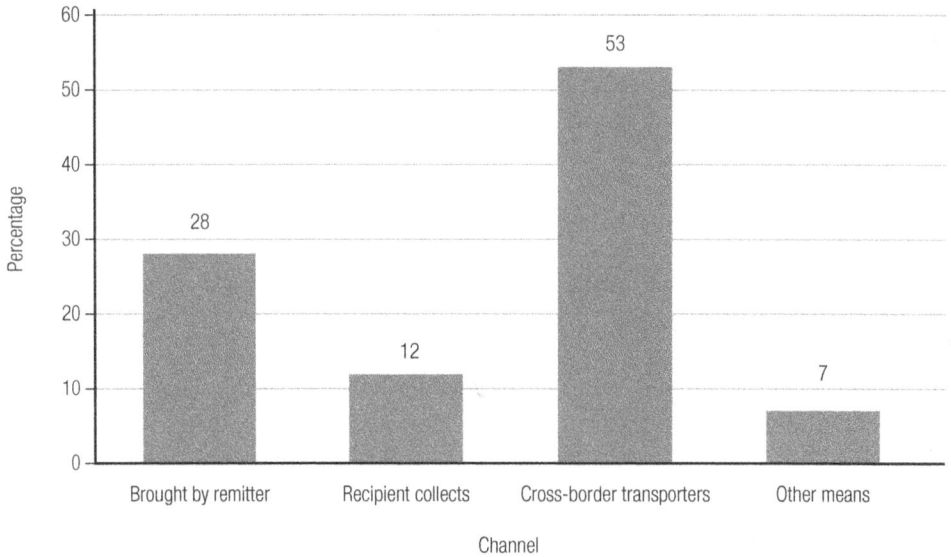

Most of the remittances are sent through informal channels. These include cross-border transport operators, personal delivery by the remitter, or collection by the beneficiary (Figure 8.3). The preferred method of channelling both cash and goods is through cross-border transport operators. These operators, popularly known as *omalayisha*, carry people, goods and money. One of the reasons for using this channel to send remittances is that there are no banking facilities in the area. Banks are found in Plumtree, which is 100 kilometres away. A postal agency that used to offer banking facilities closed a year before the study, citing prohibitively high rentals for the premises from which it was operating. Using banks or the postal service to send remittances would be both costly and inconvenient, as recipients would have to travel to Plumtree to collect them. The cost includes transport, accommodation and food if one has to spend a night in Plumtree, which is often the case because of transport problems. At the time of the research, there were no buses going directly to Plumtree passing through Ward Seven. Residents who wanted to go to Plumtree had to use a route that went via Bulawayo, making the trip much longer and more expensive than normal. The other reason for preferring informal channels is the undocumented status of most of the migrants originating from this area. Undocumented migrants often avoid formal and official ways of doing business.

There are two types of cross-border transport operators: full-time and part-time. Part-time operators are those who have jobs in South Africa and provide transport on weekends, holidays, or when they are on leave. These operators charge a fee of R20 for every R100 they deliver. The charge for transporting goods is determined by weight. There are no standardised methods of determining weight, such as scales; rather, the weight is determined by lifting the parcel and 'feeling' its weight. Although the charge can be negotiated, the transport operator has more power in the negotiation process than the remitter.

Cross-border transport is a lucrative business. Besides the profit they generate in the transport business, the operators also make money by doubling as foreign currency dealers. The advantages of using them to send remittances are mainly speed and convenience. In the absence of banks and other formal channels for transmitting both cash and non-cash remittances, they provide a fast and convenient channel. Trust plays a crucial role in the use of this channel. The choice of transport operator is influenced by kinship relations, friendship ties and neighbourhood ties, among other considerations. It takes about half a day for transport operators to drive from Johannesburg to Ward Seven. The remitter is therefore assured that his or her remittance reaches the recipient the same day it is sent. Although both remitters and recipients complained about the operators' exorbitant charges, this is a cheaper and more convenient option than receiving remittances through banks and the postal service because of travel-related costs to access these facilities. In many cases, these operators deliver the remittances to the recipient's doorstep. This provides convenience, particularly in the case of non-cash remittances, which are often bulky.

The major problem with using cross-border transport operators is the fees they charge. Respondents complained that the 20 per cent fee is exorbitant. Arriving at a charge for non-cash remittances is an arbitrary procedure. Factors such as kinship relations and friendship influence the charge. Remittances sometimes do not reach their intended beneficiaries at all or are delayed. There is no insurance against loss or damage of property, and the operators are also at risk of robbery and murder.

Remittances brought personally by migrants are few. These may be in addition to those sent through other channels such as cross-border transport operators. Bringing remittances in person ensures that the correct amount of money and goods is delivered to the intended recipients and reduces the possibility of remittances not reaching their intended beneficiaries. The disadvantage of this method is that the frequency of the remittances is tied to the frequency of the migrant's home visits. If the migrant has a regular visiting pattern then the recipients are assured of receiving the remittances regularly, which helps them plan and budget for their use; if not, this creates uncertainty for the recipients who cannot plan and budget on the basis of the expected benefits.

Beneficiaries who go to collect remittances are mostly the migrants' spouses, although their parents and children may also do this. In many cases, parents and children go to collect remittances where both spouses are migrants. The advantage of this mode of transmitting remittances is that both remitter and recipient know the amount of money and the goods that have been transferred, thus reducing the possibility of the remittances being delayed or not reaching their intended beneficiaries at all. The cost of travelling and the problems of meeting visa requirements make this the least preferred method of sending or receiving remittances. The value of the remittance is rarely sufficient to compensate for the costs involved.

Most of the problems experienced in receiving remittances involved disputes with cross-border transport operators. These problems include the late delivery of remittances, remittances being lost, wrong parcels or amounts of money being delivered and damage to goods in transit. There are more problems in receiving cash than there are with non-cash remittances. The temptation to convert remittances into own use by third parties, often with the intention of paying the owner back later, is higher in the case of cash than non-cash remittances.

6. Remittance Use

Remittances are an important source of income for households in the study area. They are used mainly to provide for households' basic needs, including food, clothing, shelter, education and healthcare. Sander and Maimbo (2003) describe investment in education, heath care and nutrition as investment in human capital. Almost all the remittance-receiving households (98,8 per cent) mentioned food as one kind of remittance. This indicates the precarious food security situation in the area where most of the household income is spent on food because harvests are very low and barely last to the next harvest season (Hobane, 1999). School fees and healthcare were also mentioned by the majority of the households (78,8 per cent and 65 per cent respectively) as uses of cash remittances (see Table 8.1).

A significant number of remittance-receiving households (58,8 per cent) mentioned investment in livestock. Cattle are reared mainly as a source of income, although they also provide milk and are occasionally slaughtered for meat. Investing in cattle is no longer a sustainable option because of the recurrent droughts, coupled with growing human and livestock populations. As more migrants invest in cattle, great pressure is placed on grazing land and pastures which are affected by the droughts. The Commission appointed by the President at the end of the Fast-Track Land Reform programme concluded that the programme had not led to a significant decongestion of rural areas.

Table 8.1: Uses of Remittances

Remittance use	Number of remittance-receiving h/hs	Percentage
Food	79	98.8
Fees	63	78.8
Medical expenses	52	65
Livestock	47	58.8
Building and consumer goods	25	53.8
Agricultural inputs	43	31.2
Business	8	10
Other	31	38.8

Remittances are also invested in buying other livestock such as donkeys, goats, sheep and chickens. Donkeys and goats are more drought-tolerant than cattle and can therefore survive in harsh climatic conditions. Donkeys provide draught power, while goats and other smaller livestock such as sheep and chickens are kept for meat but occasionally sold to raise income, particularly for emergencies such as medical and funeral expenses. Unlike the decision to sell cattle, which is often that of the head of the household (usually a male migrant), the decision to sell smaller livestock may be taken by other members of the household (usually wives or children of migrants) as needs arise. This also applies to the decision to slaughter smaller livestock for meat.

Investment in agricultural production other than livestock rearing was mentioned by 31,2 per cent of the remittance-receiving households. Cattle and donkeys are an investment in crop production as they provide draught power. Remittances are also used to purchase seed, fertiliser and agricultural implements such as ploughs and hoes. Investing in crop production is not a sustainable option as crops often fail because of the persistent droughts. Only 10 per cent of the remittance-receiving households mentioned investing their remittances in formal businesses. Most of the businesses are traditional rural businesses such as general dealer shops, grinding mills and bottle stores.

Some of the remittance money is invested in buying scotch-carts which are a major means of transport in many rural areas. Scotch-carts (usually drawn by donkeys) are a very versatile form of transport. They are used for transport for daily needs such as fetching water and collecting firewood and also as ambulances and hearses. Bicycles, another important means of transport, are often imported from South Africa. These are used to run errands and are also a useful means of transport for schoolchildren, particularly secondary schoolchildren who would otherwise walk long distances to and from school.

Building houses and purchasing consumer goods were mentioned by 53,3 per cent of the households. Some migrants have built beautiful homes, installed solar power, drilled boreholes and bought consumer goods such as radios, TVs, VCRs and furniture, mostly purchased in South Africa.

Recipients also use part of their remittances for paying debts and contributing to burial societies, funeral expenses and wages for workers. Migrants with aged parents and those with children back home usually hire domestic workers to take care of their parents and children. In the case of households where all or most of the adult male members are migrants, labour is often hired as herd boys and to assist in agricultural activities.

Although a number of migrants have acquired a variety of skills such as brick-laying, carpentry and welding, there are no formal established businesses specialising in these trades. Their activities are informal, micro-scale and seasonal, making an insignificant contribution to employment creation. There is very little investment of remittances at the community level. In the past, migrants have made individual contributions towards refurbishing a mortuary at the local hospital, school development projects and sporting activities. These contributions have been ad hoc and largely uncoordinated.

Remittances from migrants working in South Africa therefore constitute a large proportion of household incomes and have a significant impact on the livelihoods of communities in the southern parts of rural Zimbabwe. Although a large proportion of the remittances is used for basic needs, remittances also help improve the standard of living for remittance-receiving households (Stein, 2003). However, the development potential of these remittances is yet to be fully exploited. This is largely because there has been no attempt to develop an environment that would encourage the flow of remittances and their use in investment. There is no proactive policy to influence the flow and impact of remittances from undocumented migrants working in South Africa.

In May 2004, the Reserve Bank of Zimbabwe introduced the Homelink (Kumusha/Ekhaya) facility through which Zimbabweans in the diaspora could send their remittances back home. As of the end of July 2004, a total of US$23,6 million had been transmitted through the Homelink facility. The Monetary Policy announced in December 2003 also provides for opportunities for non-resident Zimbabweans to invest back home. Their investments are recognised as foreign investment, thus allowing them to fully repatriate their profits and dividends to their countries of temporary residence. Zimbabweans living abroad are also allowed to operate individual foreign accounts – a move which is aimed at encouraging non-resident Zimbabweans to internalise their investments through depositing their profits and dividends in foreign currency accounts with local authorised dealers.

The Reserve Bank Governor and his team visited the UK, the US and South Africa to market the Homelink facilities to Zimbabweans living and working in those countries. While this crusade was successful in the UK and the US, in South Africa it met with opposition. While some sections of the diasporan community in South Africa, mostly the professional class, welcomed the idea and even pledged to work with the Governor in his much-publicised economic turnaround strategy, there were animated demonstrations by some migrants who expressed scepticism over the facility. Homelink encouraged migrants to send their remittances through formal channels, which clearly excluded those migrants who, for various reasons, did not want to do this. Undocumented migrants are unlikely to use formal channels for sending remittances, and for those who might want to use them there are no banking facilities in many of the rural areas from which these migrants come. The 29 licensed local money transfer agencies (MTAs), of which 18 were fully operational by July 2004, have yet to spread their operations to the remote rural areas.

The lack of a proactive approach to dealing with migrant remittances, especially those sent through informal channels, limits their use in productive activities with the potential for sustainable development. For remittances to contribute to the kind of development which would have long-term impacts on migrants' households and communities, there is need first to recognise the current contribution of migrant remittances, and secondly for the government, migrant groups, non-governmental organisations and the private sector to collaborate to find ways to encourage the flow and effective use of remittances.

Such collaborative arrangements have proven successful in other countries. Mexico, for example, has a '3 plus 1' programme where the federal government, the state and the municipality supplement each dollar of remittances invested by a migrants' hometown association in their community of origin by contributing one dollar each (Meyers, 1998; Orozco, 2003; McKinley, 2003). Similarly, in El Salvador, some municipalities have matching funds, where local public works programmes are financed partly by local municipal funds, partly by central government and partly by migrant remittances (Meyers, 1998).

The International Organisation for Migration (IOM) is implementing programmes in countries such as Guatemala, Colombia and Brazil aimed at enabling remittances to be used to their full potential for poverty reduction and development (McKinley, 2003). For example, in Guatemala, the IOM is implementing a programme which involves a specific banking service, a communication system between villagers and migrants and a marketing platform for the purchases and sales from the community to national and international markets, and in Colombia a programme which involves the creation of a social investment fund for funding productive small-scale projects for vulnerable populations.

The role of migrant hometown associations in contributing to the development of their communities of origin has been recognised in some countries (Lopez et al., 2001; Orozco, 2003). Migrant hometown associations have acted independently and in partnership with governments to help their communities of origin (Orozco, 2003). Zimbabwean migrants have well-established and well-organised burial societies based on their village of origin. These burial societies could be used to channel collective remittances to their communities of origin.

7. Conclusion

Further research is required to clarify and elaborate on the findings presented in this chapter. The areas where it is needed include the identification of obstacles to the transmission of remittances, a comprehensive understanding of the regulatory and policy framework that has a bearing on the transmission and investment of remittances, and an estimation of the value transmitted by migrants in remittances. Research specifically targeting migrants themselves is required so as to appreciate the problems they face in sending remittances, especially through formal channels both in the host country and in the country of origin.

Both the volume of remittances and their use are likely to be influenced by the regulatory and policy environment in the country of origin. There is a need for thorough understanding of this environment, since it is likely to influence the volume of remittances as well as the way they are used. An assessment of available opportunities for investment, which migrants and their relatives at home might not be aware of, needs to be undertaken.

Remittances from migrants in South Africa contribute significantly to the welfare of many households in the southern districts of Zimbabwe. They contribute to improved standards of living and better access to healthcare and education and, to a lesser extent, are invested in productive activities. However, for the developmental potential of remittances to be fully realised, there is need for collaborative effort involving the government, migrant groups, the local community, non-governmental organisations and international organisations to seek ways of encouraging the flow and creating an environment for more sustainable investment of remittances.

Acknowledgements

The author expresses special thanks to the Council for the Development of Social Science Research in Africa (CODESRIA) for funding the research.

References

ADAMS Jr, R, 1991, The effects of international remittances on poverty, inequality and development in rural Egypt. Research Report 86, Washington DC: International Food Policy Research Institute.

BALLARD, R, 2003. Processes of consolidation and settlement in remittance-driven Hawala transactions between the UK and South Asia. Presentation at a World Bank/DFID International Conference on Migrant Remittances: Development impact, opportunities for the financial sector and future prospects, London, 9–10 October.

BLACK, R, 2003. Soaring remittances raise new issues. *Migration Information Source* feature story.

CHIMHOWU, A, PIESSE, J & PINDER, C, 2003. Assessing the impact of migrant remittances on poverty. Paper presented at the EDIAS conference on New Developments in Impact Assessment for Development, Organised by the Institute for Development Policy and Management (IDPM) University of Manchester and Women in Sustainable Enterprise (WISE) Development LTD, 24–25 November.

CRUSH, J & WILLIAMS, V, 2002. Labour migration in southern Africa: contemporary trends and issues, a preliminary review. Paper presented at the ILO Tripartite Forum on Labour Migration in Southern Africa, Pretoria, 26–29 November.

GAMMELTOFT, P, 2002. Remittances and other financial flows to developing countries. Working Paper 02.11, Centre for Development Research, Copenhagen.

HOBANE, AP, 1999. The commercialisation of *Gonimbrasia Belina* in Bulilima-Mangwe district: problems and prospects. Unpublished MPhil thesis, Harare: Centre for Applied Social Sciences.

INTERNATIONAL LABOUR ORGANISATION/ SOUTHERN AFRICA MULTIDISCIPLINARY TEAM (ILO/SAMAT), 1998. Labour migration to South Africa in the 1990s. Policy Paper No. 4, Harare.

KANYENZE, G, 2004. African migrant labour situation in Southern Africa. Paper presented at the ICFTU-Afro Conference on Migrant Labour, Nairobi, 15–17 March.

LOPEZ, FH, ESCALA-RABADAN, L & HINOJOSA-OJEDA, R, 2001, Migrant associations, remittances and regional development between Los Angeles and Oaxaca. Research report Series No. 10, North America Integration and Development Centre, University of California, Los Angeles.

MCKINLEY, B, 2003. Migrants' remittances in the Americas: trends and policy options for RCM countries. Paper presented during the 8th Regional Conference on Migration, Cancun, Quintana Roo, Mexico, 29–30 May.

MEYERS, DW, 1998. Migrant remittances to Latin America: reviewing the literature. Inter-American Dialogue/ Tomas Rivera Institute Working Paper.

OROZCO, E, 2003. Remittances and markets: new players and practices. Inter-American Dialogue (IAD) and Tomas Rivera Policy Institute (TRPI), April, Lahti, Finland.

PATON, B, 1995, Labour export policy in the development of southern Africa. University of Zimbabwe, Harare.

RATHA, D, 2003. Workers' remittances: an important and stable source of external finance. World Bank, Global Finance, Washington DC.

SACHIKONYE, LM, 1998. Rethinking about labour markets and migration in Southern Africa. In Sachikonye, LM (ed.), *Labour markets and migration in southern Africa*. SAPES (Southern Africa Political Economy Series) Trust, Harare.

SANDER, C & MAIMBO, S, 2003. Migrant labour remittances in Africa: reducing obstacles to developmental contributions. Africa Working paper Series, The World Bank.

STEIN, E, 2003. Development role of remittances: the case of Central Americans in the US. Paper presented at the International Conference on Migrants: Development Impact, Opportunities for the Financial Sector and Future Prospects, London, 9–10 October.

TAYLOR, JE & FLETCHER, PL, 2001. Remittances and development in Mexico: the new labour economics of migration: a critical review. *Rural Mexico Research Review*, Vol. 2. Institute of Governmental Affairs, UC Davis University of California.

VAN DOORN, J, 2002a. Migration, remittances and small enterprise development. International Labour Organisation (ILO) Background Paper, Social Finance Programme Employment Sector. Geneva: ILO.

— 2002b. Migration, remittances and development. *Labour Education*, 4(129): 48–53.

ZINYAMA, L, 1990. International migration to and from Zimbabwe and the influence of political changes on population movement, 1965–1987. *International Migration Review*, 24: 748–67.

— 2000. Who, what, when and why: cross-border movement from Zimbabwe to South Africa. In McDonald, D (ed.), *On borders: perspectives on international migration in Southern Africa*. New York: St Martin's Press, pp. 71-85.

9 MIGRATION AND DEVELOPMENT IN MOZAMBIQUE: POVERTY, INEQUALITY AND SURVIVAL

FION DE VLETTER

1. Introduction

Southern Mozambique has been a significant labour exporting area for more than 150 years (Harries, 1995; Katzenellenbogen, 1982; Jeeves, 1985). However, apart from migration occurring from Tete Province to Southern Rhodesia in the early 1900s, the rest of Mozambique has supplied almost no external labour migration and experienced comparatively little internal labour migration. Such a regional dichotomy allows for interesting comparisons, especially in regard to the impact of migration on household accumulation and wealth. In the 1980s, household differentiation was clearly evident in southern Mozambique, largely because of the fairly significant wage differentials between relatively skilled and unskilled mineworkers (First, 1983). Although many migrant-sending households clearly benefited from migration, the majority of these remained impoverished and became wage-dependent as their capacity to produce subsistence crops diminished. External work opportunities and conditions for migrants, especially after the abolition of apartheid, have become much more varied, leading to a much higher degree of household differentiation than prevailed from the mid-1800s to 1990 (de Vletter, 2000).

This chapter demonstrates that rural southern Mozambique, an area relatively bereft of resources and traditionally less productive agriculturally than other regions of Mozambique (due to poorer soils and erratic weather patterns), is now more developed and better off (at least in terms of average income and levels of wealth) than other rural areas. This difference is largely attributed to labour migration and the transfer of significant volumes of remittances.

Although migrant worker households are often seen as better off than non-migrant supplying households, there are, indeed, significant numbers of the former that are vulnerable to poverty. These households are usually deficit agricultural producers, being largely dependent on migrant remittances. In turn, with the increasingly harsh attitude to unskilled illegal migrants in South Africa, their employment situation has become less and less secure (Crush, 1999). Although external migration is the preferred employment option for many Mozambicans, it represents the option of last resort for many others simply because of the limited employment absorption capacity of Mozambique's formal economy. In South Africa, employment is available for almost anyone willing to risk the consequences of illegal entry and prepared to be exploited, meaning that the remittances or accumulated wages brought home are likely to be minimal.

This chapter undertakes an inter-regional analysis (based on the results of a national survey of some 4000 rural households) of the south, centre and north of Mozambique, demonstrating clear developmental differences that are largely attributable to many years of remittances channelled to the mainly rural areas of southern Mozambique.

2. Methodology

This study draws mainly from the results of two surveys: the National Roads Administration (ANE)/Austral Survey of Rural Households (1999–2001) and the Southern African Migration Programme (SAMP) Migration and Remittances Survey (MARS) (Pendleton et al., 2006) described below. Supporting data was drawn from the 1996 SAMP Survey of Mozambican Miners (de Vletter, 1998). The rural household study was used because it incorporated detailed questions on migrant labour and looked at a broad range of variables to determine household wealth. The results of the MARS provide important new revelations on migrant remittance patterns which help us better understand the influence of migration on development and household differentiation. Details of the three surveys are provided below.

ANE/Austral Survey of Rural Households (1999–2001)

The National Roads Administration (ANE), in collaboration with the consulting company – Austral Consultants (Austral Consultoria e Projectos) – conducted a comprehensive rural household survey covering all regions of Mozambique along selected sections of rehabilitated secondary roads. The sample consisted of approximately 4000 households. These households were visited annually over a period of three years (1999–2001), with the primary objective of measuring the socio-economic impact of road rehabilitation. The survey provided an excellent opportunity to also collect detailed economic data for rural households, including comprehensive information on migrant labour. Regions were defined as follows:

- South: Provinces of Maputo, Gaza and Inhambane, as well as Maputo City
- Centre: Sofala, Manica, Zambezia and Tete
- North: Nampula, Niassa and Cabo Delgado.

SAMP Migration and Remittances Survey (2004)

The SAMP MARS was conducted in Botswana, Lesotho, Malawi, Mozambique, Swaziland and Zimbabwe. The survey interviewed only households with external migrants and focused on remittance patterns and migration history. The Mozambique survey consisted of 726 households located in the south. The survey areas were randomly sampled and included households in rural and urban areas.

SAMP Survey of Mozambican Miners (1996)

An earlier survey of mineworkers was undertaken by SAMP in Mozambique (de Vletter, 1998). The study interviewed 455 miners during the months of August and September 1996. Interviews were conducted at the Teba/Wenela depots at Ressano Garcia and Johannesburg as well as the depots of the recruiting agency Algos, which recruits mine and farm labour. In addition, a separate survey instrument was used for interviewing 160 miners' wives in the provinces of Inhambane, Gaza and Maputo.

3. Wage Employment and Migration Patterns in Rural Mozambique

The ANE study found that one-quarter of all households have at least one member engaged in wage employment but the distribution of wage-worker supplying households is highly skewed. More than half (55 per cent) of the rural households of the south had members engaged in wage employment, compared with only 18 per cent in the centre and 7 per cent in the north. Furthermore, the wage employment opportunities available for the south are overwhelmingly located at a considerable distance from the households. In the north and centre, more than half the wage workers are employed in the same district as their households (73 per cent and 58 per cent, respectively). Of the households with wage workers, 75 per cent in the south have absentee workers (compared with 32 per cent in the centre and 41 per cent in the north). Reflecting the relative imbalance of male adults, the percentage of female-headed households with wage workers is only 42 per cent, compared with 60 per cent for male-headed households.

Of households with a wage worker, most of those in the south have more than one worker in wage employment (averaging 1,6) while almost all in the centre and north have around one (1,1 and 1,3 respectively). Households in the south are therefore more dependent in two ways: in terms of the proportion of households involved in migrant labour and the extent to which households with wage workers participate in wage employment. Of all the wage workers, 42,5 per cent could be considered commuter workers, i.e., workers who normally sleep at the household.

Almost one-tenth (9,6 per cent) of all households were found to have seasonal workers (usually employed according to agricultural needs) who worked an average of five months a year. Seasonal work opportunities were concentrated in the south and centre (with 14,3 per cent and 11,6 per cent of households providing seasonal workers respectively, compared with barely more than 1 per cent in the north).

Reflecting the higher wages in South Africa (and to a certain extent wages in Maputo), the ANE survey found that more than two-thirds (67,6 per cent) of the households in the south have workers earning the equivalent of more than US$60 per month compared to only 13,7 per cent in the centre, while more than half of the households of the centre have wage earnings of less than US$12, or considerably less than the minimum wage.

Historical and other factors have ensured that large numbers of workers from the rural south are employed outside Mozambique (de Vletter, 2000). More than half (53 per cent) of the wage employees coming from households of the south work outside the country. In very sharp contrast, both the centre and north have almost no workers migrating abroad, having, respectively, only 3 per cent and less than 1 per cent of their workers outside Mozambique. Despite the strong dependency on South African employment, economic development within southern Mozambique has managed to absorb almost half (47 per cent) of the workers coming from the rural areas of the south. Most of these workers are located outside their districts, in contrast to the large majority of workers who are located near their households in the centre and north.

The MARS study found that 66 per cent of the adult population earn a cash income of some sort and that more than half of this 66 per cent (55 per cent) are external migrants. Virtually all (94,1 per cent) of the external migrants work in South Africa and the vast majority (93,1 per cent) are male. Almost half (47,3 per cent) of the external migrants are aged between 25 and 40. More than half (54,9 per cent) of the external migrants are married, with 15 per cent cohabitating and 26 per cent unmarried. Significantly, more than half (50,7 per cent) of the migrants are sons (and in a few cases daughters) of household heads, while just over a third (34,9 per cent) of the migrants are actually household heads (coming from just over half of the households). Almost half (46,1 per cent) of the household population were either students (22,8 per cent) or too young to work (23,3 per cent).

External migrants are generally poorly educated: only 15,2 per cent of the external migrants have secondary education, most (70,5 per cent) have primary education, while 8,2 per cent have no education at all. Sectorally, mine work still dominates. Of the 860 migrants whose place of work is known, 38 per cent work on the mines. The informal sector is the second most important (at 14 per cent), followed by the manufacturing industry (7.8 per cent) and working in a shop (3.6 per cent). A further 3,6 per cent are professionals. The remainder occupy a variety of different jobs (Table 9.1). The agricultural sector is surprisingly under-represented (at less than 2 per cent) since many irregular migrants entering South Africa are thought to get caught up in agricultural work in Mpumalanga Province before moving on to other work (Mather, 2000).

The rate of internal migration for domestic employment from rural households in the south of Mozambique is almost as high as that of external migration. However, the number of household members from external migrant-sending households working as migrants within

Mozambique is very low. The MARS data shows that 19,1 per cent of the total household population lives outside of Mozambique and only 3,7 per cent of the household population lives away from the household in another part of Mozambique. This suggests that migrant-sending households tend to send migrants either abroad or within Mozambique, but rarely in combination.

Table 9.1: Sectoral Distribution of External Migrants		
Main work place	No.	%
Factory	67	6.4
Mine	329	31.3
Shop	31	2.9
Office	14	1.3
Government	5	0.5
Informal	120	11.4
Domestic	13	1.2
Farm	15	1.4
Profession	31	2.9
School	5	0.5
Other	230	21.9
Don't know	191	18.2
Source: MARS		

4. Migration and Household Wealth Patterns

Evidence collected from the ANE survey shows stark disparities between the three regions in terms of household income and assets (wealth). The south, poor in natural resources and more prone to drought and floods than the other regions, has labour migration (both external and internal) as its most important economic feature, distinguishing it from the centre and north. On average, households from the south are better off materially than those in the rest of the country. However, there are still many poor and vulnerable migrant-sending households in the south. Remittances are often low and unpredictable, and subsistence production is marginal and susceptible to a changeable climate.

One of the best indicators of household wealth (and some would argue welfare) in Mozambique is the material used for building houses. The ANE survey found that one of the biggest contrasts between the regions was in housing (Table 2). In the south, almost a quarter (23,8 per cent) of the households have constructed their principal houses with cement blocks. In the centre this drops to 5,4 per cent and in the north to less than 1 per cent. The type of roofing shows even greater variation: in the south almost two-thirds (64,6 per cent) of the houses have non-thatch roofing (mainly zinc sheets). In the centre 86,9 per cent of the houses have thatch roofs and in the north almost all (98,8 per cent). Other notable regional differences were the source of lighting and the use of rivers or springs as the principal source of water.

Table 9.2: Indicators of Living Conditions			
Variable	South (%)	Centre (%)	North (%)
Cement walls	23.8	5.4	0.6
Thatch roof	34.1	86.9	98.1
Cement floor	52.0	10.1	1.9
Source of lighting – kerosene	85.9	52.8	39.6
Cooking fuel – firewood	94.9	90.5	94.0
River/spring as principal source of water	17.9	49.9	61.1
Source: ANE			

Households of the south own significantly more livestock than those in the other regions, with the greatest disparities being in cattle ownership (Table 9.3). Much higher percentages of the households in the south also own common household goods and assets (Table 9.4). Households in the south are also much more inclined to make investments than those in the other regions (Table 9.5). More than half the male-headed households in the south had invested more than the equivalent of US$40 in the previous year, compared with considerably lower percentages in the centre (39,1 per cent) and north (17,7 per cent). Female-headed households tended to invest less, but in similar regional proportions to male-headed households. Most of the investment went into construction or renovation of houses and relatively little into agricultural activities or transport. Not only is the proportion of households undertaking investments significantly greater in the south, the value of the investments is also higher. More than a quarter of the households in the south invested values in excess of US$400 in housing, agricultural equipment, transport and animals. In contrast, virtually none of the investing households of the centre and north had reached such levels.

Table 9.3: Ownership of Livestock						
Type of livestock	South		Centre		North	
	%	Average number	%	Average number	%	Average number
Cattle	18.5	6.4	4.8	7.7	0.1	2.0
Goats	52.7	5.2	38.8	9.3	21.7	6.1
Pigs	42.3	2.9	22.8	4.9	6.3	3.3
Chickens	72.6	11.4	68.1	10.2	-	8.3
Source: ANE						

Table 9.4: Selected Inanimate Asset Holdings			
Type	South	Centre	North
Solar panel	17.6	0.6	0.2
Bicycle	35.1	51.7	40.1
Pick-up truck	20.0	0.8	0
Car	7.8	0.6	0.1
Tractor	1.9	0.3	0
Refrigerator	14.2	1.5	0
Television	11.7	1.9	0
Video	10.6	0.6	0
Music system	35.9	14.3	3.6
Generator	3.9	0.1	0
Grain mill	12.6	0.6	0.1
Plough	17.6	2.5	0.1
Watch	66.7	34.0	10.1
Water tank	12.8	1.6	0.1
Large water drum	59.1	9.2	2.1
Source: ANE			

Table 9.5: Investments (above 500 000 MT) Made in Last Year (% of households)			
	South	Centre	North
Male-headed	54.1	39.1	17.7
Female-headed	35.4	24.8	10.0
Residence	35.8	16.0	6.7
Transport	6.9	12.0	5.6
Agricultural equipment	4.8	2.7	3.6
Animals	8.6	2.4	1.1
Source: ANE			

An attempt was made to consolidate numerous variables (including wage income, investments, housing materials, assets, farming techniques, size of farm, etc.) and to convert them into 'wealth points' (see the Appendix for details of the variables that were selected and their point distribution). As expected, the distribution of wealth points is highly skewed towards poverty, with the vast majority of households considered poor. More than three-quarters (77,3 per cent) have less than 50 points and half have less than 25 points (the average being 36,8). Only 5,5 per cent had more than 100 (Table 9.6).

Levels of wealth vary considerably amongst the regions. More than half the households in the south are in the highest quartile (Table 9.6). By contrast, almost half the households of the north are in the lowest quartile and barely 5 per cent in the highest quartile. Although there are indeed stark differences between the regions, the wealth point distribution is distorted by the fact that self-consumed production is not included. Because cash income is a substitute for self-consumption for many households in the south, and is relatively easily measured and incorporated in the wealth point calculation, a more realistic depiction would show a downward adjustment for the south and an upward one for the north and centre.

Table 9.6: Distribution of Wealth Points by Region (%)				
Quartiles	Region			Total
	South	Centre	North	
1st quartile (lowest)	11.6	24.4	48.0	26.7
2nd quartile	12.8	27.9	28.9	24.1
3rd quartile	23.7	28.6	17.4	24.6
4th quartile (highest)	51.9	19.1	5.7	24.6
Total	100	100	100	100
Source: ANE				

There is a greater concentration of female-headed households in the lowest quartile. More than a third (35,7 per cent) of female-headed households fall into the lowest quartile, compared to just under a quarter of the male-headed households. Somewhat surprisingly, however, there appears to be an almost equal chance among female- and male-headed households of being in the highest quartile (25,3 per cent for male-headed and 21,6 per cent for female-headed).

5. Remittances and Poverty in the South

As this chapter has shown, inter-regional household welfare comparisons provide convincing evidence of a significant wealth disparity between the households of the south and those of the centre and north. Within the south itself, however, this does not mean that there is not significant differentiation between households. Migrant-sending households are probably better off than non-migrant-sending households, a hypothesis currently being tested in another SAMP survey (the Migration and Poverty Survey [MAPS]). However, the MARS survey shows that even among migrant-sending households there is considerable differentiation. Levels of remuneration vary considerably from household to household; this is a function of the income-generating capacity of the migrant, level of education and years of experience. Earning capacity and remittances are also affected by the sector of employment (the privilege certain households enjoy in gaining access to the mining sector and the legal status of the migrant). Differentiation is also strongly influenced by the degree of commitment of migrant workers to remit money or goods to their households. Many migrants are working under such exploitative conditions that they do not have sufficient surpluses to remit.

The MARS survey of external migrant-sending households found that remitted cash is the most widespread source of household income (76 per cent of households) followed by remitted goods (64 per cent) (Table 9.7). Income from wage work (largely internal) was cited by a third of the households (34 per cent). Migrant contributions provide the overwhelmingly largest share of household income (Table 9.8), although almost a quarter (22 per cent) of migrant-sending households do not receive cash income from migrant workers. Most migrants send money home either once a month or once a quarter (Table 9.9). The average value of remittances received is closely correlated with the frequency with which money is sent. Households receiving remittances on a monthly basis averaged about US$825, compared with US$123 for those receiving once a year.

Table 9.7: Household Income from All Sources (by frequency)			
	Responses	% of households	% of responses
Wage work	243	33.5	13.6
Casual work	103	14.2	5.8
Remittances – money	548	75.5	30.6
Remittances – goods	466	64.2	26
Income from farm products	161	22.2	9
Income from formal business	30	4.1	1.7
Income from informal business	157	21.6	8.8
Pension/disability	23	3.2	1.3
Gifts	22	3.0	1.2
Other	23	3.2	1.3
Refused to answer	11	1.5	0.6
Don't know	4	0.5	0.2
Total	1791		100
Source: MARS.			

Table 9.8: Household Income by Source and Value			
	No.	Mean	Median
Wage work	149	$1016.19	$608.70
Casual work	44	$226.67	$65.22
Remittances – money	438	$523.99	$347.83
Remittances – goods	266	$393.79	$217.39
Income from farm products	115	$103.84	$39.13
Income from formal business	8	$779.89	$391.30
Income from informal business	84	$255.72	$130.43
Pension/disability	15	$263.45	$86.96
Gifts	12	$60.94	$26.09
Other income	11	$226.48	$52.17
Total income	579	$936.91	$528.26
Source: MARS.			

Table 9.9: Frequency and Value of Money Remittances			
	No.	Mean	Median
Twice or more per month	13	$630.77	$365.22
Once a month	135	$862.39	$782.61
More than twice in 3 months	37	$327.09	$304.35
Once in 3 months	147	$0.02	$326.09
Once every 6 months	68	$201.62	$163.04
Once a year	82	$123.40	$65.22
At end of the contract	4	$240.22	$197.83
Other	67	$494.16	$304.35
Don't know	15	$435.65	$478.26
Source: MARS			

The earning potential of Mozambican migrants in South Africa is affected by four basic factors. First, wages vary considerably among sectors in South Africa, even for unskilled or semi-skilled migrants. Farmworkers are notoriously badly paid. In contrast, the mining sector is relatively well paid. Secondly, the migrants' education and experience affects their job prospects. Thirdly, migrant social networks influence labour market accessibility. Finally, the legal status of the migrant influences job access and security. Miners have a degree of security unknown to irregular migrants working in sectors such as construction and services.

About one-third of the MARS migrants work in the mining sector and earn substantially more than those engaged in other sectors. Miners also have better facilities for transferring wages and goods. In addition, they are subject to a system of deferred pay which ensures that the majority of their pay packet can only be drawn in Mozambique. In sum, households with mine migrants tend to be considerably better off than other households. As Table 9.10 shows, miners are second only to the small number of professional migrants when it comes to remitting home. At the other end of the scale, it is likely that many migrants from poorer households are working irregularly and under exploitative, low-paid conditions.

Apart from sector and legal status, earning capacity is largely determined by the level of education and work experience. The vast majority (at least 70 per cent) of migrants have only primary education and 8 per cent have none at all. The survey showed distinct differences in the average annual amounts of cash remitted by level of education (Table 9.10). There is a big difference between the amounts remitted by those with only primary education and those with secondary education, the former sending an average of US$784 and the latter US$1072.

The MARS survey found that the most common method of remitting both money and goods is taking them back personally or through friends, despite significant changes in transfer technology. The most important changes relate to improved banking facilities for miners using TEBA Bank and the pre-paid delivery services of Kawena Distributors. Kawena, formerly limited to serving mineworkers, now offers facilities in various cities and towns in South Africa to anyone wishing to deliver goods to any accessible household in southern Mozambique or to one of a large network of warehouses. With time, more sophisticated transfer mechanisms will be increasingly used by Mozambicans working in South Africa.

Table 9.10: Annual Cash Remittances by Level of Education and Sector			
	No.	Mean	Median
a. Education			
None	40	$444.60	$304.35
Primary	424	$426.32	$269.13
Secondary	82	$582.36	$347.83
Don't know	28	$492.45	$428.26
b. Main workplace			
Factory	37	$390.09	$304.35
Mine	249	$537.22	$434.78
Shop	20	$462.15	$201.09
Office	5	$427.22	$243.48
Government	1	$434.78	$434.78
Informal	48	$312.57	$158.70
Domestic	6	$323.19	$304.35
Farm	5	$241.30	$239.13
Professional categories	16	$842.93	$304.35
School	2	$67.39	$67.39
Other	124	$402.84	$173.91
Don't know	43	$338.52	$152.17

Regardless of the methods used, of major importance to the determination of remittance flows is still the degree of commitment by the migrant to transferring wages or goods. Commitment seems to be closely linked to gender, marital status, age and relationship to the household head. Annually, household heads send considerably more (US$1000) than their sons/daughters (US$625) or spouses (US$560), and males send more than females (US$840, compared to US$688) (Table 9.11). Cash remittances also increase by age, up to the 40–59 cohort, but decrease thereafter. Married migrants predictably send home much more money than non-married (almost twice as much).

Household expenditure estimates derived from the MARS survey are at best indicative. Table 9.12 shows the frequency of the types of expenditures incurred in the previous month. Food was by far the most important (89 per cent of households) followed by fuel (mainly wood and paraffin) (47 per cent), transport (45 per cent) and education (44 per cent). Other important categories included utilities (of particular importance to urban households), clothes, alcoholic drinks and medical expenses.

Table 9.11: Money Sent Home: Average Amount over a Year by Migrant Type

	No.	Mean	Median
Relationship			
Head	285	$570.31	$417.39
Spouse/partner	26	$316.91	$219.57
Son/daughter	224	$341.41	$173.91
Father/mother	3	$628.99	$608.70
Brother/sister	27	$317.01	$173.91
Grandchild	3	$333.33	$434.78
Son/daughter-in-law	2	$165.22	$165.22
Nephew/niece	5	$456.96	$217.39
Other relative	1	$380.43	$380.43
Gender			
Male	553	$457.65	$304.35
Female	23	$374.64	$152.17
Age			
15 to 24	55	$247.57	$152.17
25 to 39	292	$457.21	$304.35
40 to 59	119	$612.53	$434.78
60 and over	9	$472.71	$304.35
Don't know	99	$372.19	$217.39
Marital status			
Unmarried	79	$264.92	$160.87
Married	367	$498.29	$347.83
Cohabiting	109	$474.51	$330.43
Divorced	7	$298.14	$260.87
Separated	3	$236.23	$304.35
Widowed	4	$196.20	$109.78
Don't know	1	$260.87	$260.87

Source: MARS.

In terms of value spent, the largest average amounts were spent on building activities (about US$150), although relatively few households (13 per cent) spent money in this category. The second highest expenditure was on food (US$70), which was also the most frequently cited expenditure. The third highest average value was for special events (US$50) such as weddings and funerals.

Food was by far the most dependent on remittances (78 per cent claiming that remittances were 'very important'). Remittances were also considered to be 'very important' for cattle purchases, school fees, clothing, transport costs, vehicle purchase and maintenance, informal sector trading and farm labour costs. They were felt to be 'important' to the survival of the household in a significant majority of cases for food (73 per cent), medical treatment (64 per cent) and cash income (75 per cent).

Table 9.12: Monthly Household Expenses			
	No.	% of households	% of responses
Food and groceries	648	89.3	20.4
Housing	5	0.6	0.2
Utilities	291	40.1	9.1
Clothes	262	36.1	8.2
Alcohol	240	32.6	7.5
Medical expenses	229	31.5	7.2
Transport	323	44.5	10.2
Cigarettes, tobacco, snuff	43	5.9	1.4
Education	319	43.9	10.0
Entertainment	15	2.1	0.5
Savings	84	11.7	2.6
Fuel	338	46.6	10.6
Farming	82	11.3	2.6
Building	97	13.4	3.0
Special events	80	11.0	2.5
Gifts	41	5.6	1.3
Other expenses	33	4.5	1.0
No expenses	8	1.1	0.3
Refused to answer question	43	5.9	1.4
Total	3181		100
Source: MARS			

The relevance of these findings for household differentiation is that expenditure on food and other basic needs overwhelmingly dominates the budget of external migrant-sending households. Comparatively few households (mainly those with miners and a handful of others with members in higher income jobs) therefore have the capacity to invest in housing, cattle or vehicles.

One of the more interesting findings to come out of the MARS study relates to the borrowing patterns of the respondent households. The need to borrow can be seen as an important indicator of vulnerability. A significant 42 per cent of the households said they had borrowed money during the previous year. Of those borrowing, half borrowed from family, 37 per cent from friends and 2 per cent from employers. The main reasons for borrowing money were to buy food (33 per cent), for health care (22 per cent) and for funerals (5 per cent). Financing companies are hardly present, with the exception of a few microfinance operators (having almost no presence in the rural areas and usually lending according to small business needs).

Loans are for the most part used for 'survival' issues, i.e., food and health. These are typical periodic needs of poor households, especially for those who have to rely on irregular remittances. A big advantage for many remittance-receiving families is that they are probably seen as a lower risk for loans than subsistence households with less reliable cash flows. Schooling and business loans are also quite common and are possibly linked to the household's ability to repay.

6. Household Differentiation

Household economic differentiation can best be highlighted through poverty analysis. A common poverty indicator takes the percentage of food expenditure relative to overall expenditure. The MARS survey found that the average percentage of expenditure devoted to food is 57 per cent. 'Relatively poor' households were defined as those spending between 60 and 79 per cent of their total expenditure on food and 'extremely poor' as spending between 80 and 100 per cent. The results show that almost a quarter (25 per cent) of the households can be considered to be relatively poor and slightly less (22 per cent) extremely poor. These findings should be qualified for two reasons. The first is that many households depend to a significant extent on self-produced household consumption that is not measured in the above analysis. This would mean that food 'expenditure' is even higher than indicated and that the level of poverty is, in fact, worse than indicated. On the other hand, the proportion of expenditure devoted to food may have been exaggerated, given that most households were interviewed during the month following traditionally high consumption periods, namely, Christmas and New Year.

Other surveys, such as the Lived Poverty Index, suggest a high level of poverty amongst a significant portion of migrant-sending households. The MARS survey found that 24 per cent of the households are often without food and 11 per cent are often without medical care. Although these households are very dependent on cash income, 37 per cent claim to have been often without cash and 33 per cent several times without cash.

Despite the difficulties of getting accurate figures relating to poverty indicators, the data suggests that many external migrant-sending households are indeed very poor. These findings underscore what earlier work on Mozambique demonstrated, i.e., that there is a high degree of economic differentiation among migrant-sending households, ranging from the elite, who benefit from several migrants with relatively high mine wages or professional salaries, to households that are forced to send members to work under poor conditions for lack of suitable employment in Mozambique (First, 1983).

7. Conclusion

The rural areas of southern Mozambique have fewer resources and are agriculturally poorer and more vulnerable to climatic instability than those of the centre and north. Yet, as this study has demonstrated, the pool of economic assets of the average rural household in the south is far greater than that of other regions. This disparity can largely be explained by the phenomenon of wage migration. Although a significant number of households in the south have migrant and commuter members working for wages in the domestic economy (mainly in the industrial enclave of Maputo-Matola), the most significant flow of wage-seeking labour has been, and continues to be, to South Africa.

Early migration may have been largely influenced by push factors such as hut tax, chibalo labour (the colonial system of forced labour), drought and famine. Later, however, employment in South Africa, particularly on the mines, was the preferred income-generating choice of Mozambican men from the rural (and often also urban) areas. Free transport, board and lodging and a virtually quarantined life allowed miners to save most of their wages. Compulsory deferred pay (a system of forced savings) further ensured that miners would return to their homes with comparatively large amounts of money and goods. Such remittances were generally used, at least initially, for improving the household's quality of life (through the construction or furnishing of cement-walled homes). Remittances were also used for savings (normally in the form of livestock) or investment. Traditionally, one of the most common investment choices was to buy a pick-up truck (bakkie) for transport purposes (often hired out) or a pump for irrigated agriculture. Now, with the proliferation of vehicles in the rural areas and limited irrigable areas, there is a greater tendency to invest remittances in informal sector trade activities undertaken by resident family members. For many years, import duty exemptions for miners gave them further accumulative advantages over other Mozambicans. Although no longer enjoying such privileges, Mozambicans in South Africa can take advantage of distribution services that provide reliable and cost-effective delivery of a large variety of goods direct to their rural base.

Much of southern Mozambique's external migration history took place during periods when black workers, especially foreigners, were subjected to the most exploitative of conditions. South Africa's migration system was the economic modus operandi of the apartheid system. Yet despite the degradation and oppression of such work Mozambican men streamed into South Africa, usually offering a supply much greater than the absorption capacity of a mining industry wary of excessive dependence on one source. Mine work still offered the best of the economic options for the majority of rural work seekers from the south and allowed them to build up their rural home base, but at considerable social cost.

Mozambican miners may collectively be seen as a wage elite. Households with several generations of miners are likely to have built up assets and a home-based production capacity that would put them well above the economic status of other households with a more recent involvement in mine migration. Households with miners with greater skills, longer service, or more than one miner, may have relatively high earnings. However, a significant proportion of mine-sending households could be considered to be poor. Differentiation between households is even more poignant when looked at across the entire range of migrant-sending households.

Despite Mozambique's economic growth rate being one of the highest in Africa over the past few years, much of this growth is linked to the development of highly capital-intensive 'mega' projects with limited absorption of unskilled workers. The urban informal sector, which has hitherto absorbed considerable numbers of the unemployed, has become less attractive for the rural labour surpluses as increasing competition makes economic survival more difficult. Such limitations within the domestic economy, recently exacerbated by the current drought in the south, have forced many rural dwellers to seek employment in South Africa.

This chapter has demonstrated that the overall economic impact of migrant labour has been positive in southern Mozambique. It has also shown that the nature of migration has changed significantly over the past 15 years, with the eclipsing of mine migration and the increasing numbers of young Mozambican men chasing a limited number of jobs. It is therefore likely that, in coming years, as the amounts of wages remitted are reduced (because of lower earnings) and the mechanisms available for doing so become more limited than they are for miners and workers in other, more privileged, wage sectors, the economic benefit for Mozambicans of working as migrant labourers in South Africa may diminish substantially.

Acknowledgements

I would like to express my gratitude to the National Roads Administration (ANE) and the consultancy company Austral Consultoria e Projectos, Lda, for allowing the use of household interview data collected during a survey of rehabilitated roads during the period 1999–2001.

References

CRUSH, J, 1999. The discourse and dimensions of irregularity in post-apartheid South Africa. *International Migration* 37: 125–49.

DE VLETTER, F, 1998. *Sons of Mozambique: Mozambican miners and post-apartheid South Africa.* SAMP Migration Policy Series No. 8, Cape Town.

— 2000. Labour migration to South Africa: the lifeblood for southern Mozambique. In McDonald (Ed), *On borders: perspectives on international migration in Southern Africa.* New York: St Martin's Press, pp. 46–70.

FIRST, R, 1983. *Black gold: the Mozambican miner, proletarian and peasant.* New York: St Martin's Press.

HARRIES, P, 1995. *Work, culture and identity: migrant laborers in Mozambique and South Africa, c1860–1910.* Cape Town: David Philip.

JEEVES, A, 1985. *Migrant labour in South Africa's mining economy: the struggle for the goldmines' labour supply, 1890–1920.* Montreal and Kingston: McGill Queen's University Press.

KATZENELLENBOGEN, S, 1982. *South Africa and Southern Mozambique: labour, railways, and trade in the making of a relationship.* Manchester: Manchester University Press.

MATHER, C, 2000. Foreign migrants in export agriculture: Mozambican labour in the Mpumalanga Lowveld, South Africa. *Tijdschrift voor Economische en Sociale Geografie,* 91(4): 426–36.

PENDLETON, W, CRUSH, J, CAMPBELL, E, GREEN, T, SIMELANE, H, TEVERA, D & DE VLETTER, F, 2006. *Migration, remittances and development in southern Africa.* SAMP Migration Policy Series No. 8, Cape Town.

Appendix: Wealth point determinants

Wealth point determinants for ANE survey		
Determinant	Cohorts	Point allocation
1. Size of Machamba (fields)	< 1 ha	0
	1–2ha	5
	2–5ha	10
	5 ha +	20
2. Value of crop (000 MT per annum)	<200 (but greater than 0)	1
	200–500	2
	500–1000	4
	1–2000	8
	2–5000	16
	5–10 000	30
	10 000–20 000	40
	>20 000	50
3. Improved seeds	Yes	10
	No	0
4. Fertilisers	Yes	10
	No	0
5. Pesticides	Yes	10
	No	0
6. Livestock	Per goat owned	1
	Per head of cattle	5
7. Monthly wages (000 MT)	Don't know, but > 0	5
	<200	5
	200–500	10
	500–1000	20
	>1000	30
8. Monthly non-agricultural income (000 MT)	Don't know but >0	2
	<50	2
	50–100	4
	100–200	8
	200–500	16
	>500	20

9. Animals sold during past 12 months (000 MT)	<200	1
	200–500	2
	500–1000	4
	1000–2000	8
	2000–5000	16
	5000–10000	30
	10 000–20 000	40
	>20 000	50
10. Investments (annual) (MT)	.5–1m	5
	1–3m	10
	3–5m	20
	>5m	30
11. Housing materials	Cement block	40
	Other	0
	Cement/tiled floors	5
	Other categories	0
	Water piped in or out of house/well in yard	10
	Other categories	0
	Electricity supplied	30
	Electricity not supplied	0
12. Other assets	Solar panel	5
	Generator	5
	Water pump	20
	Grain mill	20
	Plough	5
	Refrigerator	5
	Radio	2
	Music system	3
	Television	5
	Video	5
	Watch	1
	Boat	15
	Fishing net	3
	Bicycle	3
	Motor cycle	20
	Pick-up truck	50
	Car	50
	Truck	80
	Tractor	50
	Water tank	3
	Drums (200 litres)	1
	Other large water containers	1
	Cool box	1

10 POVERTY, GENDER AND MIGRANCY: LESOTHO'S MIGRANT FARMWORKERS IN SOUTH AFRICA

THERESA ULICKI AND JONATHAN CRUSH

1. Introduction

Previous studies have highlighted the history and persistence of poor working conditions on many South African farms (Marcus, 1989; Jeeves & Crush, 1997; O'Conchuir, 1997; Crush et al., 2000; Department of Labour, 2001; SAHRC, 2003). During the 1990s, eastern Free State vegetable farmers became increasingly reliant on migrants from neighbouring Lesotho to meet their seasonal labour needs (Johnston, 1997; Sechaba Consultants, 2004). This trend coincided with a major downsizing of the mine labour force in South Africa, hitherto the major employer of Basotho migrant workers (Seidman, 1995; Sechaba Consultants, 1997; Crush et al., 2001). However, there was no simple process of transfer of unemployed migrants from one sector (mining) to another (farming). Rather, decisions on who would migrate were mediated by domestic relationships and household poverty within Lesotho. One of the major casualties of mine retrenchments and the drying-up of remittances has been women, not men (Coplan & Thoalane, 1995). Women and girls with domestic skills but little formal training have been forced into the labour market. Their options are very limited – confined, in the main, to domestic work in Free State towns and labour on Free State farms.

This chapter is based on the findings of a Southern African Migration Programme (SAMP) survey of 152 Basotho farmworkers (including 40 undocumented workers). The farms concerned were located in six different districts in the eastern Free State: Ladybrand, Clocolan, Ficksburg, Fouriesburg, Bethlehem and Reitz, and ranged from 250 hectares to 5 000 hectares in size. The labour force varied from 35 employees to 1 300, with the number of Basotho employees ranging from 12 to 889. Supplementary interviews were undertaken with Free State farmers and farmers' unions, labour and home affairs officials in both countries and representatives of SAAPAWU (South African Agricultural Plantations and Allied Workers' Union) and the National Union of Farmworkers (NUF). Documentary sources include the Labour Agent's agreements entered into by the government of Lesotho and farmers, farm-workers' contracts, and the inspection reports by Lesotho Ministry of Labour representatives in Welkom, South Africa.

2. The Regulatory Framework

There is a pervasive assumption in South Africa that all Lesotho citizens working in the country are (with the exception of contract miners) illegal. This is certainly not the case. South Africa has had a bilateral treaty with Lesotho (signed in the 1970s and still in force) allowing South African employers to recruit temporary labour in Lesotho on legal contract (Crush & Tshitereke, 2001). Before the 1990s, the treaty was used only by The Employment Bureau of Africa (TEBA) and various smaller companies recruiting exclusively for the gold and coal mines. With the expansion of the market gardening industry in the Free State, there was a need for a mechanism which would allow farmers to recruit labour legally in Lesotho. The bilateral treaty served the purpose well.

Farmers or their agents recruit labour at the Labour Offices of the Ministry of Labour in Lesotho. They must obtain what is called a 'no-objection' or BI-17 permit from the Department of Home Affairs in South Africa, which they bring to Lesotho. They are issued with a Labour Agent's Licence permitting them to recruit a certain number of workers from a specific district. A separate licence is issued for each district in which the farmer may recruit. Licences are valid for either six months (R75) or one year (R150). Farmers are also required to pay R10.15 for each farmworker recruited. A contract is completed for each recruit that stipulates the terms and conditions of employment, including rate of remuneration, type of accommodation and type of medical service provided.

Farmers' contracts with the Lesotho government specify that they must provide free transport to and from the place of employment, free accommodation, three free meals daily and medical care. However, the Lesotho Ministry of Labour neither sets minimum standards for accommodation, meals and medical care nor ensures that farmers adhere to the conditions laid down in the contracts.

Approximately 7–10 000 Basotho per annum are recruited legally through Lesotho's Ministry of Labour. One-third of the farmers interviewed use the services of a recruiter, generally another farmer, to hire Basotho. The largest agency in Maseru, Lesotho – Agrilabour – recruits approximately 2 000 Basotho each year for asparagus and potato farmers. Technically, before a Labour Agent's Licence is issued to a farmer, the Lesotho labour representative in South Africa should inspect the farm in question, although this rarely happens. For one district labour official, the reason was simple: 'We do not have enough manpower or such funds to see to it that these requirements are actually being met.' According to the Labour Commissioner, Lesotho must 'rely on the decency of farmers for the meals and accommodation.' Labour officials reported that on the few occasions when inspections were actually carried out and recommendations made that a farmer's recruiting licence should not be renewed, the recommendations were ignored.

The Lesotho Ministry of Labour's inspection of farms is wholly inadequate. The Welkom office, which is responsible for inspecting places of employment for Basotho in the whole of the Free State, including the mines, has a staff of three. In the 13-month period from September 1997 to October 1998, for example, these labour representatives inspected a total of three farms, although reports only exist for two. The labour representative stated that the office is provided with insufficient information to perform more inspections: 'Because we don't have the proper particulars of name and telephone number, only the physical address, we are afraid really of being shot if we come without calling.' When inspections were conducted, they were hampered by the fact that labour representatives were not issued copies of the farmers' contracts, so they did not know if the conditions which had been stipulated were being adhered to. Furthermore, district labour offices and the labour representative in Welkom said it was difficult to determine on which farms inspections and improvements were necessary as farmworkers rarely lodged formal complaints.

The Government of Lesotho encourages Basotho to seek employment on Free State farms through the labour offices, rather than to 'cross the river' (a euphemism for working illegally). However, only 28 per cent of farmworkers interviewed believed the government had done enough to try and ensure adequate working conditions for its citizens on Free State farms. They complained that there were too many people at the labour office competing for jobs, that labour officials did not act on workers' grievances, and that farmers hired through the labour offices only in peak seasons, whereas if a person went on their own, work could be found year round. On the other hand, workers stated that if they were recruited through the labour office it was more difficult for farmers to cheat them, that they could be contacted through the labour office in the event of an emergency, and that they had the labour office to turn to in the event of a grievance.

Undocumented Basotho labour is certainly still used, especially on border farms. About a quarter of the survey respondents had worked or were working as undocumented farmworkers in the Free State. Interestingly, women seem less likely to work on farms 'illegally' than men: only 19 per cent of female respondents had been undocumented workers compared to 33 per cent of male respondents.

Lesotho and South African labour officials reported that farmers come to Lesotho with trucks in search of workers. When crossing the border back into South Africa they cover the truck with a tarpaulin and are never searched. When the season and the work are almost finished, the farmer calls the police to report that there are 'illegal aliens' on the farm. The farm is raided – often in the middle of the night – and the Basotho migrants are arrested and deported back to Lesotho. Workers do not have enough time to collect their belongings and are often not paid their wages. Lesotho labour officials believe these incidents are a result of collusion between border officials, the South African police and farmers.

Undocumented workers fall into six categories: (a) those who go to South Africa on a 14-day visitor's stamp, search from farm to farm until they are hired, and return every 14 days to Lesotho to have their stamp renewed; (b) those who have family members who have found employment for them on a farm; (c) those who are initially employed through the Lesotho Labour Office and then seek work on their own after their contract has expired; (d) those who live in Lesotho and cross the border daily; (e) those hired by farmers who have come to Lesotho in search of illegal Basotho labour; and, a growing trend, (f) those who live 'unofficially' in South Africa in townships along the border and are recruited there by farmers. About half of the undocumented workers interviewed fell into category (d). They live at home, some within walking distance of their workplace, while others must find daily transport. Generally, these migrants do not cross over at a formal border post.

Migrants must weigh up the advantages and disadvantages of undocumented migration. Unlike migrants in Zimbabwe and Mozambique, they have a legal option readily available and are not loath to use it. In the survey, migrants were asked for their views on the advantages and disadvantages of using the district labour offices (Table 10.1). As primary advantages of the contract system, they cited the protection offered and free transport. On the other hand, they found the system too inflexible for their needs, too competitive and the process too lengthy. Some clearly also thought that the protection offered by the labour office was more apparent than real.

Table 10.1: Advantages and Disadvantages of Contract System	
Advantages	Percentage of responses
Labour office can settle disputes	20
Free transport to farms	18
Whereabouts of farmworker known in event of emergency	17
Easy to get employment	14
Farmer cannot cheat workers	8
Written contracts	6
Job security	6
Accommodation provided	3.5
Assured of wages	3
Medical care if ill	1
Employment is legal	1
Food is provided	1
Lesotho government benefits	0.5
Compensation if injured	0.5
Higher wages	0.5
Disadvantages	Percentage of responses
Labour office is non-responsive to complaints	19
Too much competition for jobs	17
Difficult to terminate contract	15
Have to wait for farmers to come to labour office	15

Recruiting process takes too long	11
Cannot see family for a long time	9
Labour officers treat workers badly	4
Cannot choose employers	4
Money deducted for transport	2
Accommodation is bad	2
Labour officers are exploitative	2

Migrants openly acknowledge the problems associated with undocumented status. They explained that, besides averaging a lower wage than farmworkers recruited through the labour offices, looking for a job is a costly procedure; they are easily cheated of wages, in which case there is no recourse; and they run the risk of being arrested. Over half of the undocumented workers (53 per cent) said they had only a verbal agreement with their employer concerning wages, working hours and accommodation. An additional 10 per cent had written agreements but in nearly half of these cases the agreements were not adhered to. Unsurprisingly, the primary problem was wages. Nevertheless, the benefits outweigh the risks for these individuals. Many are able to live with their families, all have the freedom to change employers at will and to work throughout the year and they do not require a passport.

Workers recruited through the district labour offices in Lesotho may also unwittingly become 'illegal migrants.' Farmers who have finished with Basotho labour but whose contracts have not yet expired 'transfer' their labour force to other farmers. Besides contravening the conditions of the original contract, this practice places Basotho workers in a vulnerable position. For example, the second farmer may not adhere to the conditions stipulated in the original contract and workers run the risk of arrest by police and immigration officials. As the Labour Commissioner reported:

> There was a case in June where there were a lot of people deported. So I said where are your passports and one man said here it is. They were all recruited from Quthing, all of them. And then I said, 'No, how can you be recruited when you were all deported' and then he said, 'We were recruited by one farmer and then when we were finished the work he transferred us to another farmer' and that is why they were caught by the police and deported. So one farmer recruited them from Quthing – he had a licence – and then he finished his job quickly and then he transferred his licence to this farmer and then they were caught. This is very common.

The next section of the chapter considers exactly who in Lesotho is recruited to work on the Free State farms. The evidence suggests that they are the most vulnerable and marginalised members of Basotho society.

3.   Basotho Farmworkers: A Gendered Profile

Typically, discussions of Basotho migrant workers in South Africa focus on male migrants (Ulicki & Crush, 2000). However, the farmworkers interviewed for this study were 47.5 per cent female. Information provided by farmers, recruiters and the Lesotho District Labour

Officers and gathered from a previous study (Johnston, 1997) indicated there were many more women than men working on Free State farms as seasonal labour. Nine of the 15 farmers interviewed said they do not hire any men from Lesotho and all but two stated that the majority of their Basotho workforce is female (Table 10.2).

Table 10.2: Percentage of Workforce on Farms that is Female	
Percentage – female	No. of farms
100	9
90	1
50	2
40	1
Unknown	1
Majority female*	1
* Exact percentage unknown	

There were significant differences between the men and women who seek work on the farms:

- The respondents in the survey had worked on Free State farms for one to 24 seasons, with a large majority being recent employees. Men were more recent additions to the farm workforce, averaging 2.4 seasons compared to the women's 3.7, and 85 per cent of the men had worked for three years or less, compared to 66 per cent of the women.

- Female migrant farmworkers tend to be significantly older than the men. In the main, farmwork is the lot of older women (often widowed or divorced) and younger (unmarried) men. Men in Lesotho have traditionally gone to work in the mines at a relatively young age. For most this is no longer an option owing to the drastically decreasing number of mine jobs available to Basotho. Young men with no mine experience seem to be more inclined to take up farmwork than their mine-experienced, older counterparts.

- About half of all farmworkers interviewed were married. However, many more men in the sample were single (31 per cent compared to 7 per cent of women), while many more women were widowed (26 per cent compared to 3 per cent of men). About 40 per cent of the respondents stated that they were head of their household – 53 per cent of the male and 28 per cent of the female respondents.

- Both male and female farmworkers have limited formal education and few alternative employment opportunities. Roughly 11 per cent of all respondents reported no formal schooling – 16 per cent of the male and 5.5 per cent of the female respondents – and only 5.5 per cent had completed Junior Certificate and 1.5 per cent the Cambridge Overseas School Certificate. Only 26 per cent of the interviewees had completed primary school (one-third of the women and one-fifth of the men).

Farmworkers tend to be drawn from the most marginalised segments of Basotho society. Here too there were gender differences. The majority of respondents (around 60 per cent) said they are the only wage earners in their households, despite this income being low-wage and primarily seasonal. When not working as seasonal farm labourers in the Free State, 31 per cent (primarily male) were unemployed and engaged in no income-generating activity. Many women undertake supplementary informal sector activity such as selling vegetables (12.5 per cent), beer brewing (5.3 per cent), piece work (4.6 per cent), herding (3.3 per cent), carrying parcels (2.7 per cent) and sewing (2 per cent).

Only 24 per cent of the respondents reported having a regular (as opposed to seasonal) wage earner in their household, a figure substantially lower than the 54 per cent of households with a regular wage earner in a 1994 Lesotho Poverty Study (Gay & Hall, 1994). When the figure is disaggregated by gender, the women appear at more of a disadvantage than the men: only 10 per cent of female headed households had a regular wage earner in their household compared to 27 per cent of male headed households.

To many Basotho, the primary measure of wealth and security is livestock ownership. While 69 per cent of households in Lesotho own livestock, only 49 per cent of farmworker households surveyed were livestock owners. Predictably, female-headed households had a lower rate of livestock ownership than male-headed households, at only 29 per cent as compared to 54 per cent. Nearly 60 per cent of respondents reported having no access to fields in Lesotho. Of those who do have access, only 33 per cent owned the implements necessary to plough their fields.

Although employment on Free State farms is, for the most part, seasonal and many workers endure exploitative conditions, for many households it can make the difference between destitution and survival. The quantitative data suggests that only the desperate go to work on South African asparagus farms. The absence of jobs in Lesotho, lack of food and the loss of mine jobs were the three most common reasons cited for migration (Table 10.3). This is confirmed by the qualitative evidence collected in this survey through the stories told by individual farmworkers: they go only as a last resort and when the economic situation of their household is especially dire.

Table 10.3: Reasons for Working on South African Farms	
Response	No. of respondents*
No jobs in Lesotho	100
Family had nothing to eat	15
Could not get or lost mine job	14
Quit previous job due to poor conditions	7
Nepotism and corruption mean no jobs in Lesotho	7
Usual income earner ill or died	5
Need money for school fees	5
No other income earner in family	3
Need money for hospital fees	1
Better pay than in Lesotho	1
Abandoned by spouse	1
Enjoy working outside Lesotho	1
* More than one answer per respondent was accepted.	

Gender differences in the economic and demographic profile of Basotho farmworkers are echoed on the farms themselves. There are two main categories of work: fieldwork and work in the processing and canning factories. Half of the sample (39 per cent of women and 60 per cent of men) worked in the fields as pickers. A greater proportion of women (53 per cent) than men (11 per cent) worked in factories, cutting, canning, cleaning and packaging asparagus. Some 11 per cent of men (but only 3 per cent of women) also worked harvesting potatoes. Other jobs included cleaner, cook and supervisor; although the numbers of these were small (Table 10.4).

Table 10.4: Farm Job Categories		
Category	% of females	% of males*
Harvest asparagus only	28	54
Asparagus factory	53	11
Harvest asparagus and other produce	11	6
Harvest potato	3	11
Harvest pumpkin	1	0
Can peaches	0	1
Cleaner	0	4
Cook	3	1
Loader	0	5
Supervisor	1	3
Office	0	1
Tractor driver	0	1
Shepherd	0	1
* Figures do not add up to 100 % due to rounding.		

The majority of Basotho on Free State farms are hired as seasonal workers (some 83 per cent of the sample worked for four months or less at a time). There is little discernible gender difference here – 81 per cent of men and 86 per cent of women worked on a seasonal basis only. The remaining 17 per cent who worked between five and 12 months per year were not necessarily employed by only one farmer; many respondents reported seeking work on other farms once their initial contracts expired.

Farmers themselves expressed a distinct preference for female workers, both in the factories and the fields. They indicated that a female labour force was more placid, easily controlled, and problem-free: women are 'better workers', 'more reliable and responsible than men', 'less complicated' and 'more humble.'

3.1   The 'wages' of work

Working conditions on the farms are onerous and poorly rewarded. The respondents in the survey worked for an average of ten hours per day, six-and-a-half days per week during the season. Many said they work split shifts or until everything in the fields or factory is harvested or packaged. This means a work day that is inconsistent and unpredictable – perhaps five hours one day and 13 the next. The general pattern for those harvesting was to begin at about 5 a.m., break for breakfast/lunch mid-morning and work an afternoon shift until all the produce was harvested. In peak season this pattern was extended and work sometimes continued until midnight. In the factories, workers tended to work two five-hour shifts with five hours in between. Again, in peak season these hours could be extended. Although those in factories might only work ten hours, their working day began at 5 or 6 a.m. and only ended at 8 or 9 p.m. which is a 15-hour day.

The average monthly income for farmworkers at the time of the survey was R225.29, with the highest paid earning R600 per month. Others earn as little as R60 per month. Women averaged R234.49 per month, while the men earned slightly less at R216.22. The maximum monthly seasonal wage was the same for both men and women, but the minimum monthly wage for women was higher at R120 compared to R60 for men (Table 10.5).

Table 10.5: Monthly Income of Farmworkers (Rand)		
Wages	No. female %	No. male %
60	0	1
90–109	0	4
110–129	1	2
130–149	0	4
150–169	11	8
170–189	2	8
190–209	7	8
210–229	12	6
230–249	18	16
250–269	7	3
270–289	1	0
290–309	5	4
333	1	1
367	1	0
400	0	2
433	1	0
500	0	1
600	1	1
Unknown	4	11

The reported average daily wage was R8.05. Farmers claimed it was R10.90 but there were differences in perception. In one case, for example, the farmer stated that his workers averaged R400–600 per month but workers on that farm reported an average of only R313 per month.

A large majority of workers were only paid their wages on the day they left the farm to return to Lesotho – without the interest that had accrued. During the course of their contract they were paid R10 or R20 every two weeks to purchase necessities. Lesotho officials saw this as a method of control, preventing workers from leaving during a contract:

> The monies that these guys have worked for, they deduct them and keep them until the end of the contract – sort of some deferment of wages – which in the contract is omitted. But in fact, even if someone is being ill-treated, they cannot leave their workplace.

Farmers, on the other hand, took the paternalistic view that this system benefits workers who otherwise would not have any money to take home with them. As one farmer noted disparagingly, 'If she gets it here, she drinks it.'

Unsurprisingly, the majority of farmworkers said their wages were unsatisfactory. As many as one-third claimed their wages were too low to meet even the basic needs of their families. Another 40 per cent said they did not believe that the rate of pay was commensurate with the workload. Many respondents said it is often unclear how much they are supposed to be paid, or that they are cheated. Each farmworker is supposed to have the terms of the contract fully explained by labour officials at the District Labour Offices in Lesotho, but only 55 per cent reported that this was done. Of those, half said the information was incorrect:

> Even though I do not know how to read and write, I know the farmer cheats us. One cannot be paid R400 for three months yet every working day is equal to R10.

> They do not tell us anything. We only overhear the farmer telling the labour office that 'I will pay the workers R10 per day and they will also get bonuses.' But these were just dreams. The wages are not as stated and there is nothing like a bonus when we get to the farm.

A major source of conflict and confusion is that workers rarely seem to be paid according to the stipulations of their contracts. Most farmers reported that they pay their workers on a piecework basis and one-third of farmworkers stated they are paid according to what they produce. However, an examination of contracts showed that most did not stipulate a piecework but rather a daily rate. Interviews with farmworkers and officials indicated that the practice of not paying the wage stipulated in the contract is widespread. As one District Labour Officer noted:

> You know this practice of paying 20 cents per kilo or whatever is not negotiated at our office. When I was at Mohale's Hoek that was the first time I heard about that. The workers were complaining that their wages were lower … It is breaking the contract to use that pay method.

Adding to the confusion were overtime rates and deductions. Over 40 per cent of respondents claimed that they work overtime hours, but were either not paid overtime wages or their wages did not correspond to the number of overtime hours worked. Only 16 per cent stated they were paid overtime wages, although few knew how much they actually received for overtime:

> We worked extra hours, but we were never paid overtime wages, rather the farmer would only say 'thank you.' We tried to complain but the farmer told us that it was his farm and not Mandela's.

> We are not sure if we get overtime because we get our money at the end of the contract. We do not ask as he does not want to talk to us. Even when we have complaints, we just keep quiet ... But we find we are paid the same even if we have worked overtime. Sometimes we think that we will be paid much as we have worked a lot of overtime, but we find that we are still paid the same.

According to farmers' contracts with the government of Lesotho, employers are required to provide Basotho farmworkers with free transport, accommodation, medical care and meals. However, 30 per cent of the farmworkers said these are deducted from their wages. Lesotho's Labour Representative responsible for inspecting Free State farms agreed: 'There are too many deductions, like for medical and rent ... Wages are also deducted if workers stay in the clinic for too long.'

The respondents also claimed that money was deducted from wages in the form of fines or penalties. They said that wages were withheld for breaking equipment or toilets, poor work, damaging produce, taking too long in the toilet, damaging clothing and fighting. They were also not paid for rainy days when they could not work, or for days they were assigned other duties: 'You find that some days he gives us different jobs to what he hired us for. For example, he said we had to go and cut trees and never paid us for that day. He said we were helping ourselves as that wood would be used by us.'

3.2   Living and working conditions

The majority of seasonal farmworkers (85.5 per cent) said they lived in accommodation provided by the farm. After wages, this was the area they felt needed most improvement. Only 44 per cent of respondents found their accommodation satisfactory (61 per cent of women and 29 per cent of men). However, a judgement of 'satisfactory' does not necessarily indicate habitable accommodation since it depends largely on expectations. For example, one worker who classified his accommodation as 'satisfactory' was actually living in a storeroom with 20 other workers, none of whom were provided with mattresses or beds. Others were more direct in their evaluation of living conditions:

> We live in shacks. These are stables where animals used to be kept. The roofing is very old and we encounter problems during harsh weather ... To bathe, we need to fetch wood from the bushes to make a fire. There are no toilets, we go to the bushes ... The food is not well cooked.

> Accommodation is not satisfactory at all. The mattresses are very old, smelly and have lice. There are no beds and these mattresses are very thin and we put them on dirty floors. Moreover, there are no lights in some hostels and we must buy candles with our own money.

The most common complaints about accommodation are listed in Table 10.6. Farm inspection reports by Lesotho's Ministry of Labour contain numerous negative comments: 'uninhabitable for human beings', 'the bedding was so dirty that you [the farmer] did not even want to get inside the hostels – you were waiting outside during our inspection', 'unhealthy with no ventilation', 'what is called a hostel for the employees is something out of this world', and so on.

Table 10.6: Stated Reasons for Dissatisfaction with Accommodation	
	No. of responses*
Crowded	21
No beds or mattresses	18
Cold but no heaters	15
Unsatisfactory or insufficient food	10
Theft	10
No electricity	9
Not weatherproof	8
Previously used as stables	8
No toilets	6
Poorly maintained	6
Dirty and unhygienic	5
Noisy	5
Sex in hostel	5
No security	5
Dirty mattresses	3
Younger and older workers stay together	3
Water is dirty	3
Unhygienic toilets	3
No windows or doors	3
Have to share bed	1
Basotho and South Africans stay together	1
*More than one response was accepted from respondents.	

Visits to farms by the research team revealed that the quality of housing varied a great deal from farm to farm. On the best farms, there was adequate electrified hostel-type accommodation with ablution blocks with running water. On others, accommodation consisted of tents in the middle of fields with no water or proper cooking facilities. Dwellings were rarely built specifically for the purpose of housing seasonal workers. Rather, stables, sheds or perhaps storage rooms were converted into seasonal accommodation.

Service and sanitation facilities are also inadequate on most farms. Seventy per cent of farmworkers reported using pit latrines and only 19 per cent had access to flush toilets. On one farm, there were only two pit latrines for 140 workers. Nearly all the farmworkers reported access to water primarily from a communal tap, pump or tank, but 93 per cent had no hot water. Provision of electricity was less common – 37 per cent of farmworkers had no electricity in their dwellings.

In terms of the Lesotho Government's Contract of Foreign Service for migrants, farmers are required to provide workers with three cooked meals per day. Only 15 per cent of interviewees reported that they were given no meals, which suggests a reasonably high level of compliance. Quality of food is another matter entirely. Only two per cent of respondents judged the meals they receive to be satisfactory. Inspection reports and interviews revealed that the food provided was often insufficient, nutritionally unbalanced and unpalatable. Some farmworkers boosted their rations with purchased food.

Workers said they often began their first shift before 5 a.m. without any breakfast and might only be fed two meals per day – breakfast/lunch at the mid-morning break and dinner after the afternoon shift. Few farms had proper kitchens. Meals were generally cooked on open fires in three-legged pots. On one farm where kitchen facilities were examined, 100 meals were cooked over an open fire in a shed with no running water. While conditions vary enormously, cooking facilities tend to be better in the larger corporate-owned farms. Meat and fruit were rarely provided.

Lesotho Government contracts also stipulate that farmers must provide Basotho farmworkers with free medical care. The medical care available to farmworkers ranged from clinics on the farm to doctors and hospitals in town. On some farms, workers were immediately dismissed if sick or injured. The majority (79 per cent) stated that in the event of illness they received no wages and only 20 per cent of employers actually paid for medical expenses. Most respondents claimed that medical fees were paid by the farmers but then deducted from their pay. Farmworkers said that rather than forfeiting wages by not working they preferred to work when ill. Furthermore, those farmers who paid for medical costs were selective as to which illnesses were covered. Sexually transmitted diseases were considered 'self-inflicted' by farmers – as were injuries from fights – and were therefore not the responsibility of the farmer.

Occupational health and safety experts consider commercial farming in South Africa to be among the most dangerous of occupations. Virtually all farming operations use pesticides or poison. On these farms, only 42 per cent of respondents said they received protective clothing. Of those who did, nearly one-third stated that the clothing was in poor repair, or that key pieces, such as gloves and face masks, were missing. Nearly 40 per cent of workers used dangerous chemicals and/or machinery, but half of these said they received no training or only unsatisfactory training.

In the event of a serious injury or death, the majority of respondents (61 per cent) stated that workers received no compensation from the farmer, even if the farmer was directly or indirectly to blame. Some farmers deducted the medical costs of injuries from workers' wages. Some Basotho working legally on South African farms are eligible for South African Workers' Compensation; however, payment can take years. In order to be eligible for compensation, the death or injury has to be work-related; however, the Ministry of Labour in Lesotho suspects farmers report many deaths as 'natural' when a work-related injury or illness may actually be the cause.

The standard of treatment at work was low. Overall, 15 per cent of respondents reported physical abuse (19 per cent of men and 11 per cent of women) and 32 per cent reported verbal abuse (36 per cent of men and 28 per cent of women). While it is likely that only a minority of farmers are guilty of such abuses, the numbers are still unacceptable and all such acts are illegal. In total, nearly 40 per cent of all farmworkers interviewed reported some kind of abusive treatment from farmers. One farmworker commented that abusive language was so common it ceased to have any impact: 'Insulting and offensive language is used so often on the farm that we are used to it, so that we hardly feel offended when insulted, rather we laugh.'

The stated reasons for abusive treatment differed widely, but included working more slowly than expected, making mistakes, complaining about work-related issues and eating produce. Hitting and kicking were the most common forms of physical mistreatment reported. But they were not the only kinds. One farmworker testified that a farmer forced him and another worker to hold a hot iron bar which burnt their bare hands. The farmer laughed and called them 'stupid fools.'

3.3   Freedom of movement

Farmers in the Free State complain about two things. First, they maintain that South Africans will not work on the farms and they are forced to hire from Lesotho. In fact, the benefits of hiring impoverished Basotho migrants outweigh any incentive to improve conditions to attract South Africans. Secondly, farmers complain that Basotho labour is too expensive and costs them extra. These costs include payment to the Ministry of Labour in Lesotho and transport, housing and food on the farms.

Once they have recruited their workers and transported them to their farm, farmers must ensure they retain them, i.e., that their Basotho farmworkers do not vote with their feet and move on to another farm seeking greener pastures. The easiest way of doing this is to retain their labourers' passports. As many as 68 per cent of the workers surveyed said that they are not allowed to keep their passports during their contract. Farmers claimed that they retain Basotho workers' passports to prevent them from getting lost or stolen, or in case of an inspection by Lesotho's Ministry of Labour or South African immigration officials.

Farmworkers do not accept the farmers' explanation. Half said it was a tactic to prevent them from 'escaping' back to Lesotho or going in search of jobs elsewhere. The legal implication for Basotho farmworkers travelling without their passports was a source of concern for the Ministry of Labour in Lesotho, as was the legality of farmers confiscating workers' passports. The Labour Commissioner commented as follows:

> I think it is illegal. A passport is issued to a particular person and it should be kept by that person it has been issued to. But I'm sure it is common for foreign labour where employers say 'I've got you here, you can't run away.' For me, I am not surprised to hear this. It is to avoid their movement.

The majority of farmworkers are on three- to four-month contracts in the Free State. Nearly 20 per cent said they were not permitted to return home at all and another 22 per cent said they could only go home if they had a particularly good reason, such as a death in the family. The practice of confiscating documentation is clearly also used to control the movement of workers in their off-duty hours. Fully 40 per cent of workers stated that they were not permitted to leave the farm even during their free time. While one-third could offer no explanation, others said the farmer had told them it was dangerous to leave the farm (19 per cent), that workers commit criminal acts and farmers are held responsible (10 per cent) and that other farmers would shoot them if they are found on their property (10 per cent). Clearly, many of these explanations are merely scare tactics by farmers to keep migrant workers on the farm.

Flexibility and mobility are important to farmworkers who wish to avoid or escape unacceptable conditions or find a better deal (Table 10.7). But once they have fixed on a particular farm, they try to return to the same one each year. Almost two-thirds of the survey respondents had worked on only one farm. As a group, though, they had experience of 42 different Free State farms. Familiarity and acceptable treatment by the farmer are the major determinants here (Table 10.8).

Table 10.7: Reasons for Working on the Same Farm	
Reason	Percentage*
Satisfied with farmer	34
Used to the farm	33
Farmer is kind	9
May be worse elsewhere	7
Farm is close to Lesotho	5
Enjoy work	3
Work is not seasonal	2
Wages are better	2
Was cheated elsewhere	2
Do not know other farms	2
Unknown	2
*Figures do not add up to 100% due to rounding.	

Table 10.8: Reasons for Not Working on the Same Farm	
Reason	Percentage
Went to farm which was hiring	49
Looking for better wages	18
Looking for better working conditions	10
Farmer was cruel	5
Not on good terms with farmer	2
Enjoy challenge of new farm	2
Farmer did not pay	2
Farmer no longer hiring men	2
Looking for easier work	2
Food was bad	2
Farm was sold	2
Found longer contract	2
Farmer didn't have money to pay	2

4. Grievance Procedures

Three-quarters of the farmworkers surveyed stated that there was no grievance committee on the farm where they worked. Those committees which do exist are limited in their ability to deal effectively with the grievances of seasonal Basotho workers because of how they are structured. Many of the committees are limited to permanent (therefore primarily South African) employees, conduct meetings in Afrikaans only (thereby limiting Basotho participation), allow only workers who have worked on the farm a certain number of years to participate and have no female members. On one farm where 81 per cent of the staff is seasonal Basotho and female, the grievance committee is comprised entirely of permanent, male South Africans. Here the grievance committee doubles as a disciplinary structure and dispenses corporal punishment to offenders. According to one respondent:

> [Fighting] is against one of the regulations which says that whenever we have disputes amongst ourselves, we should report to the committee. The punishment for women [who fight] is to be beaten by the committee members.

Many of the so-called 'grievance committees' deal with disputes between workers rather than employee dissatisfaction with work conditions. In fact, few farmers will admit the possibility that workers are dissatisfied with employment conditions. One, for example, noted that:

> Before they come to the farm they know what they are going to get, what are the conditions. If it is a problem with one or two men or women, I just send them back to Lesotho and they can't come back to the farm. You see, everyone working here gets 0.8 kilograms of mealie maize a day and milk and meat, so there couldn't be a problem.

In contrast, the farmworkers interviewed had no shortage of work-related grievances, which suggests that they were not expressing their grievances, grievances were not being reported by supervisors to farmers, or farmers were not being honest when responding to the question. A study by Heunis and Pelser (1995) found that the majority of farmers in the Bloemfontein area addressed workers' grievances by maintaining an 'open-door' policy. In other words, they wanted workers to approach them directly with any problems. A similar situation was found in this study. On farms where there are no grievance committees, grievances are dealt with in an arbitrary fashion 'based on the farmer's perception of himself [or herself] as a sort of father figure' or perhaps as 'chief of the village.' As one farmer commented:

> The committee is the way it should be, but that is not the way it always works. They are having difficulty to keep the committee going. With the traditional system, the chief of the village, he is the headman and his word is law, but he is approachable and that way it works better actually. I think I can solve their problems with the authority of the committees, even if they elect them themselves. There is more respect for the chief. The call me the chief of the work. I prefer the more direct method of personal involvement. You can do that if you speak their language.

'Open-door' policies are also ineffective because employees risk retaliation and victimisation, as they are very well aware:

Everybody is afraid of the farmer and no one can complain to him because if you do he will give you your passport and you will have to walk to Lesotho.

We are expected to report our concerns or complaints to the farmer; however, because he is the one ill-treating us, there is nowhere we can complain.

When I have a complaint I do not tell the farmer because it is the same if I tell or if I do not tell him, so I find it useless.

Less than a third of workers (30 per cent of females and 29 per cent of males) said they felt they could approach the farmer with a concern. Respondents who said relations were 'poor' focused on the failure of the farmer to listen and the 'cruel and abusive' behaviour of farmers and supervisors (Table 10.9). Those who thought that relations were good cited the farmer's friendliness or lack of intrusiveness.

Table 10.9: Labour Relations on Farms	
Reasons why relations are poor	No. of respondents *
Farmer won't listen to complaints	10
Farmer is cruel and abusive	9
Supervisor is cruel and abusive	6
Farmer is racist	6
Fear of farmer's ability to dismiss at will	5
Little interaction with farmer	5
Workers cannot leave farm	2
South African workers treated better	2
Farmer yells excessively	2
Misunderstanding due to language differences	1
Poor wages	1
Farmer does not fulfil promises	1
Reasons why relations are good	No. of respondents *
Can discuss problems with farmer	15
Little interaction	10
'No apartheid'	5
Farmer is friendly	4
No physical or verbal abuse	3
Farmer tries to solve problems	2
Farmer speaks Sesotho	2
Working conditions have improved	1
* More than one answer per respondent was accepted, but not all respondents gave a reason.	

Of the 152 farmworkers interviewed, only one belonged to a union. Many stated that there was no time for unions or that the contract was short term and organisation was not feasible, and many expressed fear of being dismissed for union involvement. According to some, labour organisation of any form is discouraged or even forbidden by the Lesotho District Labour Offices where they are recruited. Those responsible for recruiting in Lesotho tell farmworkers they have been hired to work and there are many who are willing to replace them. One recruit complains, 'It is as if we are sold.' Furthermore, there is a real lack of knowledge regarding unions amongst the respondents. Savings societies, grievance committees and even the South African Department of Labour's local manpower office were all mistakenly identified as unions by respondents. Farmers are opposed to the extension of collective labour legislation to agriculture.

The final question is whether the contract system and the Lesotho Labour Offices offer protection and a means of redress. The workers were uniformly negative on this point. Respondents reported that they have no effective advocates despite the fact that Lesotho's Ministry of Labour supposedly represents their interests. Furthermore, while labour officials in Welkom are responsible for inspecting farms and protecting the interests of the Basotho working on these farms, it appears they do little of either.

5. Conclusion

This chapter contributes to the growing literature on conditions on commercial farms in the post-apartheid period. Commercial farming is sometimes heralded as one of the success stories of the post-apartheid economy. It is clear, however, that much of South Africa's economic 'success' in this area continues to be built (as it has been in the past) on the backs of migrants from neighbouring countries.

By focusing on the personal profiles, experiences and perceptions of Basotho migrant farmworkers in the Free State, this chapter shows that Basotho working on Free State farms are predominantly older women, who are amongst the poorest citizens of Lesotho and who generally see farmwork in South Africa as the only option available to them. Almost without exception, the farmworkers interviewed testified that they endure exploitative employment conditions; including wages below the Minimum Living Standard; unhygienic and crowded living conditions; and abusive treatment from farmers and supervisors. The mutual mistrust exhibited by Basotho farm labourers and Free State farmers undermines productive labour relations; furthermore, the farmers' determination to deny their labour force basic rights and freedom of movement often results in abusive treatment. Conditions on many farms have changed little since the end of apartheid. The state and the unions have a major task on their hands if they are to undo this scenario.

References

COPLAN, D & THOALANE, T, 1995. Motherless households, landless farms: employment patterns among Lesotho migrants. IDRC Migrant Labour Working Paper, No. 18.

CRUSH, J, LINCOLN, D, MARIRIKE, C, MATHER, C, MATHEBULA, F & ULICKI, T, 2000. *Borderline farming: foreign migrants in South African commercial agriculture.* SAMP Migration Policy Series No. 16, Cape Town.

CRUSH, J & TSHITEREKE, C, 2001. Introduction to special issue: evaluating South African immigration policy after apartheid. *Africa Today,* 38(3): 1–14.

CRUSH, J, ULICKI, T, TSEANE T & VAN VUUREN, E, 2001. Undermining labour: migrancy and sub-contracting on the South African gold mines. *Journal of Southern African Studies,* 27(1): 5–31.

DEPARTMENT OF LABOUR, 2001. *Report on determination of employment conditions in South African agriculture.* Pretoria: Department of Labour.

GAY, J & HALL, D (eds), 1994. *Poverty in Lesotho, 1994: a mapping exercise.* Maseru: Sechaba Consultants.

HEUNIS, J & PELSER, A, 1995. Basic labour practice in commercial agriculture: the need for formalisation. *South African Journal of Sociology* 26(2): 62-8.

JEEVES, A & CRUSH, J, 1997. *White farms, black labour: the state and agrarian change in southern Africa, 1910–50.* Pietermaritzburg: University of Natal Press.

JOHNSTON, D, 1997. Migrant workers in the Free State. *South African Labour Bulletin,* 21(6): 64–5.

MARCUS, T, 1989. *Modernising super-exploitation: restructuring South African agriculture.* London: Zed Books.

O'CONCHUIR, R, 1997. *Farm worker conditions of employment on Free State commercial farms.* Bloemfontein: Free State Rural Committee.

SECHABA CONSULTANTS, 1997. *Riding the tiger: Lesotho miners and attitudes towards permanent residence in South Africa.* SAMP Migration Policy Series No. 2, Cape Town.

— 2004. How can you tell the sun not to shine? behavioural surveillance survey report. Maseru: Ministry of Labour.

SEIDMAN, G, 1995. Shafted: the social impact of down-scaling in the OFS goldfields. In Crush, J & James, W (eds), *Crossing boundaries: mine migrancy in a democratic South Africa.* Ottawa: International Development Research Centre, pp. 176-84.

SOUTH AFRICAN HUMAN RIGHTS COMMISSION (SAHRC), 2003. Final report into human rights violations in farming communities. Braamfontein: SAHRC.

ULICKI, T & CRUSH, J, 2000. Gender, farmwork, and women's migration from Lesotho to the new South Africa. *Canadian Journal of African Studies,* 34(1): 64–79.

11 ANXIOUS COMMUNITIES: THE DECLINE OF MINE MIGRATION IN THE EASTERN CAPE

XOLA A. NGONINI

1. Introduction

One of the major unaddressed questions in the migration and development literature is what happens to development when migration goes into decline. The South African mining industry provides an excellent test case as it has shed over 200,000 jobs in the last decade. Many rural sending areas have had to contend with the impact of returning ex-miners. This chapter examines the case of the Eastern Cape, long dependent on mine migration yet also one of the poorest regions of the country.

In the past three decades, numerous studies have been undertaken on the role migrants play in the economy of the sending areas, as well as the effects of migrancy on the family and household (Beinart, 1979; Bundy, 1979; Murray, 1981; May, 1984; Muller, 1984; Spiegel, 1987). More recently, scholars have examined the impact of restructuring in the mining industry on the mining environs and, to some extent, in Lesotho and other southern African countries (Crush & Yudelman, 1991; Steinberg & Siedman, 1995; Chirwa, 1997; Crush et al., 1999, 2000). However, none of this recent literature examines the effects of mining restructuring in the former Transkei – the most underserviced and impoverished of the Bantustans and one of the key sources of migrant labour for the mining industry (Steinberg & Seidman, 1995). This chapter seeks to fill this lacuna in the literature by presenting data on the effects of restructuring in the former Transkei.

2. Methodology

Ex-migrant workers look to the future with fear and hopelessness, shrouded by uncertainty, but marked by a nostalgic reverie of what could have been a route to 'modernity.' Against this background, the research examined the links between the ex-migrants and their communities and the mining industry. To understand the impact of retrenchments required immersion in the realities of anxious communities caught in the throes of restructuring industries. The author thus spent time with the ex-migrants and their families gaining insights and trying to understand the situation they were in. The study had a three-pronged approach of unstructured interviews, participant observation and social biography of migrant workers.

The unstructured interviews were conducted with ex-migrants to gather their individual perceptions of, and reflections on, the turn their life had taken as a result of retrenchment. However, in rural areas, unlike urban ones, employment is also a socially observed function, open to the whole community. The author therefore also interviewed ex-migrants' dependents, and community members who knew them, and observed what kind of work they had done while employed, to see how retrenchments had affected the ex-migrants' social lives. The aim was to reveal the sufferings and felt needs of the actors in a social group by seeing them as the result of structural conflicts in the social order.

The villages studied, Nyanisweni and Dutyini, are in the southeast of the coastal Pondoland region in the former Transkei. Nyanisweni is ten kilometres and Dutyini about 40 kilometres from the town of Mbizana. Both fall under the Mbizana Municipality, which is under the OR Tambo District Council – a compendium of various municipalities, such as Ntabankulu, Ingquza, Mhlontlo, King Sabata Dalindyebo, Nyandeni and Port St Johns – with an 80 per cent unemployment rate. According to StatsSA (2005), Mbizana has a population of 1 604 411 and covers an area of 2411 square kilometres.

The Eastern Cape is the poorest province in South Africa. It includes the former homelands of Transkei and Ciskei and has a population of 6,2 million people. Its poverty levels are the highest in the country, with an estimated 80 per cent of the population living in poverty, and it has an unemployment rate of 80 per cent. The former Transkei is the poorer of the two former homelands. Nearly 80 per cent of the homesteads have no running water, more than 50 per cent have no electricity and 58 per cent are further than five kilometres from a health clinic. Poverty is deeply rooted in this province, with 27 per cent of households earning less than R400 per month and only 11 per cent earning more than R1500 per month (PSLSD, 1993; CSS, 1995; May et al., 1998). The majority of the people have no schooling and 60 per cent of the children who attend school have to walk a long distance to get there (StatsSA, 2005). The economic growth of the new era has increased the demand for skilled workers but, conversely, made the older, unskilled migrant labourers redundant.

According to Malherbe (2000), 53 districts in this province rely heavily on mining as a source of employment, income and financial security. In 15 of these districts, one in every three African males with a job works in the mining industry; in another 38 districts, at least one in six men works on the mines (Malherbe, 2000). Thus, the report concludes, 'virtually the whole of Transkei falls in these two groups' (Malherbe, 2000). James (1992) states that in the 1970s and 1980s about 500 000 migrants were recruited from the Transkei region.

As Figure 11.1 shows, in the 1970s the number of new recruits increased. All 28 magisterial districts of the former homeland were traditional suppliers of labour, each district supplying about 5000 workers (Crush & James, 1995: 136). However, the graph also shows the decline in recruitment from this region as a result of retrenchments in the industry.

Figure 11.1: Recruitment Patterns from the Eastern Cape

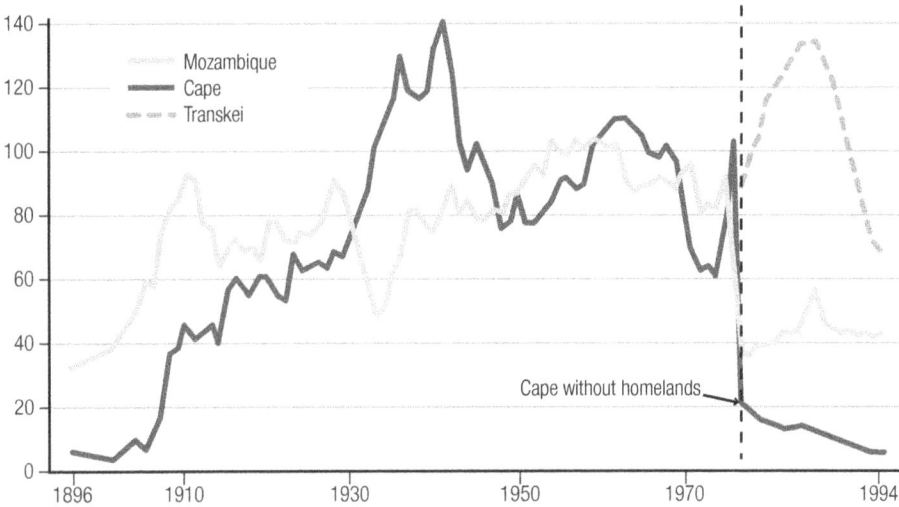

3. Socio-Economic Conditions in Nyanisweni and Dutyini

Dutyini has a population of 9085 and Nyanisweni 10 285 (StatsSA, 2005). Although these two villages are in the same district, their social, economic and political structures are vastly different. Nyanisweni is a site of political activism and has the potential to stake a claim on resources from the municipality, while Dutyini has none. Such differences have a bearing on the type of livelihoods it is possible to pursue. Dutyini village is further away from the town of Mbizana and is thus not accessing the fruits of democracy – piped water, electricity, library, tarred roads, clinics and so on. Those who have access to electricity are based in the town of Mbizana and surrounding villages such as Nyanisweni. Figure 11.2 shows the disparities in access to resources in Mbizana. It shows that here the majority still use candles for lighting, a few use gas and very few use electricity. Most of the people in Dutyini are still using candles for lighting, wood for heating and natural water for drinking. Mbizana has two hospitals (Greenville and St Patrick's) and 18 clinics. The main hospital (St Patrick's) is within walking distance of Nyanisweni, but for residents of Dutyini it is 40 kilometres away. Thus Nyanisweni has easy access to hospital services, for example, the ambulance, because there are telephones and the road is tarred. In Dutyini, by contrast, there are no telephones.

Figure 11.2: Power Resources Available to Households in Mbizana

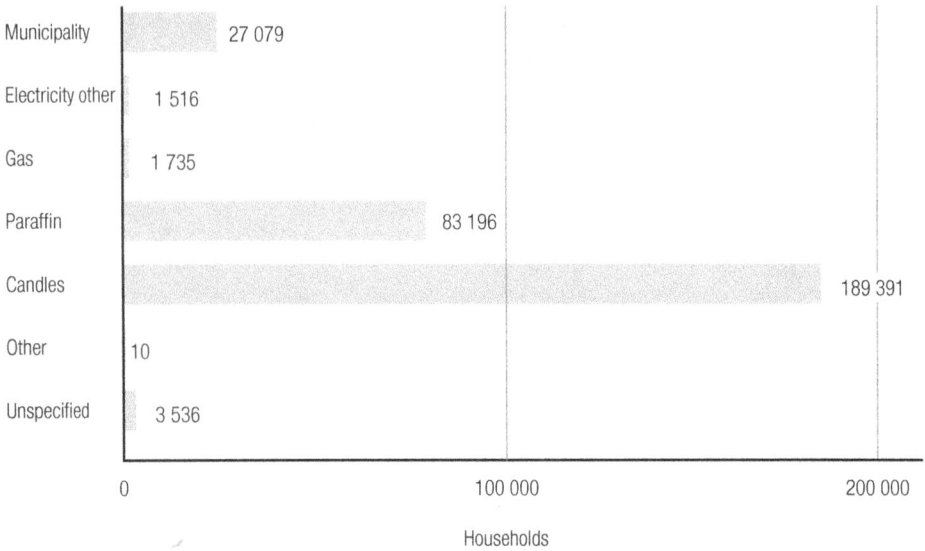

Power Resource	Households
Municipality	27 079
Electricity other	1 516
Gas	1 735
Paraffin	83 196
Candles	189 391
Other	10
Unspecified	3 536

Households

While Nyanisweni could be described as a poor rural area, Dutyini falls into the category of ultra-poor as defined in the Project for Statistics on Living Standards and Development (PSLSD). According to the PSLSD findings, the poor have an income of less than R300 per month and the ultra-poor less than R178. Dutyini residents' livelihoods have been largely from migrant wages, whereas Nyanisweni residents have various sources of livelihood ranging from part-time jobs in towns to work on the mines. People who live in Nyanisweni speak of deriving income from collecting scrap material and working for the municipality and the government. Some of them work in retail shops as cleaners, security guards and, if they are lucky, as cashiers. However, they also complain that the wages are too low to meet their needs.

There is no municipal transport system servicing the villages, neither the ones close to Mbizana nor the remote ones. Since the closure of the Transkei Road Transport Corporation (TRTC), the former homeland bus service, no alternative transport system has been made available. Needless to say, with the closure of the TRTC, hundreds of families were left stranded. Dutyini is serviced by old trucks purchased from the proceeds of migrant labour. Apart from this, some people use horses for transport.

4. Findings and Analysis

The migratory tradition was that the homestead head took an *ijoyini* (mine work contract) to either initiate or consolidate the homestead. After 10 to 20 years on the mines, the first-born followed in his footsteps. In the past, older miners used to negotiate for their sons. It became the norm that if a father worked on the mines, the sons would definitely go there as well. Now the system has changed, as one ex-Elysburg mine worker explained:

> When I started working on the mines, I was not asked if I had a certificate or not. They only checked my weight and height. And if you had strong muscles you were more likely to be taken without questions. But now, when we apply they tell us about some certificates we need to produce, and also to demonstrate that we can read and write. These things were not asked for before.

When these men were on the job, their families were proud of them. The common parlance of the time was, 'My son and I are industrial workers or mine workers' (Ngonini, 2001). One Lesotho migrant, cited in Moodie (1994: 18), declared 'We are the bulls of the mines.' During this time of *ijoyini*, skills were not important – they would be acquired on the job. All that was crucial was the weight and height of the migrant worker. So, desperate for cash, migrants who were not strong and heavy would wrap chains around their waists to increase their body weight.

Underground workers were respected and feared because of the physique they developed and the 'mystique' they acquired through drilling, loading the underground train and so forth. Most of the disabled ex-migrants the author interviewed said they had worked underground, and most of the widows said that their husbands were *mshini* boys (drillers). Because of hard work on the mines, leave periods were normally taken during the rainy season. Migrants who worked underground were the lowest paid and most vulnerable of the mineworkers. Socially, in their villages they commanded high cultural capital – they were respected for what they knew and could do.

The migrant labour system appears to have had a Janus-faced impact. On the one hand, it permitted the homestead and its people to survive, which is different from having a decent livelihood. On the other, it gradually erased the idea of working the land and thus living independently. It also inundated rural areas with manufactured goods, thus diminishing rural people's need to farm.

Mhle (not his real name) took *ijoyini* in the 1970s, and from that date never considered himself a farmer. He saw himself rather as an industrial worker who digs for gold underground. Migrants of the 1970s were more cosmopolitan than their predecessors and this cosmopolitanism has been transmitted to youngsters. One older ex-miner mourned the fact that today's children do not know how to farm and see no future in it, perceiving it as a waste of time:

> When the kids return from schools, they do not want to work in the gardens. They say we should buy food from the shops, they do not understand the extent of poverty here because they are just from high school – where they were eating meat and vegetables, rice, all that fancy stuff.

Migrants bought aprons and blankets for their in-laws to strengthen homestead relations. However, behind the jubilation of this kind of work were the debilitating accidents, which migrants did not foresee. In the minds of the ex-migrants, lost limbs were a glaring reminder of the dangers involved in mine work. Koki, who worked for Leudoran Mines, showed me his experience that he carries around every day; it is the only thing other than documents that he still has as evidence of his stint on the mines:

> Look here [showing me his right hand from which two fingers are missing], I

never got money for this injury, now I cannot lift heavy material. I have no pension. I am forced to rely on my wife and after every time I lift something heavy this thing bleeds.

Migrants who have lost limbs now depend on family members for help in carrying out their daily duties such as eating, washing and moving around. One woman commented on the difficulty she faces in her homestead – caring for her husband, who is virtually immobilised by injuries from the mines:

We, females, suffer a lot. When our husbands were on the mines we struggled to make the ends meet. For they sometimes took time to send money and you could not sit on your laurels waiting for that manna – you needed to improvise. Now they are back, some with fractured legs, cut hands, in fact some are crippled. We have to nurse them. My husband lost the left leg as well as the left arm. He cannot do a damn thing. He has no money, no job. The mines just dumped him here at home.

Migrant labour was necessary not only for survival but also to secure respect in the community. Those who bought blankets, aprons and horses were highly esteemed. Hence, working on the mines became an entrenched way of life, and a prized possession. In particular, building and maintaining *umzi* (the homestead) depended on perpetual migrancy. Men initially migrated to make money to build and maintain it, and once they had built it they assumed that migrancy would support them forever. And every young man who got married paid *lobola* (bride price) with remittances from the mines rather than with cattle. When cattle were used, they were purchased with the same remittances. Migrant wages in Mbizana made a number of traditional functions possible, such as circumcision ceremonies and weddings. The monetary contribution made it possible for migrants' homesteads to buy oxen, goats and sheep to provide meat for the feast.

5. Ex-Miners' Economic Practices and Income-Generating Opportunities

A strong relationship exists between local economic practice and income. Thus, the more diversified the economic practices, the better the income. In Mbizana there are no industries; the only job opportunities are the retail shops. The majority of people survive because of the informal sector. Several of the ex-migrants the author interviewed have 'gone green' – they now cultivate potatoes, cabbages and spinach. The leader of the 'green' ex-migrants is a man who was retrenched in 1995 and has been unemployed since then. Frustrated by waiting and hoping for the next employment opportunity, Nqoyi stated:

I have given up on looking for a job. My wife left me in 1990 and I have been living alone ever since. Because of the difficult experience of not having a source of income, I decided to start farming, just to provide supper for us.

Three other ex-migrants were lured by his success. However, he has a problem of theft, since his garden is not fenced and he does not have money to buy fencing material to keep out the people who help themselves in his garden at night. For men like him, ready to do anything yet aware of being skilled at nothing, always available to do anything and totally subject to everything, there is nothing solid, nothing certain and nothing permanent (Bourdieu, 1990: 66).

There is a perception that Pondoland produces one of world's best varieties of marijuana (locally 'weed' or dagga). In oral discussions, the elders always speak about dagga being sold to tourists who visit the area, some of them from overseas. Most of the homesteads the author visited in Dutyini used it as their source of income. It is the cheapest of all crops to grow. Grown mainly around shrubs and in forests, it does not need fertilisers and hoeing, so it leaves the farmer with more time to devote to other crops. The main farmers and best entrepreneurs of the crop are women, but they are also victims of police arrests. They showed me dagga farms in the forests. Nomzamo, a mother of eight children, commented:

> I have been arrested five times in the past two years. First I was arrested at night on my way to Durban and then Gauteng. I get more money in Durban and Gauteng than when I sell it locally. Here a box of matches [the villagers use a matchbox to measure the quantity of marijuana] would cost R2 but in Durban and Gauteng I can charge R15 or more.

Another source of livelihood diversification is commercial sexual relationships. These take place between better-off men and poor or ultra-poor females, in most cases at midday and after hours, when men are on drinking sprees, oscillating between drinking spots. The men who engage in this form of exploitation or sexual predation know very well that these women care about their children and thus are forced into this business to support them. As Mandlovu says:

> Poverty can cause you to do all sorts of bad things, from witchcraft, pilfering and sleeping with other women's husbands. Most of us have secret boyfriends [amaqabane] who give us money to buy food for iintsapho [family]. If there is no work, no food in the house – what would you do?

The risk of disease is high, as many of these 'secret boyfriends' are migrants, mostly to KwaZulu-Natal and Gauteng, two provinces with a high prevalence of HIV/AIDS. In Dutyini there is neither a clinic nor provision of condoms. Consequently, in the past three years St Patrick's Hospital has recorded the highest incidence of HIV infection of any hospital in Pondoland. HIV, according to St Patrick's staff, is concentrated in the most inaccessible places. Where it hits, people deny that it is HIV; rather they decry it as witchcraft and embark on killing neighbours and relatives. Large numbers of migrants have perished. Mbizana and other traditional sources of migrant labour in the former homelands have the highest levels of migrancy-related HIV/AIDS. Kati, an elderly former migrant, remarked:

> In our times, only the old were prone to death, but now we are are burying young people every weekend. What moves me is that they leave children behind and we are old and going to die soon. What is happening is shame.

This respondent started counting the number of people who have succumbed to the deadly disease in a short period of time. In some cases, entire families have been wiped out by it. These families are haunted by not only the reality of retrenchment and unemployment, but also by the risk of dying from HIV-related illnesses for which there is no remedy.

Kuckertz (1990) argues that remittances made a number of socio-cultural functions possible, such as weddings, circumcision ceremonies, and so forth. However, in the wake of massive retrenchments, elders lament that now they only talk about death and there are hardly any jubilant social events like *ukthombisa* or *ukwaluka* (female and male initiation).

The family structured around a permanently employed male breadwinner is now under severe assault. The traditional family was the basic unit of production, and agriculture involved all members of the family. In these villages, many homesteads are now split over numerous sites and have to diversify survival strategies and work in a number of places. Mandlovu said:

> I wake up very early in the morning, around 4 a.m., to work in the garden in sum-
> mer, and thereafter without even taking a break, I go to ask nurses or teachers
> if they have a laundry that needs to be done. I do this so as to pay fees for my
> children because since their father was retrenched they are routinely sent home.

Women are becoming the major social actors, and the burden of family responsibility has been shifted to them. Over the past few years, the cost of living has increased dramatically, school fees have gone up and school uniforms have become expensive. As another respondent remarked, 'If your kids don't have the uniform, then they can't be in the classroom.' Sadly, this happens at a time when these parents have realised the importance of getting an education. Lack of income has destabilised many families.

With the loss of jobs, many homesteads complained about poor diet and shortages of food. Migrant families say they used to eat meat almost every day when the heads of the home-steads were still employed. Food is one of the things that keep the family intact in the rural areas. Now, however, for most families, as the old Xhosa adage goes, 'the cat sleeps on the hearth,' meaning cooking does not take place because there is nothing to cook. As a conse-quence, relatively young women have decided to leave their husbands and either go back to their original homesteads or migrate to KwaZulu-Natal. Nolizwe, aged 28, said, 'If he can't provide food and money for us I don't know why I have to stay with him because he is never going to get a job here. The only thing I see is *yindlala* [hunger, poverty].'

Most women stated that what they hear from their husbands is *'Ayikho'* (meaning 'There is nothing'). These women then decide to migrate to Durban to work as street fruit vendors if they fail to secure a factory or domestic job. Their husbands complain that they do not come back with money; rather some come back pregnant and do not want to stay with their husbands any more. Rhadebe, who worked at East Driefontein, said:

> My wife left for Durban in 1997; she told me that her friend had found her a job.
> She only came back in 1999 pregnant and to fetch the kids from me. This dev-
> astated me very much, such that I cannot sleep properly since they left because
> I do not know what is happening to my children.

Elderly women seek employment in Mbizana from nurses and teachers who pay them pitiful wages. One said that she works as a domestic worker and she gets paid R20 a day.

Two ex-migrants suffered strokes while they were still employed and were compelled by their health conditions to stop working and come back to live with their families. Upon 'retiring' they were given severance packages, which they used to purchase tractors. These tractors earned them some money initially, but since they lacked business acumen they did not make much profit. Chagi, who worked at Zulwini mine, stated:

> When I came back I bought a red tractor from Kokstad, and initially I made money, but as time went by I did not see where it was going, people started not paying on time or not paying at all. They told me that their husbands or sons have not sent money. What you would see next is the disappearance of the wife to look for her husband, but never to come back.

In many homesteads, family heads have disappeared for fear of being embarrassed and losing their dignity in the family and their society in general. They choose to stay on the mines in the hope of getting another job. But even in those places, they do not find sustainable employment. This has affected the migrants' dependants. A large number of children have been withdrawn from school because their parents are unable to pay fees. Some students have completed Grade 12 but cannot further their studies because there is no one to fund them. One frustrated pupil said:

> If these unsympathetic mine owners had not retrenched my father I would be doing mechanical engineering at a university now. When we go to the bank, they ask for a pay slip, yet my father does not work and thus I do not qualify for a loan.

Food associations (*imihlanganiso*) have mushroomed over the last few years as buffers against poverty and to establish social networks. These organisations are based on contributions of R30 to R50 per month. However, the ultra-poor complain that it is very difficult for them to participate in such schemes. One migrant stated that it took his homestead almost six months to save R30 for the association and by then they had to pay R100 because of interest. As a result they were expelled. These associations need to be nurtured and supported financially by the state. It is also important to note that *imihlanganiso* are very functional during the festive season. Women collect money throughout the year and then, in December, they buy food in bulk and congregate to divide it among the members.

During the heyday of migrancy, migrant workers were treated with high esteem. The impression created in the rural areas was that they were scooping gold with their helmets and were thus rich. In Bourdieu's terms, they commanded both cultural and economic capital in the minds of the people of the villages. With retrenchments, all of this dignity (cultural capital) has dissipated. Loss of employment has serious implications for status and dignity within the family and the community at large. Ex-migrants have become the most unimportant people in the countryside. Ngutyana, who was employed by the Kloof Mine, said:

> Since I lost my job, I do not have the respect I use to command when I was working. Then, when I came back I use to buy people beers, drinks, blankets for old people, sweets for children, but now I cannot afford to buy myself even a loose cigarette.

These were traditional patriarchal villages, where men had the last word. However, the crisis in the migrant labour system has shaken the edifice upon which patriarchy was based – men as the sole breadwinners and wives staying at home. Many migrants have decided to live in 'hiding' because they cannot accept the situation they find themselves in; consequently they are always stressed and depressed because they are in a state of denial. The retrenched have limited options and were not given counselling. They keep repeating 'What am I going to do?', 'How am I going to make a living?', 'I do not know how to do anything else!'

Some ex-migrants are presumed mad because of depression. Most migrants have difficulty in dealing with the situation and are living in denial. Many families have broken down as a result of retrenchments, as some people decided to migrate to better places like Natal. These migrants say that their wives complain that they cannot stay because 'I have no money [andinamali].'

There are at least two things that frustrate the retrenched migrants. Firstly, loss of jobs and regular income with the concomitant loss of dignity and status in the homestead, and secondly, confusion emanating from worries about their dependants, not being counselled and not knowing what to do next. Kehla, an ex-Dolfontein worker, said that he received certified training which he cannot use to get a job in the village: 'I have the drilling and blasting certificate, but I cannot use these things here. I can only be a security at the gate with my knobkerrie.'

Peku, who worked at Western Deep Levels Mine, now works as a security guard at a local shop. He earns R200 per month, with which he has to feed nine people. Those who bought goats, sheep and cattle have had to sell their livestock to educate their children and state that they are no longer important people in society since their herds have decreased. Men feel abandoned by the mine labour system; their prospects have shrunk and they have become superfluous and burdensome. Nkosi, an ex-mineworker from Libanon mine, sums up their sentiments:

> My wife once told me that things were easier for her while I was away and now things have become more complex since I am here at home doing nothing. I am only a burden, and in fact I am just like one of the children she has to feed. I felt so terrible, because what she was telling was true.

His wife does laundry in town for nurses and sometimes works in other people's gardens just to ensure that the children have something in their stomachs when they go to sleep. One migrant said that his wife told him that she was going to leave if he did not do something about their poverty. Reflecting on the effects of being unemployed, Candlovu stated emphatically:

> You know indlala inamanyala [hunger breeds evil]. I never thought to myself that I could steal anything. But now I am forced by the circumstances. I cannot find a job. Children need to eat and I decided to steal. I have stolen three goats and a pig. I slaughtered them and sold them in town, to make money for food and school fees.

This former migrant's three daughters have been sent away from school and are saving money to go to Durban to look for employment. Currently, women mainly take care of the farming and cultivation, while the men tend to run away to drink, 'to drown their sorrows.'

Entrepreneurial strategies have been used quite extensively by some ex-migrants, to the point that one can say that there are at least two types – consumer migrants and entrepreneurial migrants. The latter tend to open general dealer shops and cafés and buy tractors to rent out to the local people, while consumer migrants just spend their money. However, many of those who opened shops have since failed and gone into debt with the local wholesaler. Studies in Lesotho reveal that ex-migrants fail to diversify their business undertakings (Philip, 1995; Crush et al., 2000). They have a copycat approach to business, which renders them victims of small Shylocks. When Shylock comes to cut off his pound of flesh for their failure to honour the agreement, the ex-migrants do not have an adjudicator to instruct him not to spill blood. In this case, the pound of flesh is the valuables inside the homestead; thus ex-migrants resolve to abandon their homesteads.

In the late 1970s and early 1980s, pensions and remittances became the main sources of income for the majority of homesteads (Wilson & Ramphele, 1989; May et al., 1998). But in the 1990s, pensions came to replace the remittances. A homestead with pensioners is better off than a family that relies on social and kin networks based on *ukunkinkqa*, begging with a basin for mealie meal, samp (crushed maize), sugar and tea. Homesteads which embark on *ukunkinkqa* have fewer assets, such as livestock, education and skills; absolutely no one is earning an income and alternative sources are thus not available. In most of these homesteads, wives use multiple relationships as a way to siphon money from those who are working. As Makhumala stated:

> Since he does not work, and I cannot find a job in town, besides it's too far, I have decided to date a joyini [a miner] because he is still working and does give me money, which I use to buy basic things for the homestead.

One ex-migrant told me that he lives on his mother's pension. Ndende, who worked at Carletonville, said:

> There is nothing I do here; I depend on my mother's pension. So every time I make sure that I know the pay date so that I don't miss out. Because this is the only way I can share and be able to buy drink for my friends.

The increased reliance on pensions has had a negative effect. Because of the severity of poverty in these homesteads, pensioners are forever indebted to the shops, so that by the time they receive their grant they have already spent 90 per cent of it. Rather than improving the purchasing power of rural areas, pensions compound the problem through heavy dependency on pensioners and putting off finding a solution to problems.

It is not only pensions that have become a means of achieving a livelihood; most participants said they use the child maintenance grant to support their families. This grant is earmarked for children under the age of seven, but now it serves a bigger role of maintaining not only the child but the entire homestead. Pension grants and child grants enable poverty-stricken homesteads to farm the gardens. However, they do not provide a sustainable livelihood but rather defer the crisis. When a child turns eight, the family is no longer entitled to the grant and they must find a way around that. Similarly, when a pensioner passes away, the family must devise another means of getting an income. But most families do not report to the magistrate that the pensioner has died; rather they will report that he or she is unable to walk and thus one of the family members is collecting the grant for him or her. As a result, there are 'ghost' pensioners.

The rural economy of Mbizana since the late 1980s has been shifting from migrant remittances towards a greater dependence on welfare grants. With this shift, the amount of land and the capacity to farm have diminished and cultivation has shifted to gardens (Bank, 1999). Early studies in Pondoland report that the region was conducive to agriculture because of wet weather (Kuckertz, 1990; Beinart & Bundy, 1980). Some even went so far as to argue that it was the richest region in the former Transkei homeland (Beinart, 1994). Now, the majority of farm fields have reverted to grazing lands – a result of financial deficiency rather than a move towards modernity.

Vimbela is a typical example of someone who has gone from being a productive farmer to living from hand to mouth. He had four farm fields about ten to 15 kilometres from his house. In the village, he was rated as the best farmer. When he got retrenched things changed for the worse. He could no longer afford to farm all his fields, so he lent some to his relatives who soon abandoned them because they were too short of money. As he said:

> I used to reap about five to eight tonnes of mealies in good season from all my farm fields [amasimi]. Children would not sleep on an empty stomach. We would drink traditional sorghum beer and be merry. That is not the case anymore.

Normally, families who reap excellent harvests have strong cattle for ploughing and hoeing. Vimbela told me that he only farms certain contours in the field below his homestead. Since he sold and slaughtered most of his livestock, he cannot get kraal manure to supplement fertilisers, which he says have become very expensive.

Thus, grazing lands have expanded at the expense of croplands, and the expansion of grazing lands has coincided with the shrinking of the livestock. There is now more grazing land than livestock to graze it, with the result that more areas are now overgrown with bush, providing hiding places for thieves. This situation is partly the result of forced resettlement and destruction of the rural subsistence economy, but the mine retrenchments and their effect on former migrants and their families have also been a major cause.

6. Conclusion

For centuries, the South African economy has relied on the mining industry, and the mining industry has depended on unskilled labour from impoverished rural areas. This chapter has shown the ways in which the social economy of the villages of Dutyini and Nyanisweni have been reconfigured by the permanent return of the migrants, thus exploring the rural impact of large-scale retrenchments and the decline of migration.

The chapter has illustrated the negative impact of retrenchments on the migrants' well-being and their loss of standing in the community. Men who used to function as breadwinners have difficulty adapting to the new conditions in the villages: they feel sidelined and emotionally and psychologically alienated from their rural communities. These ex-migrant workers have lost not only income; the emasculating experience of losing a job denies them any possible claims on the future.

While they have become sedentary, women have emerged as the new migrants, as the ex-miners are ill-equipped to work in other sectors or to apply mine skills at home. Without the earnings from the mines, poverty has increased and funds for educating children are unavailable. Money for investment in agriculture has declined and cropland is rapidly being converted to under-utilised grazing lands. Entrepreneurial skills are lacking, so attempts to use severance packages in business development usually fail. Many households formerly dependent on remittances are now dependent on pensions and child welfare grants. The intended beneficiaries of both forms of grant no longer benefit in the same way. The conclusion is thus that although migration did not provide a route out of poverty, its absence is making the poor a lot worse off.

Acknowledgements

Funding for the research towards this chapter was provided by the Sociology of Work Unit, Department of Sociology, University of the Witwatersrand.

References

BANK, L, 1999. Men with cookers: transformations in migrant culture, domesticity and identity in Duncan Village, East London. *Journal of Southern African Studies*, 25(3).

BEINART, W, 1979. Production, labour migrancy and chieftaincy: aspects of the political economy of Pondolond ca.1860–1930. School of Oriental and African Studies. London: University of London.

— 1994. Twentieth-century South Africa. Oxford: Oxford University Press.

BEINART, W & BUNDY, C, 1980. State intervention and rural resistance, 1900–1965. In Klein, MA (ed.), *Peasants in Africa*. Beverly Hills, California: Sage, pp. 285–9.

BOURDIEU, P, 1990. *In other words: essays towards a reflective sociology*. California: Stanford University Press.

BUNDY, C, 1979. *The rise and fall of the South African peasantry*. London: Heinemann.

CENTRAL STATISTICS SERVICES (CSS), 1995. *Income and expenditure survey: Eastern Cape*. Pretoria: CSS.

CHIRWA, W, 1997. 'No TEBA … forget TEBA': the plight of Malawian ex-migrant workers to South Africa, 1988–1994. *International Migration Review*, 31(3): 628-54.

CRUSH, J & JAMES, W (eds), 1995. *Crossing boundaries: mine migrancy in a democratic South Africa*. Cape Town: Idasa.

CRUSH, J; JEEVES, A & YUDELMAN, D, 1991. *South Africa's labour empire: a history of black migrancy to the gold mines*. Cape Town: David Philip.

CRUSH, J et al., 1999. Undermining labour: migrancy and subcontracting in the South African gold mining industry. SAMP Migration Policy Series No. 15, Cape Town.

— 2000. *Borderline farming: foreign migrants in South African commercial agriculture.* SAMP Migration Policy Series No. 16, Cape Town.

DATA WORLD, 2000. Profile of Mbizana Municipality. Available at www.demarcation.org.za

JAMES, W, 1992. *Our precious metal: African labour in South Africa's gold industry, 1970–1990.* Cape Town: David Philip.

KUCKERTZ, H, 1990. *Creating order: the image of the homestead in Mpondo social life.* Johannesburg: Wits University Press.

MALHERBE, S, 2000. A perspective on the South African mining industry in the 21st century. An independent report prepared for the Chamber of Mines of South Africa by the Graduate School of Business of the University of Cape Town in association with Genesis Analytics.

MAY, J, 1984. Development and planning in the Transkei: the rural service approach. DSRG Working Paper 15. Development Studies Unit. Durban: University of Natal.

MAY, J et al., 1998. Poverty and inequality. A report for the office of the Executive Deputy President and Inter-ministerial Committee for Poverty and Inequality. Pretoria.

MOODIE, TD. 1994. *Going for gold: men, mines and migration.* Berkeley: University of California Press.

MULLER, ND, 1984. The labour market and poverty in the Transkei, with special reference to the implications of the changing spatial division of labour. A paper presented at the Carnegie Conference on Poverty at the University of Cape Town.

MURRAY, C, 1981. *Families divided: the impact of migrant labour in Lesotho.* Johannesburg: Ravan.

NGONINI, X, 2001. Waai-waai: the impact of retrenchments on rural households – a case study of Bizana. *South African Labour Bulletin*, 25(2): 35-40.

PHILIP, K, 1995. The NUM (National Union of Mineworkers) job creation and development programme. In Crush, J & James, W (eds), *Crossing boundaries: Mine migrancy in a democratic South Africa.* Cape Town: Idasa.

PROJECT FOR STATISTICS ON LIVING STANDARDS AND DEVELOPMENT (PSLSD), 1993. *South Africa rich and poor: baseline household statistics.* Cape Town: Southern African Labour Development Research Unit, University of Cape Town.

STATSSA (STATISTICS SOUTH AFRICA), 2005. Census 2001: Achieving a better life for all: Progress between Census '96 and Census 2001. StatsSA.

STEINBERG, J & SEIDMAN, G, 1995. *Gold mining's labour market: legacies of the past, challenges of the present.* Johannesburg: Sociology of Work, Wits University.

SPIEGEL, A, 1987. Dispersing dependants: a response to the exigencies of labour migration in rural Transkei. In Eades, J (ed.), *Migrants, workers, and the social order.* London: Tavistock.

WILSON F & RAMPHELE, M, 1989. *Uprooting poverty: the challenge for South Africa.* Cape Town: David Philip.

12 RESTLESS WORLDS OF WORK, HEALTH AND MIGRATION: DOMESTIC WORKERS IN JOHANNESBURG

NATALYA DINAT AND SALLY PEBERDY

1. Introduction

The lives of migrant women have generally received far less attention than their male counterparts. So, despite the long history of women's internal and cross-border migration, their
stories and lives have remained largely undocumented (Dodson, 2000). Male migrants, and
particularly mineworkers and truck drivers, have also been the primary focus of research on
the relationship between HIV and migration (Crush et al., 2002; Lurie et al., 2003; Zuma et
al., 2003; Lurie, 2004). At times, their partners – usually called 'women at risk' – have been
included in research. Other researchers have started to look at the sexual activities of women
'left behind' by their migrant male partners (Lurie et al., 2003). Yet little attention has been
paid to the vulnerability of female migrants themselves to HIV infection and their access to
healthcare and treatment.

Johannesburg is the largest city in South Africa. In 2001, over 3 225 000 people were
counted in the Census. The city is also home to the largest number of migrants of any city
in South Africa. Census 2001 found that 35,2 per cent of the population of Johannesburg
were internal migrants born outside Gauteng Province and 6,7 per cent were cross-border
migrants or had been born outside South Africa. When people think of migrant workers, they
usually think of male migrants, yet women have a long history of migration to Johannesburg.
If place of birth is used as a marker of migrancy, Census 2001 shows that in Johannesburg
women constitute a significant proportion of migrant workers in the city. For some provinces
(Eastern Cape, Free State, Northwest and Western Cape), women migrants to Gauteng exceed
the number of men (Figure 12.1).

Figure 12.1: Population of Johannesburg by Gender and Place of Birth (%), 2001

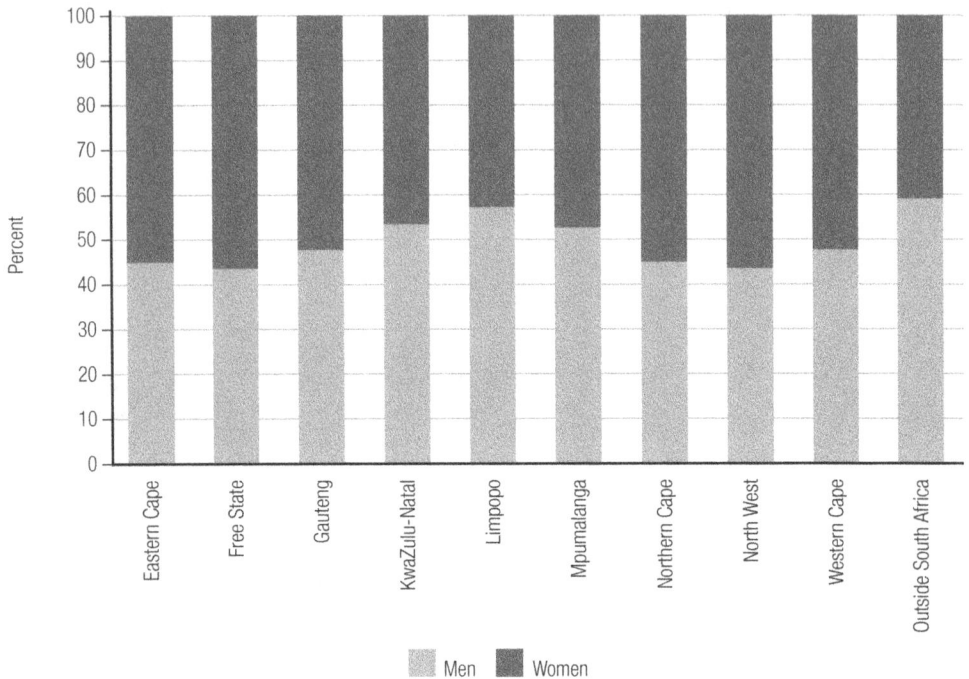

Domestic work, although often characterised as 'atypical work' in the service sector, provides significant opportunities for employment for black women in South Africa. In 2004, it was the second largest employment sector for South Africa's black female workforce, employing some 755 000 women (StatsSA, 2005). Census 2001 found that work in private households is the largest source of employment for black South African women in Johannesburg, with 88 000 women so employed (31 per cent of employed black women).

Available evidence suggests that domestic work has traditionally been, and remains, a significant area of employment for internal and cross-border female migrant workers (Miles, 1991, 1996; Cockerton, 1997). Census 2001 data obtained from Statistics South Africa (StatsSA) shows that 42 per cent of employed black women from the Southern African Development Community (SADC) who lived in Johannesburg worked in private households, although they comprised only 4,9 per cent of women working in private households in the city (StatsSA, 2004). Census 2001 also shows that some 35,6 per cent of employed black South African women born outside Gauteng Province who lived in Johannesburg worked in private households as compared to 9 per cent of employed black women who were born in Gauteng and lived in Johannesburg (StatsSA, 2004).

Many domestic workers are migrant workers. They endure poor working conditions and low incomes despite attempts by the Department of Labour to set minimum standards. Many live in isolation on their employers' properties and lack opportunities for collective action to improve their working conditions. Low incomes and arduous working conditions mean that access to health services may be limited, as time away from work may mean lost income.

Domestic workers could be at increased risk of HIV infection as a result of their gender, migrancy, social isolation, poverty, low levels of education, lack of access to healthcare services, and lack of power at work and possibly at home (Peberdy & Dinat, 2005).

This chapter explores the vulnerability of migrant domestic workers to HIV/AIDS. It is based on a survey of 1100 female domestic workers working in the Johannesburg Magisterial District (JMD) undertaken in 2004 by the Southern African Migration Programme (SAMP) and Baragwanath Perinatal HIV/AIDS Unit. The sample was identified using a cluster sampling technique from 94 randomly selected census enumerated areas in the JMD. The random selection of enumeration areas included only those areas with average household monthly incomes of over R2500 and which had more than 40 households living in detached, semi-detached or town houses. Houses where interviews would take place were then randomly selected from the selected enumerator areas. On average, 11,6 domestic workers were interviewed per enumerator area. Fieldworkers were instructed not to undertake the interview if the employer was present. Following the interview, all participants were provided with a list of clinics in the area, as well as HIV/AIDS-specific services available in the city. An average of 16,8 per cent of domestic workers in the selected households in each area could not be contacted despite repeat visits, and fieldworkers recorded a refusal rate of 18,3 per cent.

The JMD was chosen after examining the Labour Force Survey, which indicated that most areas lying outside the JMD but inside the boundaries of the City of Johannesburg report extremely low rates of employment of domestic workers. In effect, this meant that Soweto was excluded. However, the sample included a range of suburbs from Linksfield Ridge in the northwest of the city to Eldorado Park in the southeast. Owing to financial constraints, it was not possible to employ rigorous sampling techniques in the flatlands (areas of apartment blocks) of Johannesburg, so these areas were also excluded. Therefore, all enumeration areas lying in Soweto, areas with average incomes of less than R2 500 per month, areas with less than 40 households living in houses, and domestic workers employed by apartment dwellers were excluded from the survey. The survey thus provides a profile of domestic workers employed in houses in Johannesburg in areas with average incomes over R2 500. It is possible, therefore, that there may be an over-representation of women who live in and work full-time for a single employer.

2. Jobs for Migrant Women

Domestic work provides significant employment opportunities for black female migrant and non-migrant women in Johannesburg. And, as noted above, Census 2001 shows that work in private households provided employment for over 88 000 black women in the city. The census also shows that domestic service was the largest sector of employment for black women who had moved to Johannesburg from other provinces and other countries.

One of the defining features of participants in this study was that the overwhelming majority were migrant workers. So, although over 50 per cent of participants called the Johannesburg area home, some 86 per cent said they had another home somewhere else (Table 12.1). Participants with homes elsewhere showed strong ties to these homes. Of those with other homes, 72 per cent said they would rather be living there if the same job and working conditions were available (Table 12.1). Although less than 10 per cent visited their other home more than once a month, nearly 90 per cent visited at least once a year (Table 12.2). Opportunities to visit their other home may be constrained by cost, distance and time.

Table 12.1: Domestic Workers as Migrants (%)			
	Total non-South Africans	South African migrants	Total sample
Call the Johannesburg area home (N=1100)	51.5	44.3	52.2
Have a home somewhere else as well (N=1100	98.5	100.0	86.1
Would move home if could have same job there	58.2	72.8	71.9
N=945			

Table 12.2: Frequency of Visits Home (%)			
	Total non-South Africans	South African migrants	Total sample
More than once a month	1.5	7.2	6.8
Once a month	0.0	17.7	16.5
Once every few months	7.5	26.1	24.7
Once or twice a year	67.2	39.4	41.4
Less than once or twice a year	6.0	6.4	6.3
I have been just once	4.5	0.9	1.2
I have not been home yet but I would like to	7.5	1.6	2.0
Never – I cannot return home	4.5	0.2	0.5
Never – I have no desire to return home	0.0	0.3	0.3
N=945			

It is sometimes assumed that cross-border migrants from SADC countries constitute a significant proportion of domestic workers in the city. However, this study, together with Census 2001, suggests that the overwhelming majority of migrant domestic workers are internal migrants (Table 12.3). Only 68 (6 per cent) of the women interviewed were not South African citizens. When asked about the location of their other home, 6 per cent said it was in another country. Of those who had homes in other countries, all were from SADC countries. Almost 50 per cent of foreign domestic workers in the study came from Lesotho, almost a third from Zimbabwe and the rest were from Mozambique (6 per cent), Botswana (4 per cent), Swaziland (4 per cent), Malawi (4 per cent) and Zambia (2 per cent).

The majority of migrant domestic workers had grown up in rural areas, particularly those from other countries. However, many had lived in an urban area for some time. Over three-quarters had lived in Johannesburg for five years or more (Table 12.4). Unemployment seems to have been a significant motivator for moving to Johannesburg. Almost 70 per cent had been unemployed before they left home for Johannesburg (Table 12.5).

Table 12.3: Place of Birth and Place of other Home (%)

Province	Province of other home (survey)	Place of birth of black women in Johannesburg (Census 2001)
Gauteng	16.3	22.5
Eastern Cape	12.2	10.5
Free State	12.1	9.4
KwaZulu-Natal	10.9	10.9
Limpopo	10.5	15.9
Mpumalanga	6.2	5.2
Northern Cape	3.2	1.5
North West	20.4	17.9
Western Cape	1.1	1.3
Other country	6.0	5.0

Table 12.4: Length of Time in Johannesburg (%)

	Total non-South Africans	South African migrants
Less than one year	5.9	4.9
1 year	8.8	2.7
2 years	4.4	5.5
3 years	8.8	4.8
4 years	5.9	4.2
5 years	7.4	8.0
More than 5 years	57.4	69.9
N=943		

Table 12.5: Employment Status Prior to Coming to Johannesburg (%)

	Total non-South Africans	South African migrants
Employed	19.4	23.6
Unemployed	70.2	68.7
Self-employed	3.0	0.8
Student/scholar	4.5	6.3
Other	1.5	0.3
N=943		

The majority of non-South African migrant workers seem to retain relatively strong ties with their home countries, as 88 per cent regularly send money and goods there. Not surprisingly, the main reason they came to South Africa was to find a job. The choice of South Africa may have been influenced by family experience and contacts, as over half said their parents had worked in South Africa and a third said their grandparents had.

3. Domestic Workers in Profile

Who are the women who clean the homes of the city and ensure that families leave their homes pressed and tidy? The majority are of an age at which people have already established or are establishing long-term relationships and are developing families. Respondents were mostly aged between 21 and 50 (Table 12.6). The overwhelming majority (almost 60 per cent) were aged between 31 and 50. Five of the workers interviewed were under 20, while 35 were still working when they were over 60. Non-migrants tended to be older than migrants. Some 64 per cent of the former were over 40, compared with 38 per cent of foreigners and 49 per cent of internal migrants.

Table 12.6: Age (%)					
	Total non-South Africans	South African migrants	South African non-migrants	Total South Africans	Total sample
15–20 years	0.0	0.3	1.3	0.5	0.5
21–30	25.0	20.5	13.3	19.4	19.8
31–40	36.8	30.4	21.2	26.1	29.6
41–50	22.0	29.3	39.1	30.7	30.2
51–60	10.3	16.4	21.5	17.2	16.6
Over 60	5.9	3.0	3.3	3.0	3.2
N=1100					

The women live solitary lives marked by separation from family members. Although 58 per cent had a husband or partner, more than half were temporarily living apart from them. So, only 27 per cent of the women interviewed were living with a spouse or partner. Some 26 per cent were single and 16 per cent divorced, separated or widowed (Table 12.7). A third of the married women and 60 per cent of those with partners were living on their own.

Table 12.7: Marital Status (%)					
	Non-South Africans	South African migrants	South African non-migrants	Total South Africans	Total sample
Single	27.9	24.8	29.1	25.5	25.8
Divorced/separated	7.4	7.0	7.3	7.0	7.0
Widowed	8.8	8.3	13.9	9.1	9.1
Married but temporarily living apart	5.9	6.2	3.3	5.7	5.8
Married and living together	11.8	9.6	15.9	10.5	10.5
Living with partner	14.7	17.1	16.6	17.0	16.8
Partner but temporarily living apart	23.5	27.0	13.9	25.1	24.9
N=1100					

Many women are forced to live apart from their partners and spouses in their working and living arrangements. Almost 45 per cent were not allowed to have a partner stay with them where they were living, mainly because of restrictions imposed by employers. Some 17 per cent of non-migrants were temporarily living apart from their partners, which suggests that these partners are migrant workers. The majority of the 378 women who were temporarily living apart from their partners and spouses saw them fairly frequently. Some 64 per cent saw them more than once a month, and 14 per cent once a month. Nine per cent saw them only once every few months, and 8 per cent once or twice a year. Four per cent said they saw their partner less than twice a year, while four women said they never wanted to see their partners again.

Almost 70 per cent of the women had children, but were likely to live apart from them. Non-migrants were more likely to be childless (42 per cent compared to 28 per cent of migrants), but were more likely to live with children (52 per cent compared to 13 per cent of migrants). Overall, less than 20 per cent of the women interviewed lived with their children. Separated children were most likely to be in the care of their grandmothers. Almost a third said their children were not allowed to stay with them where they lived because of restrictions imposed by employers. However, although many domestic workers live alone, separated from their partners and children, this does not mean that they do not have family responsibilities. Almost 95 per cent were financially supporting other people in full or in part. The majority of dependents were their own children. Other financial dependents included parents, siblings, grandchildren and nieces and nephews and their partners.

Domestic work is often considered to be low-skilled and new entrants to the sector do not usually have to meet educational entry requirements. Certainly, this survey confirms that domestic work provides employment for women with low levels of education. Almost one-third had had no schooling or only some primary education. A further 16 per cent had completed primary school, while over 40 per cent had been to secondary school. Domestic workers are generally less educated than other women in the city. Literacy levels are important as they not only affect employment opportunities, but also may affect access to health information and ability to deal with employers and bureaucracies.

In sum, this demographic profile of domestic workers in Johannesburg indicates that many live on their own, and even those with partners and children are likely to live apart from them. Their lives are shaped, at least in part, by their profession as well as their migrant status, since where they live prevents them from living with their partners and children. Their choice of profession may be shaped by their low level of educational attainment, which may restrict their job opportunities and their access to information.

4. Worlds of Work

The South African Government has recognised that the working conditions and incomes of many domestic workers are poor. As a result, it has made efforts to improve and formalise these (Hardy & Kleinsmidt, 2004). At the time of the study, the official minimum wage for domestic workers employed in urban areas and working more than 27 hours per week was

R4,87 per hour or R861,90 per month. For those working 27 hours or less per week the minimum wage was R4,87 per hour or R569,79 per month. Maximum working hours have been set by the Department of Labour at 45 hours per week (nine hours per day for those working one to five days per week and eight hours a day for those working six to seven days per week) plus ten hours of overtime. From 2003, employers of domestic workers have had to make contributions to the Unemployment Insurance Fund for their employees.

4.1 Working conditions

These minimum standards set by the Department of Labour do not, however, guarantee that the working conditions of domestic workers are easy. Certainly, the women interviewed for this study lived hard lives and worked long hours for low pay. Their responses indicate that many employers are not meeting the statutory minimum standards of employment. The majority worked for one employer only (88 per cent) and lived at the place where they worked (64 per cent). These responses may reflect the parameters of the sample which excluded women working in apartments.

Domestic workers' employment seems to be stable, or at least long-term. Over 40 per cent of the women interviewed had been employed by their main employer for more than five years (Table 12.8). Non-South African migrants seem to have less stable employment, or were newer entrants to this sector of the labour market, as over 30 per cent had been employed by their main employer for less than a year.

Table 12.8: Length of Time Working for Main Employer (%)					
	Total non-South Africans	South African migrants	South African non-migrants	Total South Africans	Total sample
Less than 6 months	17.7	13.4	10.6	13.0	13.4
More than 6 months but less than a year	14.7	8.4	15.2	9.4	9.7
1–3 years	30.9	26.9	23.8	26.4	26.7
4–5 years	4.4	9.7	12.6	10.1	9.8
Over 5 years	30.9	41.6	37.8	41.0	40.4
N=1100					

The domestic worker's week tends to be long. On average, respondents worked 5,4 days per week (Table 12.9). Over 30 per cent worked five days per week, over 20 per cent worked a six-day week, while almost 20 per cent worked seven days per week. The data suggests that migrant workers worked the longest weeks and that non-migrant workers were most likely to work a five-day week.

Domestic workers also work long days. Some 46 per cent worked nine hours or more per day and 31 per cent worked 10 hours or more per day. Some, it seems, never go off duty. Migrant workers, whether South African or foreign, are likely to work the longest days. A significant proportion of the employers were thus exceeding the maximum working hours set by the Department of Labour. People who work long weeks and/or long days for little pay can find it hard to access healthcare, particularly if taking time off to attend a clinic results in a loss of pay.

Table 12.9: Number of Days Worked (%)					
	Total non-South Africans	South African migrants	South African non-migrants	Total South Africans	Total sample
1 day per week	10.4	7.9	9.9	8.2	2.8
2 days per week	5.2	9.4	10.5	9.6	5.9
3 days per week	7.8	7.8	10.5	8.2	7.9
4 days per week	5.2	2.8	6.4	3.3	3.7
5 days per week	32.3	29.5	34.3	30.2	34.7
6 days per week	16.9	23.7	17.4	22.8	25.9
7 days per week	18.2	17.2	7.6	15.7	18.5
Half a day per week	1.3	0.2	2.3	0.5	0.5
Other	0.0	0.1	0.6	0.2	0.1
N=1100					

4.2   Incomes and expenditure

A significant proportion of domestic workers appear to earn less than the minimum wage for urban areas set out by the Department of Labour. As the majority of women surveyed worked more than 27 hours a week, they should have been earning over R860 per month. Over 20 per cent of respondents earned less than R500 per month, and just over 55 per cent made between R501 and R1000 per month (Table 12.10) (StatsSA, 2005). The September 2004 Labour Force Survey found that nationally (including rural areas), 41,2 per cent of domestic workers earned between R1 and R500, 40,9 per cent between R501 and R1000, and 13,2 per cent between R1001 and R2500 (StatsSA, 2005).

Table 12.10: Monthly Income (%)					
	Non-South Africans	South African migrants	South African non-migrants	Total South Africans	Total sample
Less than R100	0.0	0.3	1.3	0.5	0.5
R100–500	30.9	19.9	22.5	20.2	21.2
R501–1000	47.1	56.6	51.7	55.9	55.7
R1001–1500	14.7	18.0	19.9	18.3	18.1
R1501–2000	7.4	3.4	4.6	3.6	3.8
R2001–2500	0.0	0.6	0.0	0.5	0.5
R2501–3000	0.0	0.1	0.0	0.1	0.1
Not answered/ don't know	0.0	0.0	0.9	0.0	0.7
N=1100					

One elderly woman who lived at her employer's property said she earned nothing, but was provided with food and accommodation. Almost 25 per cent received some food as part of their pay and 61 per cent had free accommodation on their employer's property. Only 5 per cent of the women had another source of income, which on average brought them a further R240 per month. Few who had children of eligible age said they received the child income grant.

4.3   Accommodation

Almost two-thirds (64 per cent) of the workers received free accommodation with their jobs. The remaining 36 per cent who had to pay for their own accommodation in Johannesburg, paid an average of R152 per month. Those who lived away from their place of employment paid an average of R175 per month for transport to work.

So, if the working week is long and hard for the majority of these women, what do they go home to at the end of a long day of cleaning up after other people? The majority go nowhere but stay at their place of employment in accommodation provided by their employer (64 per cent). Not surprisingly, migrant workers, but particularly South Africans (69 per cent), were most likely to live on their employer's property. The slightly lower proportion of non-South African migrants living in (62 per cent) is probably because they were more likely to have been employed for a shorter time and to work part-time. Only 36 per cent of non-migrants lived in.

While the majority lived on their employer's property, the remainder were most likely to live in shacks or rent a room. Most of the domestic workers who left their place of employment at the end of the day went home to a shack (16 per cent). Another 8 per cent went home to a room. Overall, more than two-thirds of respondents lived in just one room and another 11,5 per cent lived in two rooms. Some of those who live in places with more rooms were living inside their employers' houses. However, even if a domestic worker lives on her employer's property, this does not necessarily guarantee good and healthy living conditions. Almost 37 per cent of the women interviewed had no access to a bathroom with running water, and only just over half had access to an inside tap where they lived.

These women clearly work hard for a living, toiling through long days. Many never leave their place of employment at the end of the day, and wherever they live, conditions are not good. Their living and working conditions may not increase their vulnerability to HIV infection, but, if they are infected, do have the potential to compromise their health.

5. Worlds of Leisure: A Lonely Life?

Many domestic workers live relatively solitary lives and are often isolated, even though they live in South Africa's largest city. This isolation in part reflects the location of their homes and workplaces in the suburbs of Johannesburg and the length of their working weeks and days, but it also reflects their migrant status.

Of the women interviewed, almost 30 per cent of migrants and almost a quarter of non-migrants did not have any friends near where they worked. Despite their separation from family and friends, over half said they never felt lonely and only 16 per cent felt lonely often or most of the time. The loneliest times for domestic workers were the evenings and weekends. Again, this may be because their living arrangements precluded them from having friends (and, of course, partners and children) to visit. Almost half were not allowed to have visitors where they lived. Friends were primarily fellow domestic workers, other neighbours and relatives and friends from home. Sadly, and perhaps expressing the isolation of some of these workers, eight said their employer was their best friend. Finding friends in their neighbourhood meant that almost two-thirds said they saw their most important friend three or more times a week.

The social lives of domestic workers, like their working lives, are relatively constricted, at least for those who live in. Most of their social activity (whether migrant or non-migrant) took place in homes or at church and very few regularly visited a bar or a shebeen. And, despite the clusters of domestic workers often seen sitting on the grass verges of Johannesburg's northern suburbs, the street played only a small role in their social lives.

The main leisure activities for domestic workers when not working were watching television and listening to the radio (49 per cent), their two main sources of information. A further 14 per cent spent time alone. Some 12 per cent spent time with friends and only 3 per cent (33 women) said they spent time with a male friend. Domestic workers do not seem to be big gamblers in their leisure time, with only 8 per cent reporting that they had played fafee (a local gambling game based on predicting dream imagery). However, dreams of big wins are not far away, as almost half had played the Lotto (the South African national lottery) in the previous three months.

6. Worlds of Health

In South Africa, healthcare is available to South Africans through state or private services. Citizens attending state facilities are required to pay fees and pay for medicines unless they are able to prove that they cannot. Non-citizens, if identified as such, may be required to pay higher fees and deposits for services provided by the state. The policy of charging foreigners different rates varies from facility to facility. Medical aid, or health insurance, will pay for healthcare treatment (if required, and according to the plan paid for) at private health facilities. Domestic workers, because of the long days they work, and their working conditions, isolated lives and low pay, may have particular health problems and also problems accessing health care.

6.1   Health status

Just over a fifth of respondents had taken a day or more off work in the previous three months because of ill-health. Non-migrants were more likely than migrants to have taken a day off work. Their illnesses may have prompted visits to the doctor; overall 20 per cent had visited a clinic or doctor in the previous three months. Almost a hundred women (9 per cent) had been admitted to hospital in the previous year.

Participants reported that they had been told by a doctor or nurse that they currently had specific medical conditions. Some 12 per cent (133 women) reported that they had been diagnosed with a sexually transmitted disease at some point in their lives. However, overall, their most significant health problems were related to work (joint, back and limb problems). Over 20 per cent reported high blood pressure problems and more than 5 per cent that they had been diagnosed with heart problems. South African non-migrant women were most likely to have reported heart and blood pressure problems.

Domestic workers generally do not compromise their health through smoking, nor find solace in alcohol or drugs. Snuff seems to be the tobacco of choice – less than 8 per cent said they currently smoked cigarettes. The 130 women who had drunk alcohol in the four weeks prior to the interview were asked how often they had had a drink. For most, having a drink was a weekend leisure activity. Sixty per cent of those who had used alcohol drank every weekend. Another third were occasional drinkers, having drunk alcohol on less than three days in the previous month. Only one respondent said she drank alcohol every day. Three others had a drink nearly every day. These four women were all long-term Johannesburg residents.

6.2   Use of healthcare services

Usage of healthcare services suggests that, overall, these relatively healthy women can find health services if they need them. The majority choose to use allopathic (i.e. standard Western) health services for their health problems. Almost a third had been to see a doctor in the year prior to their interview. Almost 50 per cent had been to a clinic and 15 per cent had been to a hospital outpatients' department. Family planning services and clinics were the venues of choice for getting help with sexual or reproductive health issues. Almost 30 per cent of the sample had attended a family planning service in the six months prior to the interview, although less than 4 per cent had had a baby in the previous year. Only 15 per cent had visited a traditional healer, and only 48 per cent of these women had done this for health reasons. Almost half of those who had visited traditional healers for health reasons had also used allopathic services for the same problem.

What is the cost of using health services and who usually pays? Only 13 of the women interviewed were members of medical aid schemes, which would enable payment for private medical services. Thus, most would have to pay for private health services themselves. Very few employers (15) helped pay for medical treatment. Payments by domestic workers for health services suggest that state services are the most affordable, and private doctors the least. Those who saw private doctors either had medical aid or were likely to get assistance from their employers. The low usage of traditional healers may have something to do with cost. Respondents reported the cost often exceeded R100 and three women had paid traditional healers between R1000 and R3000.

6.3   Contraceptives and condoms

As noted above, over 70 per cent of respondents had children. Over 90 per cent of these women had received antenatal care from a doctor or clinic for their last pregnancy. A significant proportion had also attended family planning services in the six months prior to interview and/or had been to a clinic or doctor for sexual or reproductive health issues. Yet the majority said they are not using contraceptives and do not seem to be receiving or following any advice about using condoms. So, while only 11 per cent of respondents wanted a child at the time of interview, less than 40 per cent were using anything to delay or avoid pregnancy. Only 12 per cent of the women used condoms for contraception (Parker et al., 1998).

It could be that many of these women may not need to use contraceptives or to protect themselves from sexually transmitted infections (STIs) by using condoms because they are not sexually active. Many live apart from their partners, seeing them only irregularly, and over 40 per cent were single (although some of these women did say they had boyfriends). Respondents were asked how many sexual partners they had had in the past five years and, on average, they had slept with just 1,7 men. Thirty per cent had had two or three sexual partners. In addition, 24 had had between six and ten sexual partners and two women had had seventeen or more partners. Overall, just over half (52 per cent) were in an ongoing sexual relationship with their main partner.

Although the majority of the domestic workers appear to have only one partner, only a quarter who have long-term partners or husbands actually live with them. Women who live with partners may still be at risk of HIV infection or infection with other STIs if they or their partners are unfaithful and do not have safe sex with other partners. Those who live separately from their partners may be at risk if either they or their partners are unfaithful and have unsafe sex with their other partners (Lurie, 2004).

South Africa has very high rates of sexual violence and domestic abuse. Studies have indicated an association between sexual violence and HIV (UN, 2004). The relationships that women have may be violent – over 80 per cent said that they had been pushed, shoved, slapped and/or had things thrown at them. Some 18 per cent of all respondents had been assaulted in the previous year. And, although just over half of those said it had happened only once, almost 30 per cent said it had happened a few times and 18 per cent said it had happened many times. Three of the women had been assaulted by their employers. Fewer women reported that anyone had ever threatened to use a gun, knife or other weapon against them (10 per cent). It is unclear whether these threats came from partners or other people.

Not altogether surprisingly in the South African context, almost 6 per cent of participants, or 64 women, said they had been raped. And 6 per cent, or 66 women, had been forced to have sex with their current boyfriend, husband or other partner because they were afraid of what he might do if they refused. One woman said she had been sexually assaulted by her employer. These figures are consistent with national data, indicating that domestic workers are not at greater risk of violence than other women in the general population, but are no more protected either (Jewkes et al., 2001).

Perhaps reflecting their less restricted lives, South African non-migrant women were more likely than migrant women to have been assaulted in the previous year (26 per cent). They were also more likely to have been raped (13 per cent) or forced to have sex by a partner (9 per cent). Levels of violence reported by women in long-term relationships suggest that it may be difficult for women to negotiate condom use in their relationships (Jewkes et al., 2001). Given that the majority of domestic workers live apart from their partners, condom use may be particularly important in protecting them from infection. Disturbingly, their use of condoms in sexual relationships was low, and lower than among young women in South Africa (Parker et al., 1998).

Over 60 per cent of the women had never used a condom. Of those who had used condoms, almost 30 per cent had never used a condom with a new partner. Of those who had used a condom in the past, only 71 per cent had used one the last time they had sex. Only 65 per cent had used one the time before that. Thus, it seems that condom use is somewhat haphazard. Only 20 per cent of those domestic workers who used condoms used them all the time. Others said that they used condoms with some men and not others, while some said that they start with condoms and then stop using them.

Some of those who had used condoms but who were not using them regularly, had only ever had one partner (27 per cent of condom users). While monogamy can be seen as protection from HIV infection, it may be less effective if the partner is not faithful. Living separately from their partners may also encourage sex with multiple partners (Lurie et al., 2003). Less than a quarter of respondents did anything to protect themselves against contracting an STI. Of the 250 women who did something, the majority said they used a condom (56 per cent), and some had only one sexual partner or did not 'sleep around' (20 per cent). Others said they abstained from sex (21 per cent). A few used traditional medicine (Table 12.11). Only 12 per cent of the women interviewed did not know where to get condoms.

Table 12.11: Protection from STIs (% of those using protection)					
	Total non-South Africans	South African migrants	South African non-migrants	Total South Africans	Total sample
Use a condom	70.0	55.1	37.0	53.2	59.8
One sexual partner/ boy-friend only	15.0	16.5	14.8	16.4	13.5
Do not sleep around	0.0	1.7	11.1	2.7	2.0
Abstain from sex/ no sexual partner	15.0	19.5	29.6	20.5	20.3
Use traditional medicine (drink muti)	0.0	1.3	3.7	1.5	1.6
Healthy lifestyle/ take care of myself	0.0	0.4	0.0	0.4	0.4
Avoid high risk areas	0.0	0.4	0.0	0.4	0.4
Had an AIDS test	0.0	0.4	0.0	0.4	0.4
N=251					

6.4   Knowledge of HIV/AIDS

Low use of condoms for protection can only partially be explained by abstinence, monogamy, lack of access to condoms, or abusive or unbalanced relationships. Although the majority of the women interviewed spent most of their leisure time watching television and listening to the radio, they did not seem to be taking on board HIV education and prevention messages and information available through the media. Furthermore, a significant proportion had given birth to children in the past and used family planning services in the previous six months, while others had attended other health services. In theory, they should have had relatively good knowledge of at least some HIV/AIDS issues from health care providers.

Participants were asked if they had heard of a variety of issues relating to HIV/AIDS and whether they could explain what they were. More than 30 per cent could not explain or describe how to have sex safely. If people do not understand the importance of safe sex, or how to have sex safely, they are unlikely to be able to protect themselves or ask their partners to wear a condom. Although over a quarter of South Africa's adult population is infected by HIV, and women (because of childbirth, antenatal care and use of family planning facilities) are likely to have come into contact with healthcare workers and may even have been tested for HIV, only 45 per cent of respondents knew about mother-to-child transmission.

The domestic workers also showed relatively low knowledge about HIV treatment issues. Only 16 per cent could explain what anti-retroviral treatment is and only 20 per cent could explain treatment for opportunistic infections. Their lack of knowledge about issues related to treatment is surprising, as a significant proportion of participants said HIV/AIDS had touched their lives in intimate ways. Furthermore, the survey took place at a time when there was considerable debate in the media about treatment for HIV/AIDS and the roll-out of anti-retroviral therapy.

So, while there have been a number of campaigns around HIV/AIDS education, prevention and treatment, with these issues being integrated into popular locally produced soap operas and dramas, it seems that this group, who watch television and listen to the radio, are not being reached by these campaigns. As some commentators have noted, approaches which focus on behavioural change are often inadequate as they ignore the context within which people live and have to negotiate behaviour change. They suggest it is necessary to take into account issues of power, poverty and gender relations in people's social and working lives, so as to better understand how to enable people to act on information received, or even how to enable them to receive the information in the first place (Parker et al., 1998).

7.   Conclusion

So, how do migrancy, work, health and HIV/AIDS intersect in the lives of domestic workers living in Johannesburg? And what are the implications of this study for domestic workers and health service providers?

First, migrancy is a defining feature of the lives of the majority of the domestic workers surveyed in this study. It shapes their lives and relationships in many ways. Many, though they have lived in Johannesburg for a long time and see it as a home, are constantly looking to a home elsewhere, one where their children, and sometimes their partners, live. Over 40 per cent of the sample described themselves as single, widowed, divorced or separated (although this did not prevent them from having children and boyfriends). Further research is needed to understand whether being single provides an incentive for women to migrate for work.

As migrant workers, many live in accommodation provided by their employers. Restrictions imposed by employers prevent them being joined by their children, partners and boyfriends. Only a quarter of the women interviewed live with their partner. While living with a partner does not prevent people from having multiple relationships, it does reduce the likelihood.

Secondly, working conditions are hard. The women work long days and long working weeks for low pay. Despite attempts by the government to improve working conditions for domestic workers, many employers pay under the minimum wage and require their employees to work over the maximum working hours. Most domestic workers only have access to one room and the majority of those who live off their employer's property are living in shacks. Only a third have access to a bathroom with running water and almost half have to go outside to get water. While none of this necessarily increases their vulnerability to HIV infection, low incomes and poor living conditions do have implications for people who are living with the virus, as these may compromise their health status.

Working and living conditions, particularly for those who live in, appear to provide some protection to domestic workers as they limit their opportunities to socialise with friends and meet new partners. It seems that many live restricted lives, as most of their friends are likely to be the neighbouring domestic workers they meet at their homes or in the street. Church provides another significant opportunity for social interaction. Otherwise, the majority of these women workers spend most of their few leisure hours alone, watching television and listening to the radio.

Thirdly, the majority of these women, whatever their migrant and national status, do not have problems accessing health services. The majority use allopathic health services provided by the state. Traditional healers are used by only by a few. And almost half of those who use a traditional healer for a health problem also go to allopathic services for the same problem. They seem to have only minor health problems particular to their work, and perhaps their isolation in the workplace reduces their chance of contracting infectious illnesses such as colds and flu.

Fourthly, despite their use of health services, the majority of these women do not appear to be protecting themselves from HIV infection. A defining characteristic of this group is the lack of condom use. Over 60 per cent of the sample have never used a condom in their lives. Also disturbing is that the majority of those who use condoms use them irregularly, with only a fifth of condom users saying they use condoms all the time when they have sex. Low levels of condom use may also reflect experiences of violence in relationships.

Fifthly, health promotion campaigns do not seem to be reaching these women workers, or it may be that they are just not listening. Low levels of condom use may be related to low levels of knowledge about HIV/AIDS issues, including safe sex and inaccurate perceptions of their own personal risk of HIV infection. Almost a third were unable to describe how to have safe sex and only 11 per cent thought they might have been infected. Levels of knowledge about treatment issues were also low and only 16 per cent knew about anti-retroviral therapy. Low levels of knowledge about this therapy, and the fact that it had yet to be introduced in public health services in the Johannesburg area, may have affected attitudes to testing. Less than a third had been tested for HIV and only 26 women in the sample had tested positive. Further research is necessary to find out whether the effectiveness of campaigns which encourage voluntary testing and counselling will be increased with the roll-out of anti-retroviral treatment.

Finally, low levels of knowledge and condom use are inconsistent with the experiences of these women with the virus. Many have been touched by HIV/AIDS. Over a third knew someone who had died of AIDS; a similar proportion said a member of their family was HIV-positive or had died of AIDS; and almost a fifth had physically cared for or supported someone with AIDS. Probably reflecting their closer connections to their communities and wider social networks, non-migrant women were most likely to know someone with HIV/AIDS and to have cared for someone with AIDS.

Overall, it seems that migrancy and work shape these women's lives and affect their vulnerability to HIV. It seems that for many, particularly those who live in on their employer's property, their social lives are restricted by their working and living conditions. This social isolation may actually protect these domestic workers as it reduces opportunities for starting new relationships. Unlike many other migrant workers, it seems that the live-in status of many migrant domestic workers, and their working conditions, may mean that their chance of becoming infected by the virus could be lower than that of their non-migrant counterparts. However, this does not mean that they are not vulnerable. And, conversely, their migrant status, separation from partners and, for many, restrictions on when and where they can see their partners and boyfriends may make them more vulnerable.

The low levels of condom use, given the circumstances of their relationships and low levels of knowledge about HIV/AIDS, are of concern. The majority of these women rely on television and radio for information, and the majority attend health services at some point during the year. Therefore, it seems that these women workers in Johannesburg are not being reached by health promotion campaigns relating to HIV/AIDS education, prevention and treatment. And it may be that their isolation, socio-economic circumstances and lack of power in their working lives affect their ability and willingness to act on the information they have.

Acknowledgements

The authors would like to thank the domestic workers who took time out of their busy working days to participate in this research, and to acknowledge the financial support from DFID (British Department for International Development) and CIDA (Canadian International Development Agency) through the Southern African Migration Programme (SAMP) that made the study possible.

References

COCKERTON, C, 1997. Documenting the exodus: the dimensions and local causes of Bechuanaland women's migration to South Africa, 1920–1966. *South African Geographical Journal*, 79: 43–51.

CRUSH, J, WILLIAMS, B, GOUWS, E & LURIE, M, 2002. *Spaces of vulnerability: migration and HIV/AIDS in southern Africa.* SAMP Migration Policy Series No. 24, Cape Town.

DODSON, B, 2000. Women on the move: gender and cross-border migration to South Africa from Lesotho, Mozambique and Zimbabwe. In McDonald, D (Ed), *On borders.* Kingston and New York: SAMP and St Martins Press, pp. 119–50.

HARDY, C & KLEINSMIDT, A, 2004. *HIV/AIDS and the workplace: your rights as a domestic worker: HIV and the law.* Johannesburg: AIDS Law Project.

JEWKES, R, PENN-KEKANNA, L, LEVIN, J, RATSAKA, M & SCHRIEBER, M, 2001. Prevalence of emotional, physical and sexual abuse of women in three South African Provinces. *South African Medical Journal*, 91(5): 421–8.

LURIE, M, 2004. *Migration, sexuality and the spread of HIV/AIDS in rural South Africa.* SAMP Migration Policy Series No. 31, Cape Town.

LURIE, M, WILLIAMS, B, ZUMA, K, MKAYA-MWAMBURI, D, GARNETT, G, STURM, A, SWEAT, M, GITTELSOHN, J & ABDOOL KARIM, S, 2003. The impact of migration on HIV-1 transmission in South Africa: a study of migrant and nonmigrant men and their partners. *Journal of the American Sexually Transmitted Diseases Association*, 30: 149–55.

MILES, M, 1991. *Missing women: a study of Swazi female migration to the Witwatersrand, 1920–1970.* MA Thesis, Queen's University.

— 1996. *Migration and development in post-colonial Swaziland: a study of women's mobility and livelihood strategies.* PhD Thesis, University of the Witwatersrand.

PEBERDY, S & DINAT, N, 2005. *Domestic workers in Johannesburg: worlds of migration, work and health.* SAMP Migration Policy Series, No. 40, Cape Town.

PARKER, W, DALRYMPLE, L & DURDEN, E, 1998. *Communicating beyond AIDS awareness.* Auckland Park, SA: Beyond Awareness Consortium, 11–28.

STATISTICS SOUTH AFRICA (STATSSA), 2004, Unpublished Census 2001 data.

— 2005. *Labour force survey, September 2004.* Pretoria: Statistics South Africa.

UNITED NATIONS (UN), 2004. Facing the future together. Report of the Secretary-General's Task Force on Women, Girls and HIV/AIDS in Southern Africa. Geneva.

ZUMA, K, GOUWS, E, WILLIAMS, B & LURIE, M, 2003. Risk factors for HIV infection among women in Carletonville, South Africa: migration, demography and sexually transmitted diseases. *International Journal of STD and AIDS*, 14: 814–7.

13 RISK AMPLIFICATION: HIV IN MIGRANT COMMUNITIES

PRERNA BANATI

1. Introduction

Migration is a fundamental part of the architecture of modern day South Africa, shaping many social and cultural practices. Unfortunately, the history and geography of migration in South Africa have been characterised by intractably complex problems, compounded by poverty, inequality and HIV/AIDS. The vulnerabilities of migrant living are exacerbated by poverty and transience, and key decisions on sexual health practices are rooted in complex social–environmental contexts.

The impact of migration on the HIV/AIDS epidemic in sub-Saharan Africa, and indeed worldwide, remains woefully underevaluated. Migration is a poorly understood phenomenon, evading characterisation and meaningful measurement. Efforts to capture migrant behaviour through survey methodology do not effectively reflect its dynamism. Population-based surveys typically exclude those living in hostels, and where they attempt to ascertain the impact of migration on the household, fall short of adequate definitions. Additionally, sub-standard measurement techniques have thwarted attempts to capture health risks in migrant communities and limited the scope of quantitative analyses.

Assessing the impact of migration as a contributor to ill-health is problematic, in part because there are many confounders related to both mobility and health status, including a variety of economic variables such as poverty and income distribution, and in part because of differences in the behavioural characteristics of migrant communities. As a result, it is prudent to remember that a multitude of confounding factors can influence such links. Global links between migration and HIV/AIDS are, however, clear. In areas of the world where populations are mobile, there are clear trends towards the spread of disease.

Ecological analyses also provide insight into associations and suggest possible proximal determinants of HIV risk. A comparative study (Boerma et al., 2002; undated) of relatively high and low level prevalence areas in Kisesa, Tanzania, and Manicaland, Zimbabwe, identifies mobility as a potential risk factor for the uneven spread of HIV in rural areas. In Kisesa, prevalence among men aged 17 to 44 and women 15 to 44 was 5,3 per cent and 8 per cent respectively, while in Manicaland these values were more than three times higher: 15,4 per cent and 21,1 per cent respectively. In the low-mobility area of Kisesa, 0,8 per cent of husbands and 1,6 per cent of wives were not cohabiting with their spouses, while in the high-mobility areas of Manicaland, the corresponding values were 10,8 per cent and 52,9 per cent. Recent in-migration was a significant risk factor for HIV at both sites, and in Kisesa, those who had moved into the ward had a higher HIV prevalence than those who had been resident in the ward all their lives. Additionally, HIV prevalence was twice as high in the trading centres as in the surrounding areas. The authors suggest that higher levels of mobility and spousal separation in Manicaland may have led to greater contact with high-risk groups. Another recent study (Lagarde, 2003), conducted in West Africa where the epidemic is more attenuated than in southern Africa, shows the impact of mobility on epidemic spread. A comparison of rural communities in Senegal and Guinea-Bissau showed that mobility was a key factor for HIV spread in rural areas, in part because population movement allowed the spread of HIV, but also because of the particularly risky behaviours of mobile communities. Short-term mobility was found to be a risk factor for HIV, with male migrants being twice as likely to be infected as non-migrants.

This chapter explores the relationship between HIV risk and migration in South Africa by identifying urban informal settlements as key magnifiers of risk, increasing the vulnerability of migrants to HIV. It makes a concerted attempt to look beyond the oft-cited unidimensional relationship between HIV and migration and begins to contextualise the problem into the unique environments in which migrants live, exploring the urban informal settlement as a focal determinant of HIV risk (Banati, 2005). This approach allows a reconfiguration of the migration–HIV dialectic by ensuring a contextualisation of the HIV/AIDS problem within a broader discussion and provides a better understanding of the determinants of HIV infection in migrant communities. HIV programmatic interventions can be vastly improved when a holistic picture can be presented. To date, however, these have been typically vertical in nature. In identifying the multidimensionality of HIV risk, this study presents solutions that may fall outside of traditional programmatic interventions and have not been evaluated to date.

The next section of the chapter reviews the migration dynamic in South Africa from both historical and geographic perspectives. This is followed by a description of urban informal settlements as risk amplifiers, defining these areas as focal determinants of HIV risk in the South African context. This involves a discussion of the unique risk environments generated among migrant communities living in urban informal areas, with an exploration of high-risk sexual behaviours commonly seen in these geotypes. In conclusion, the implications for HIV programming are presented, with a view to addressing the migration–HIV dynamic within a broader development perspective.

2. Perspectives on Migration and HIV/AIDS

A cursory review of countries and their corresponding migration indices shows the association of migration and high HIV prevalence. This can be seen for the southern African region in Table 13.1. Small countries with highly mobile populations where disease spread is less contained, such as Swaziland and Lesotho, have experienced a faster growth in the epidemic, evidenced by smaller time intervals between the year widespread HIV transmission began and the year peak HIV incidence was noted. It is possible that population mobility may have contributed to the speed at which peak incidence was reached (UNDP, 2003) and shaped the nature of the epidemic.

Table 13.1: Migration, HIV Prevalence and Behaviours in the Southern African Region

Country (year widespread transmission began, peak incidence reached) (UNAIDS, 2002)	Migration patterns	% pop in urban areas (UNPP, 2000)	Median 2002 HIV prevalence unless otherwise stated (UNAIDS, 2002)	Behaviours (DHS, 1998–2003)
Botswana (1988, 1997)	Rural-to-urban migration, commonly diamond mining.	49,4	35,4% (ANC data for 22 districts). Major urban areas (40.2%) and rural districts (37%) showed little difference.	25% of men and 11% of women reported >1 sex partner in the last year. High condom use (last sex condom use >70% among men and women having sex with a non-regular partner in the last year).
Lesotho (1989, 1995)	Cross-border migration to South Africa – 50% of men aged 15–49 work in SA, mostly in agriculture or as labourers.	29,8	20,9% (2000) in 5 antenatal clinics. In Maseru, the capital, prevalence was 42,2%, while clinics in the lowlands ranged from 19–26%. In the mountains it was 12,3%.	51% of migrant workers surveyed reported sex with a non-regular partner in the last year, 36% using a condom at last sex. Among miners, 51% reported sex with a non-regular partner in the last year, 50% using a condom at last sex.
Malawi (1980, 1993)	Migration to South Africa among miners (recently stopped). Informal migration to South Africa common.	15,1	Median prevalence is 16.9% in 2001, highest in Blantyre, lower in semi-urban areas and lowest in rural sites. Prevalence appears to be declining.	In 2000, 9% of women and 33% of men reported sex with a non-regular partner in the last year, of which 39% and 29% reported condom use at last higher-risk sex respectively.

Mozambique (1985, 1995)	Rural-to-urban migration. Informal migration cross-border to South Africa. Rural SA, particularly Limpopo and Mpumalanga, attracts Mozambicans to work in sugar plantations. Major routes connecting African countries pass through Mozambique towards SA.	34,3	Nationally, 13,7%. In the capital Maputo prevalence was 18,0%. Southern sites, closer to the SA border, have higher prevalence than northern ones. Median prevalence less than half in northern antenatal clinics than southern ones (combined data for 2000 and 2001).	In 1996, 37% of men and 14% of women reported sex with a non-regular partner in the last year, of which 28% used a condom at last sex with a non-regular sex partner. Women were less likely to use condoms than men (19% and 28% respectively). Overall, low condom use is reported.
Namibia (1986, 1996)	Rural-to-urban migration for mining.	31,4	Nationally, 22,5%. Urban and rural sites did not show significantly different prevalence rates. Highest rates (>40%) are found in easternmost part, which connects with Botswana, Zimbabwe and Zambia. Epidemic still on the rise.	Information not available.
South Africa (1987, 1997)	Rural-to-urban migration to seek work. Receives many migrants from southern Africa. Large informal migrant community.	57,6	Nationally, 26,5% and is highest in the eastern part of the country, declining considerably across to the western part. The epidemic is stabilising.	4% and 14% of men and women respectively reported >1 sex partner in the last year. Among those with multiple partners, condom use was 20% and 49% respectively among those with 2 and 3 sex partners. In 1998, 16% of women reported using a condom with a non-regular partners at last sex.
Swaziland (1987, 1995)	Cross-border migration to SA, mostly for mining/farmworkers. Large informal migration into South Africa.	25,7	Nationally, 38,6% at 17 antenatal clinics. Prevalence is higher in urban sites, with sharp increase seen between 1992 and 1996.	Non-regular partners were common among long-distance truck drivers (29%) and the military (58%). Condom use at last sex with a non-regular partner was 29% and 58% respectively.

Zambia (1980, 1991)	Rural-to-urban migration. Previously for copper mining but less so at present.	39,8	Nationally, 20,4%. Higher in the south and west, and in major urban areas such as Lusaka. 2001/2 study showed prevalence in rural areas was half that of urban areas (11% vs 23%). Prevalence rates in Lusaka, Copperbelt and southern provinces bordering Zimbabwe exceeded the national average.	In 2000, 16% of women and 29% of men reported sex with a non-regular partner in the last year. In 1996, 21% of men reported sex with a commercial sex-worker (CSW) in the last year. Condom use at last sex has increased, with 33% of women and 44% of men having sex with a non-regular partner reporting condom use at last sex in 2001/2.
Zimbabwe (1980, 1993)	Cross-border migration to South Africa. Intra-country rural to urban migration.	36,0	Nationally (2001) prevalence was 30,4% in 19 sites. Little difference seen between urban and rural areas.	In 1999, 14% of women and 41% of men reported sex with a non-regular partner in the last year, of which 43% and 70% reported condom use at last sex.

In Central and West Africa, HIV-1 seroprevalence rates are considerably higher in urban centres than rural areas, with urban rates typically four to ten times higher than rural (Caldwell & Okonjo, 1968; Quinn et al., 1994). Rapid urbanisation in African cities has been linked to urban poverty and unemployment and there are additional social and economic pressures on those living in the mushrooming urban slums (Buve et al., 2002). It is important to understand that the communities in these informal areas are typically transient. This study accepts the well-founded assumption that informal housing arises from the needs of mobile communities: informal settlements indicate migrant populations. The social constructions of these areas are uniquely high-risk, with distinct behavioural dynamics, and differing sexual behaviours are an important consideration in understanding these dynamics. Commercial sex is more prevalent in urban centres, where bright lights and temptation can attract and anonymity is secured (Jochelson, 1991). Additionally, migrants to urban centres belong to different sexual networks from rural people (Weir et al., 2003). Urban migration patterns are often associated with an increase in risky sexual behaviours, particularly increased partnership rates (Coffee, 2005) and a higher rate of sex outside of marriage (Herdt, 1997). Urbanisation increases opportunities for sexual encounters, and urban residents tend to marry later and have a greater frequency of casual sexual relationships as a result.

Beyond existing differences in sexual relationships, the social and cultural milieu of one's immediate environment affects health risks. Stereotypical dichotomies of 'urbanisation, individualism and modernity' versus 'village, community and tradition' have been identified as important factors in determining migrant interactions in the urban environment (Crush, 1997). Adaptation is imperative to ensure successful migration and, as a result, changes in cultural practices, including the acceptance of sexual freedoms in urban areas, are a necessary consequence. Epidemic conditions can also arise from the 'notion of "crisis", of social disintegration', where 'critical events' can provide suitable conditions for an intensified spread of HIV (Herdt, 1997). War conditions in central Africa are oft-cited examples and, in the case of South Africa, the end of apartheid gave rise to massive population movement and social upheaval in a previously subjugated society, creating substantial disruptions and possibly contributing to the spread of disease.

While simple geographic distinctions provide an important explanatory variable in the assessment of health risk, the vulnerabilities of migrant lifestyles and their relationship to health are complicated. Heavy migrant flows, increases in female migration, highly evolved transport infrastructure and rapid urbanisation have blurred the geographic distinction with respect to health end-points, and what can be construed about the relationship between migration and health in South Africa is limited. As a consequence, a better resolved geographical representation is warranted. At the magisterial district level, 1996 South African Census data provides insights into migration patterns at an earlier stage of the epidemic. The proportion of people having lived in their usual place of residence for less than two years was highest in Gauteng and the gold mining areas of Northwest and Free State provinces. Population dynamics also showed greatest transience in the major cities of Cape Town, Durban and Port Elizabeth, as well as the coast of KwaZulu-Natal north of Durban. Additional pockets of higher transience included the farming areas of Mpumalanga and Limpopo provinces and the platinum mining areas of the country.

Figure 13.1 shows the provincial distribution of net migrant flow in the mid-1990s. Gauteng had the highest migrant flow, while the Eastern Cape had the largest out-flux of migrant workers. Net gains and losses, however, do not convey circular migration patterns. North West province showed only a small net increase in migrant workers entering the province, but it is likely that large-scale circular migration between the mines and the rural homelands is not fully captured. The schematic representation in Figure 13.2 shows the direction of inter-province migration flows. Light grey arrows indicate the source locations of the largest number of immigrants into each province; dark grey arrows indicate the second and third largest source provinces. This figure displays the complexity of inter-provincial migration, but also identifies Gauteng as a primary destination for many intra-provincial migrants. The primary migrant flows in most cases remain intra-provincial. Other types of migration form a small component of overall movement and, in fact, much more mobility occurs within provinces and from nearby settlements (Stevens & Rule, undated). However, international migration cannot be discounted as a vector of disease and the introduction of foreign migrants into local sexual networks may have initially played a part in spreading HIV.

Figure 13.1: Provincial Distribution of Net Gains and Losses Due to Migration

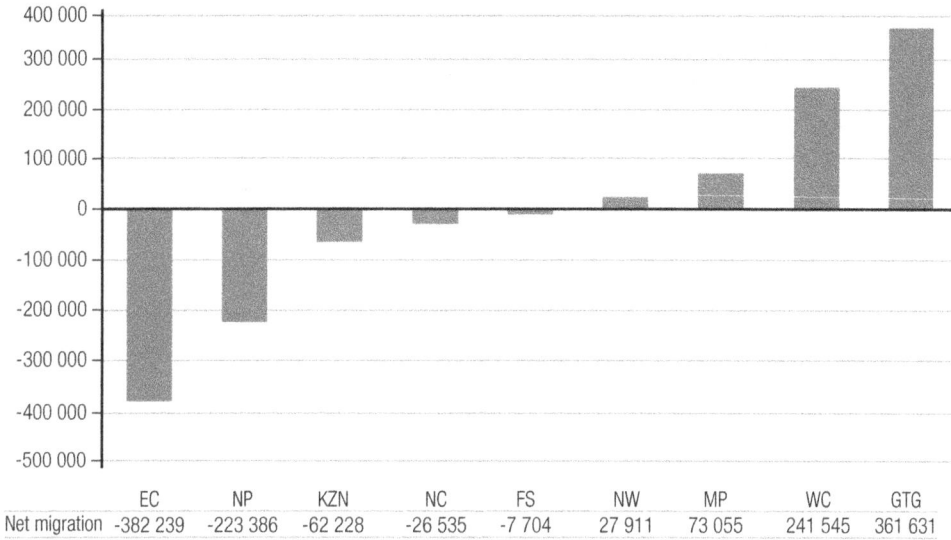

	EC	NP	KZN	NC	FS	NW	MP	WC	GTG
Net migration	-382 239	-223 386	-62 228	-26 535	-7 704	27 911	73 055	241 545	361 631

Source: Stats SA, 1996

Figure 13.2: Map of Inter-Province Migration

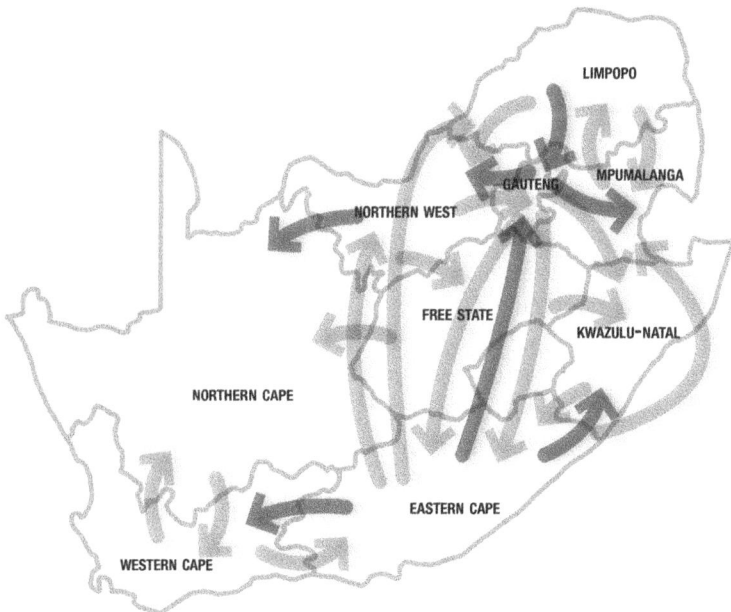

Source: Stats SA, 1996

Table 13.2 shows the distribution of types of areas from which migrants come. Bolded values identify the primary type of previous residence among women responding to the South African Demographic and Health Survey (SADHS, 1998). Among migrant women, most previously lived in the countryside, while in Gauteng most moved between (or more likely within) cities and those in the Western and Northern Cape had previous residences in urban areas. Table 13.2 reflects a type of hierarchy consistent with rural-to-urban migration, showing that much movement appears to be occurring away from rural areas, into towns and cities. An important note here is that many migrants reaching highly urbanised areas such as Gauteng or the Western Cape (and the large cities of Johannesburg and Cape Town) tend to move within or between these cities.

Table 13.2: Previous Place of Residence among Women not Living in their Usual Place of Residence				
Province	Type of place of previous residence			N
	City	Town	Rural area	
KwaZulu-Natal	32.9%	16.7%	50.4%	1 096
Gauteng	38.0%	35.6%	26.4%	534
Free State	22.0%	24.3%	53.7%	445
Limpopo	7.5%	5.5%	87.0%	401
Eastern Cape	18.8%	22.5%	58.7%	1 342
Northern Cape	26.1%	40.7%	33.2%	479
Western Cape	25.5%	48.8%	25.7%	713
North West	13.5%	36.6%	49.9%	363
Mpumalanga	2.3%	28.0%	69.8%	576
Source: SADHS (1998). Bolded values are highest.				

The distribution of migrant flows is a function of the existence of transport networks, and the capacity to carry human traffic can limit or promote migrant labour. The role of the transport industry in the HIV/AIDS epidemic in South Africa has been previously documented. While effective transport and access are prerequisites for economic growth and development, the spread of disease that occurs may consequently annul some of its positive attributes. Whiteside (1998) notes that South Africa has the greatest concentration of roads and railways, the most vehicles in southern Africa, and the busiest air traffic in Africa. It is important to recognise the impact of the flourishing transport industry on health outcomes. Figure 13.3 shows the distribution of road density per 10 000 kilometres in South Africa (CSIR, 2003). It is evident that Gauteng and the western periphery of Johannesburg have the greatest density and that most infrastructure is designed around industrial centres. This can be a useful contribution to understanding spatial variations in risk, but there are limitations, including the inability of road density to reflect frequency of transport use or numbers of passengers. In the less affluent parts of the country, the ratio of passengers to driver may be many multiples compared to that of more affluent areas. However, despite these provisos, such a distribution provides a reasonable insight into the dynamics of population movement.

Figure 13.3: Road Density Per 10 000 kms for South Africa

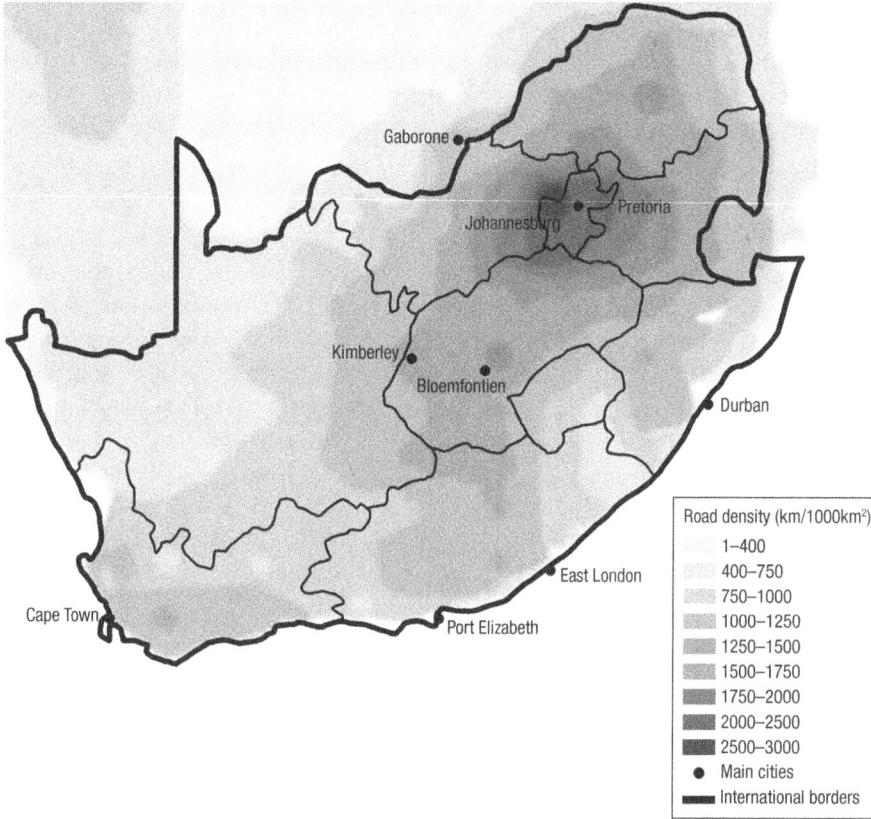

Source: CSIR, 2003

In sum, Gauteng is a province receiving many migrants, as evidenced by the density of the population who have lived there for relatively short periods and by existing migration pathways. It is also a province with a higher density of urban informal areas than labour-sending areas such as the Eastern Cape. As the following sections describe, urban informal areas are a unique geographic, social and cultural context for migrants, engendering high-risk environments for this particularly vulnerable group.

3. Urban Informal Areas in South Africa

The distribution of urban and rural proportions of the population in selected provinces, by age and gender, can be seen in Figure 13.4. The first pattern, as evidenced by the Eastern Cape, is where men and women in their twenties travel to urban areas in search of employment (Figure 13.4(a)). Upon their arrival, many take up residence in informal settlements on the periphery of the city. The average 20- to 24-year-old male is twice as likely to live in an informal settlement in a labour-receiving province like Gauteng as in a labour-sending province like the Eastern Cape. As they get older, some return to rural areas, while some move to more formal urban areas. The demographic bulge of those aged 20 to 50 living in urban areas clearly reflects this pattern. Similar patterns are seen in KwaZulu-Natal and Mpumalanga. In the second pattern, as evidenced by Gauteng, the pattern is reversed, and rural living forms a very small proportion (Figure 13.4(b)). The largest proportions of all age groups live in urban areas, with a considerable proportion of those migrating from outside Gauteng living in urban informal areas. Those under 50 are more likely to live in urban informal areas than those who are older. The demographic bulge seen in urban areas among those aged 20 to 50 is not apparent here. The third pattern occurs in areas such as Limpopo Province (Figure 13.4(c)). These areas do not have a very high migrant population and, as a result, tend to have largely rural settlements, with an almost complete absence of informal areas.

The geotype profile of the population thus differs significantly by province. Labour intensive provinces have a larger proportion of people living in urban areas in general and more specifically in urban informal areas. The majority of provinces display the common pattern of urban migration to cities among those in their productive years, reflected by a demographic bulge among those aged 15 to 49 living in urban formal and informal areas. Mostly, this reflects intra-provincial migration, which is the largest migratory pathway in South Africa. Ironically, this route has been largely ignored in the research arena, in favour of inter-province and international migration, which occur on a comparatively smaller scale. Research on longer migratory pathways has yielded very interesting results (Lurie et al., 2003). However, people working in the nearest local city are the more common migrant workers, and their characteristics and behaviours differ significantly from long-distance circular migrants, particularly in the frequency of home visits.

Figure 13.4: Distribution of Residents by Geotype

(a) Migrant Sending Area: Eastern Cape

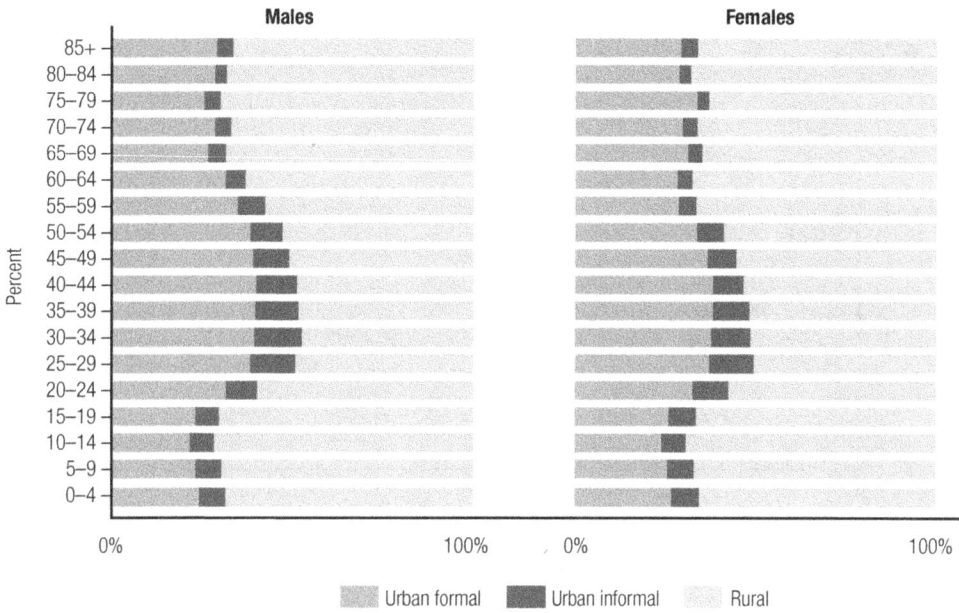

Urban formal   Urban informal   Rural

(b) Migrant Receiving Area: Gauteng

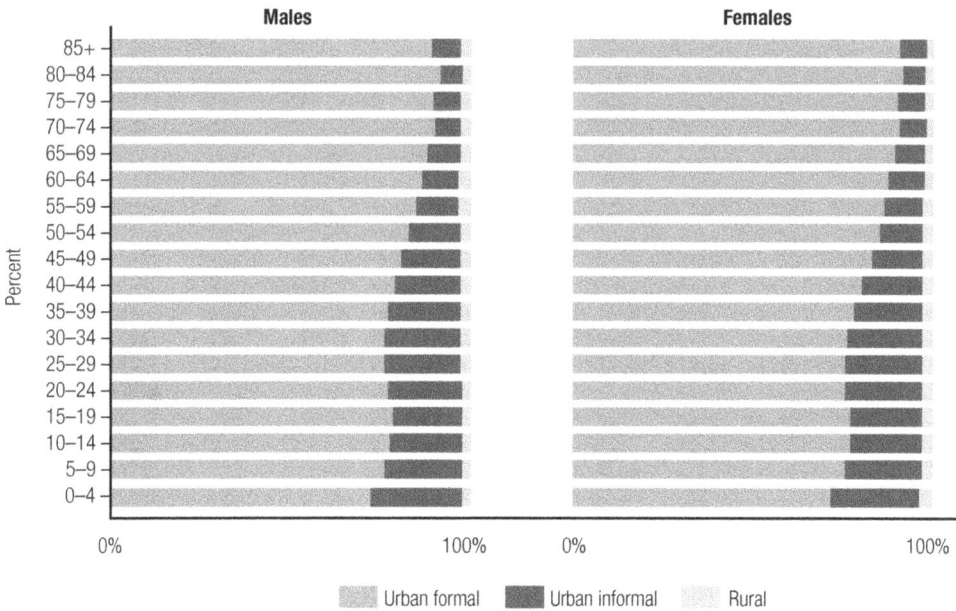

Urban formal   Urban informal   Rural

(c) Rural Area: Limpopo

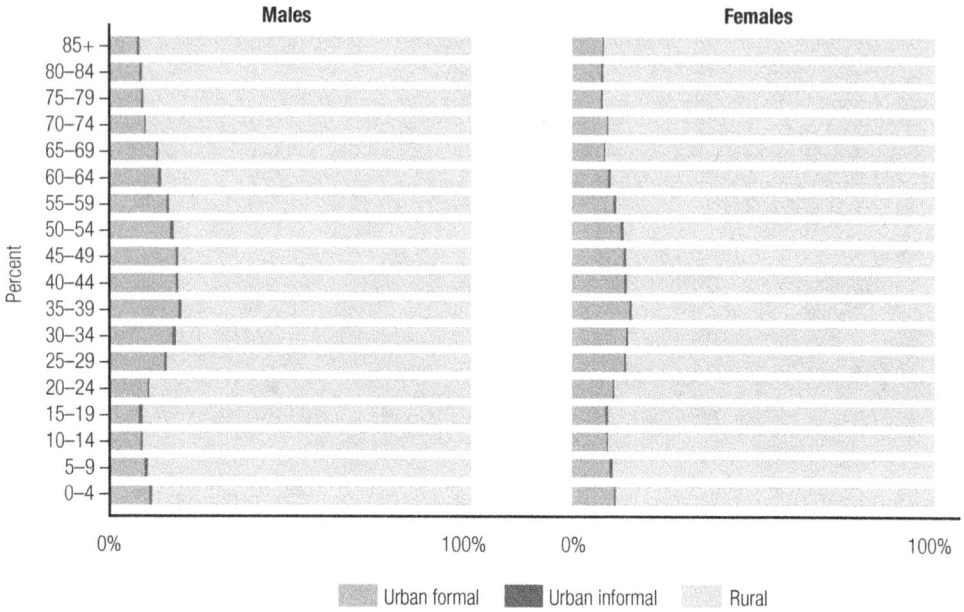

Source: StatsSA, 1996

Provinces unable to accommodate a vast influx of rural migrants into urban areas have seen an upsurge of urban informal settlements, most notably in the Free State, Gauteng and North West provinces, where the largest proportion of urban informal residents live (Figure 13.5).

Figure 13.5: Population Residing in Informal Areas

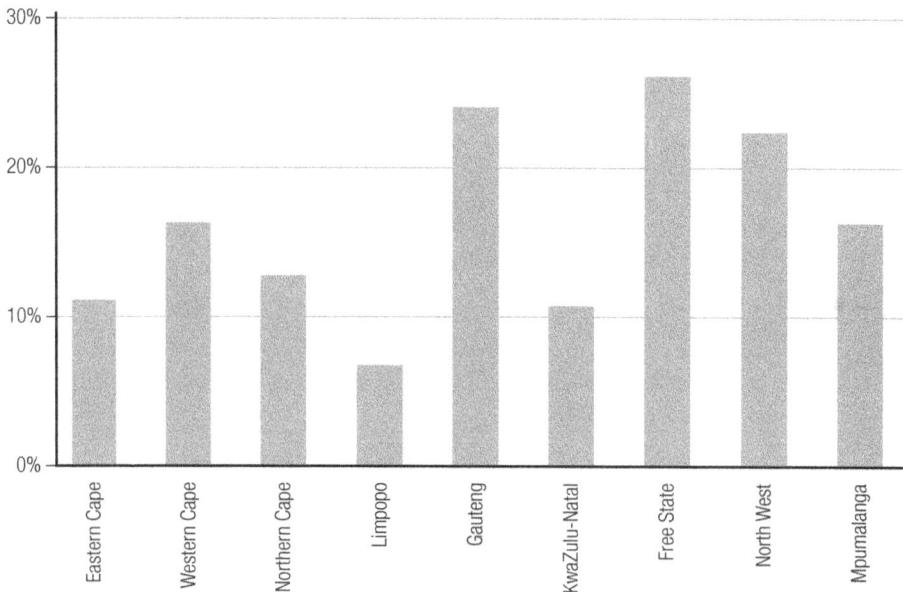

Source: StatsSA, 1996

Urban informal areas are characterised by poor housing structures with limited sanitation provision, and limited access to healthcare and other resources. Informal areas vary considerably, from poorly constructed cardboard housing structures without running water or access to sanitation to elaborately constructed brick dwellings with amenities comparable to many formal areas. The transitory nature of the informal settlement precludes the formation of the socially cohesive structures which are often associated with improved health measures (Campbell et al., 2002).

Gauteng, the province that is home to the largest number of migrant workers in South Africa, has seen a large growth in informal settlements. In 1998, 180 informal settlements were identified in Gauteng, housing in excess of an estimated one million people. Many are unemployed young people, seeking independence from their families and hoping to find work in urban centres and access to services not routinely available in rural areas (Stevens & Rule, undated).

4. Urban Informal Areas as Risk Amplifiers

HIV prevalence in South Africa is notably higher in urban informal areas. The 2002 NM/HSRC study of HIV/AIDS shows that while there is no difference between HIV prevalence in formal urban areas and rural areas, startling differences do exist between formal and informal urban areas. Table 13.3 identifies these differences. HIV prevalence in urban informal areas is over twice that of urban formal areas in South Africa, and among 15- to 49-year-olds is alarmingly high at 28,4 per cent, reflecting a 40 per cent increased risk among young people in urban informal areas compared to those in urban formal areas when correcting for behavioural variables (NM/HSRC, 2002). In nearly every province, informal urban areas present the highest HIV prevalence rates, confirming the important contribution of this geotype to increased health risks (Figure 13.6). Urban informal living is identified in this analysis as a high-risk focus area. While HIV risk remains high for this geotype in all provinces, there is a clear need for specific interventions in provinces such as the North West, the Free State and Gauteng, which have high HIV prevalence rates and high densities of urban informal settlements.

Table 13.3: HIV Prevalence by Geotype			
Geotype	N	HIV-positive (%)	95% CI
Urban formal	1 230	9.3	6.6–12.0
Urban informal	197	20.2	12.3–28.1
Tribal	524	7.0	3.9–10.1
Farms	148	8.6	1.0–16.1
Source: NM/HSRC, 2002.			

Residence type is therefore a strong predictor of behavioural risk. Results from the recent NM/HSRC (2002) study clearly show an increased vulnerability to high-risk sexual behaviours among those living in urban informal areas when compared with their counterparts in urban formal or rural areas. This type of analysis is unique, as matched quantitative data of sexual behaviours allowing for geographical stratification has not been available prior to this study.

Figure 13.6: Provincial HIV Prevalence by Geotype

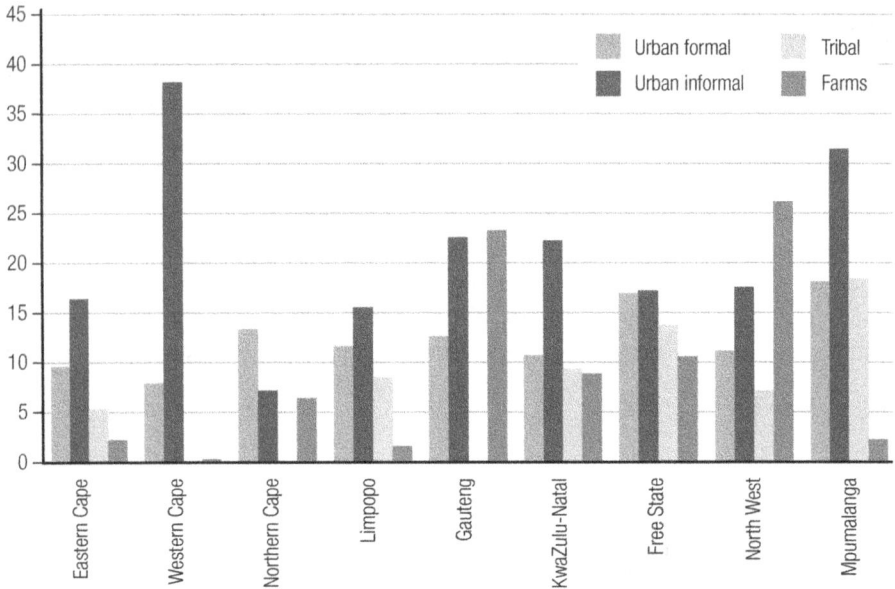

Source: NM/HSRC, 2002

Figure 13.7: Partnerships among Sexually Actives by Geotype

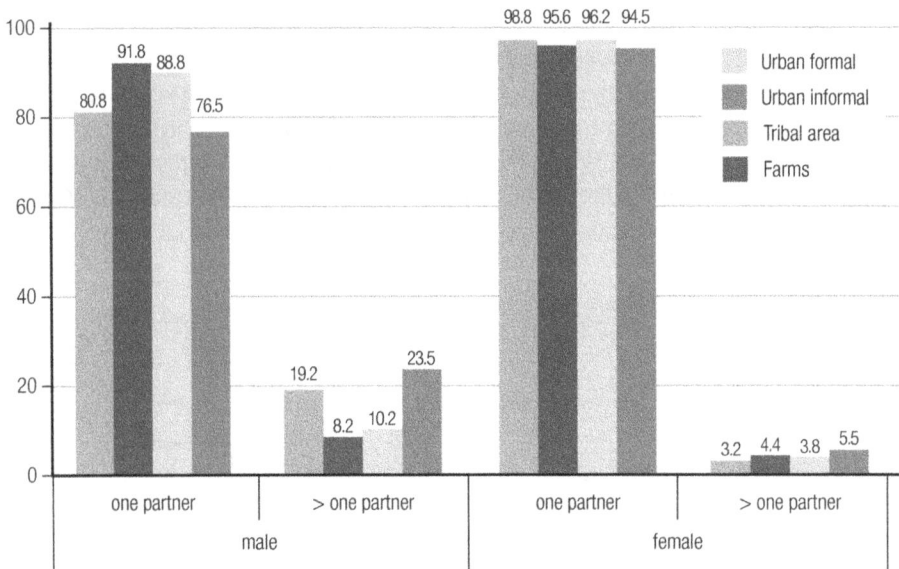

Source: NM/HSRC, 2002

While qualitative information about risk behaviours in urban townships is present in the literature, inferring health risks from this information has had limited success. Among both males and females, a greater proportion of residents of urban informal areas tend to have more than one partner (Figure 13.7). Sexual experience also differed significantly by geotype.

Among 15- to 24-year-olds living in informal urban areas, 74 per cent were sexually active, compared to 53 per cent among their urban formal counterparts (Figure 13.8). The higher curve seen in informal settlements reflects the higher degree of pressure for sexual encounters among young people living in these environments.

Figure 13.8: Sexually Active by Age and Geotype

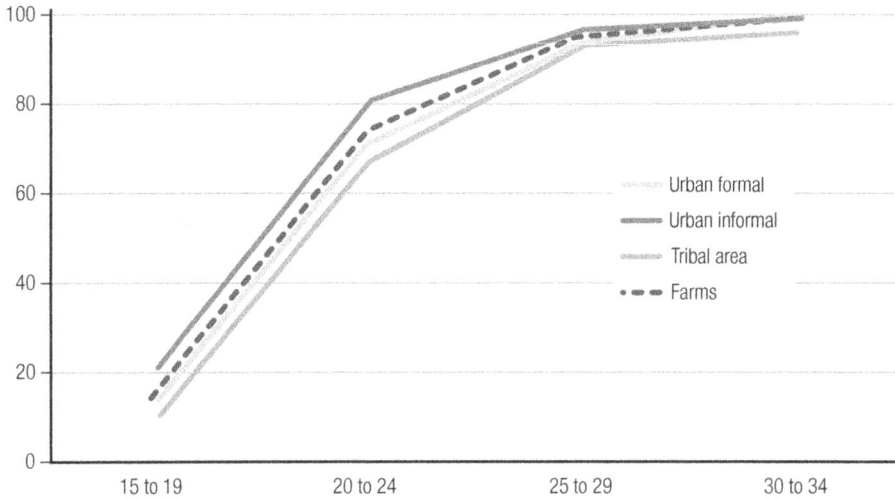

Source: NM/HSRC, 2002

The age distribution of those with more than one partner is shown in Figure 13.9 by geotype. The decrease in those with multiple partners in the 25- to 29-year-old age groups represents the increase in marriage rates in that age group. However, in urban informal areas, casual relationships persist into adulthood and such a decline is seen later than in urban formal areas, possibly reflecting the higher proportion of migrants in urban informal areas.

Figure 13.9: Proportion of Sexuality Active Youth with more than One Current Partner by Age and Geotype

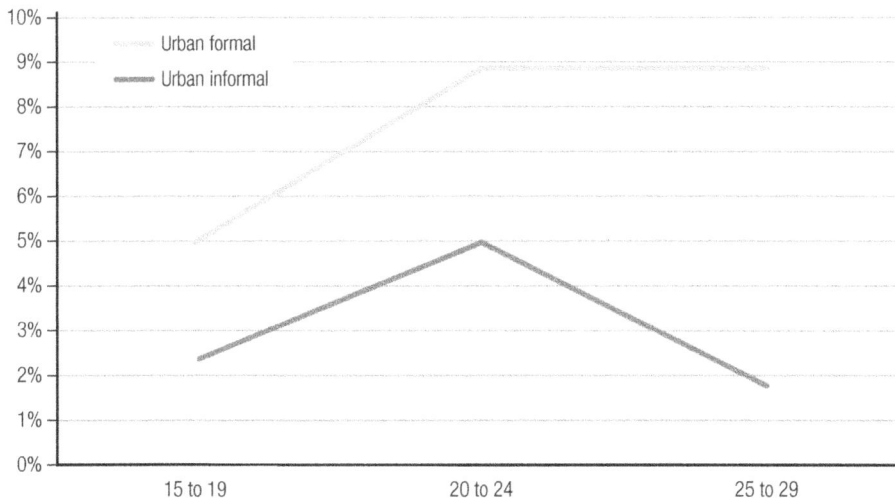

Source: NM/HSRC, 2002

A recent study (Weir et al., 2003) confirms the importance of large sexual networks as drivers of the HIV epidemic in township settings, in contrast to the commercial sex industry which is typically held responsible for propagating HIV. Sexual networks are important to this discussion as they present defined risk behaviours in distinct locales and they link locales to the accelerated spread of infection geographically. In the South African townships investigated, over a quarter of men and women had had a new sexual partner within the previous four weeks, with fewer than 10 per cent of women acknowledging an exchange of cash for sex.

As a result, commercial sex was considered to represent only a small proportion of new relationships formed in townships. The rate of new partnerships among women in townships was of an order of magnitude higher than that reported in household surveys, suggesting differing patterns of sexual behaviour in urban informal settings. High-risk environments also present greater risk avoidance strategies. Encouragingly, condom use rates are higher in urban informal areas than in urban formal areas, most notably among females, where 23,6 per cent used a condom at last sex in formal urban areas, compared with 37,2 per cent in informal areas (NM/HSRC, 2002).

In modern day South Africa, urban informal living is characterised by a volatile mix of transience, high crime rates, high unemployment and poverty, resulting in risky sexual behavioural dynamics. Migration plays a pivotal role in defining vulnerabilities in the contracting of disease as well as determining patterns of disease transmission – what Anarfi terms the 'double dynamic relationship' between migration and HIV/AIDS (Anarfi, 2005). The nature of urban informal residence uniquely exemplifies this double dynamic. These areas have a higher HIV prevalence than other geotypes, thus increasing the likelihood that new migrants will contract HIV. They also engender risky sexual behaviours, thus promoting increased HIV transmission. Low social cohesion and high crime rates, and gender, income and racial inequalities, combined with poor access to information and poor perceptions of self-determinism, are pervasive in urban informal areas. These factors build upon the migrants' disengagement from existing social support mechanisms and their insecurity in new surroundings, amplifying the already high vulnerabilities of migrant living.

Let us exemplify the above through a typical case. Nthabiseng (not her real name) is a young, unmarried, informally employed African female living in an informal urban area. Nthabiseng has recently moved from the rural Eastern Cape to an informal urban area south of Johannesburg. She has two young children who live with her mother in the Eastern Cape. She came seeking employment, hoping to send money back home. When she first arrived, she stayed with her uncle and his second wife, but when she wanted to open a fruit stand on their plot they evicted her from the property. She then rented a shack in her uncle's employer's backyard for R150 a month and began to wash clothes to earn some money. Struggling to pay her rent, she agreed to her landlord's proposition for sexual favours. The subsequent rental subsidy and her ability to find a job as a part-time domestic worker in the northern suburbs have allowed her to save about R100 a month to send home to her children. In the meantime, she is inundated by HIV/AIDS messaging encouraging condom use, faithfulness, counselling and testing. Suggesting condom use to her partner resulted in a fierce quarrel and he threatened to remove her from the plot – he says he isn't infected, citing his current fitness levels in support. Also, he has three children from his first wife and two from his second wife

– how can an infected man be so virile? She won't ask again, though she sees him at the shebeen with his girlfriends, and sometimes he brings them to his house, but she isn't sure what she can do about it. In any case, at least she manages to provide some money to her family through this arrangement.

Unfortunately, Nthabiseng's predicament is all too common among informal urban residents in South Africa. Her current living arrangements, uncertain lifestyle and lack of social support mechanisms have caused her to engage in high-risk behaviours. The sexual disempowerment she experiences is a direct function of her lack of autonomy. For Nthabiseng, interventions seeking to change her behaviour so as to decrease her risk of HIV take two forms. The first is individual intervention aimed at influencing proximal determinants of behaviour, such as helping her negotiate condom use in the context of her disempowered relationship with her sexual partner. The second is societal intervention, addressing more distal determinants of behaviour, such as working to alleviate poverty so that she no longer needs to compromise in her relationship with her landlord – or indeed to migrate to begin with. But unless these interventions take into account her environment and the impact of migrancy on her lifestyle choices, neither is likely to be successful. The example of Nthabiseng suggests that efforts aimed exclusively at individual agency or societal structure are unlikely to be successful, as they do not capture the daily contexts in which people live. What is needed is a new approach to understanding behaviour and ways in which HIV risk can be mitigated that reconcile this dichotomy. Programmatic interventions using the focal determinants approach (Banati, 2005) use the contextual environment as the entry point to understanding behaviour.

5. Focal Determinants Approach

If programmatic interventions are to help migrants, they need to be contextualised. Those that deal specifically with urban informal areas can be successful with this high-risk group. Typically, micro-agency or macro-structural interventions have worked independently of each other, but interventions based on the focal determinants approach automatically reconcile both micro and macro approaches. In South Africa, the urban informal environment is a specific locale where risk is amplified and forms a focal determinant of considerable significance. An intervention based on an understanding of not only individual behavioural limitations but also the dynamics of urban informal living can facilitate behaviour change. Social insecurity is a key concern for many of the residents in urban informal settlements, so interventions aimed at alleviating this insecurity may attenuate the high levels of risk generated in these specific contexts. Such interventions could take the form of promoting social cohesion among community members and addressing disillusionment.

The focal determinants framework (Banati, 2005) is a useful way to describe the amplification of HIV risk among migrant communities by considering the urban informal environment as a special determinant that cuts across all levels, from macro to micro (Figure 13.10). This approach reconciles the current polarisation of macro–micro approaches to HIV interventions and incorporates a third dimension to understanding behavioural environments. It defines environments as explicit determinants affecting behavioural dynamics by reviewing the environments (through physical spaces) within which people operate and by encompassing the macro and micro contexts of people's lives. The urban informal context is a distinct high-risk environment, characterised by high unemployment, disillusionment, poor housing, female disempowerment, reduced access to healthcare, low economy and a lack of social cohesion. All these factors, which interplay to amplify the risks for migrants, make urban informal areas focal determinants of risk.

Figure 13.10: Urban Informal Areas as a Cross-Cutting Focal Determinant

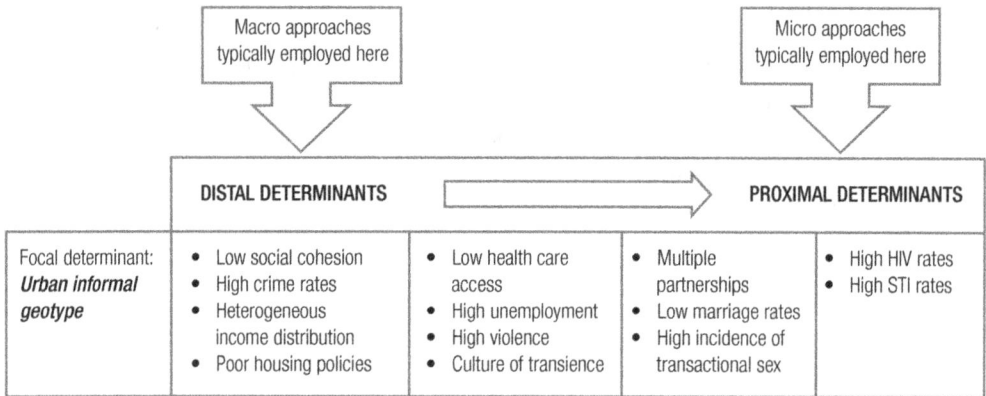

Macro approaches typically employed here			Micro approaches typically employed here

DISTAL DETERMINANTS			PROXIMAL DETERMINANTS
Focal determinant: **Urban informal geotype**	• Low social cohesion • High crime rates • Heterogeneous income distribution • Poor housing policies	• Low health care access • High unemployment • High violence • Culture of transience	• Multiple partnerships • Low marriage rates • High incidence of transactional sex	• High HIV rates • High STI rates

Focal determinants, as they amplify risk, also allow for unique risk-mitigation strategies, in the form of socially acceptable and available solutions to the high-risk environments experienced in these areas. For males in informal urban settlements, data suggests that condom use is generally an acceptable and widely used protective measure (NM/HSRC, 2005). This offers an opportunity to target specific interventions to areas where they are more likely to have impact (Banati, 2005).

6. Conclusions

The key finding of this study is the importance of understanding the behavioural patterns of high-risk groups. Migration processes also need to be seen as dynamic, but having distinct elements. Labour-sending and receiving areas have different risk profiles, represented by different risk groups. The dynamics of migrancy in labour-receiving areas are further focused through the lens of the urban informal geotype. The study stresses the importance of identifying multidimensionality within the seemingly unidimensional problem of migration. The high-risk determinants in urban informal areas amplify individual risk factors, making these areas worthy of special attention, particularly through intervention efforts. The impact of urban informal residence as a risk factor for HIV is evident. Identifying other important focal determinants through which interventions can be targeted could increase the impact of HIV programming.

The HIV–migration dynamic is complicated by many social, economic and demographic variables such as age and gender distributions, income levels, housing types, racial characteristics and education. The implications for contextualising migrant risks are critical for programmatic interventions. These cannot be designed without a thorough understanding of the complex contexts in which migrant vulnerabilities exist. The focal determinants framework presents one possible method of developing interventions that can encompass a multitude of concerns across a continuum that addresses a wide range of contextual considerations.

References

ANARFI, J, 2005. Reversing the spread of HIV/AIDS: what role has migration? In *International migration and the millennium development goals – selected papers of the UNFPA Expert Group Meeting*, Marrakech, Morocco.

BANATI, P, 2005. Scaling the epidemic: contextualized responses to AIDS in South Africa. PhD Dissertation, University of Cambridge.

BOERMA, JT, NYAMUKAPA, C, URASSA, M & GREGSON, S, n.d. Understanding the uneven spread of HIV within Africa: comparative study of biological, behavioural and contextual factors in rural populations in Tanzania and Zimbabwe. Measure evaluation, unpublished.

BOERMA, JT, URASSA, M, MNOKO, S, NG'WESHEMI, J, ISINGO, R, ZABA, B & MWALUNKO, G, 2002. Sociodemographic context of the AIDS epidemic in a rural area in Tanzania with a focus on people's mobility and marriage. *Sexually Transmitted Infections*, 78 (Supplement 1): i97 – i105.

BUVE, A, BISKIKWABO-NSARHAZA, K & MUTANGADURA, G, 2002. The spread and effect of HIV-1 infection in sub-Saharan Africa. *The Lancet*, 259: 2011–17.

CALDWELL, J C & OKONJO, C (eds), 1968. *The population of tropical Africa*. London: Longman, Green & Co.

CAMPBELL, C, WILLIAMS, B & GILGEN, D, 2002. Is social capital a useful conceptual tool for exploring community level influences on HIV infection? An exploratory case study from South Africa. *AIDS Care*, 14(1): 41–54.

COFFEE, MP, GARNETT, GP, MLILO, M, VOETEN, HA, CHANDIWANA, S & GREGSON, S, 2005. Patterns of movement and risk of HIV infection in rural Zimbabwe. *Journal of Infectious Diseases*, 191, Supplement 1: S159–67.

CRUSH, J, 1997. *Spaces of vulnerability: migration and HIV/AIDS in South Africa*. SAMP Migration Policy Series No. 24, Cape Town.

COUNCIL FOR SCIENTIFIC AND INDUSTRIAL RESEARCH (CSIR), 2003. Road density map of South Africa courtesy of Johan Maritz, Transportek, CSIR, Pretoria, South Africa.

DEMOGRAPHIC AND HEALTH SURVEYS (DHS), 1998–2003. Available at: www.measuredhs.com

HERDT, G (ed.), 1997. *Sexual cultures and migration in the era of AIDS. Anthropologic and demographic perspectives*. Oxford: Clarendon Press.

JOCHELSON, K, MOTHIBELI, M & LEGER, JP, 1991. Human immunodeficiency virus and migrant labour in South Africa. *International Journal of Health Services*, 21(1): 157–73.

LAGARDE, E, SCHIM VAN DER LOEFF, M & ENEL, C, 2003. Mobility and the spread of human immunodeficiency virus into rural areas of West Africa. *International Journal of Epidemiology*, 32: 744–52.

LURIE, MN, WILLIAMS, BG, ZUMA, K, MKAYA-MWABURI, D, GARNETT, GP, SWEAT, MD, GITTELSOHN, J & KARIM, SS, 2003. Who infects whom? HIV-1 concordance and discordance among migrant and non-migrant couples in South Africa. *AIDS*, 17(15): 2245–52.

NELSON MANDELA / HUMAN SCIENCES RESEARCH COUNCIL STUDY OF HIV/AIDS (NM/HSRC), 2002. South African national HIV prevalence, behavioural risks and mass media household survey. Pretoria: HSRC.

QUINN, TC, 1994. Population migration and the spread of types 1 and 2 human immunodeficiency viruses. *Proceedings of the National Academy of Sciences, USA, 91*(7): 2407–14.

SOUTH AFRICAN DEMOGRAPHIC AND HEALTH SURVEYS (SADHS), 1998. Macro International.

STATISTICS SOUTH AFRICA (STATSSA), 1996. Census www.statssa.gov.za

— 2001. Census www.statssa.gov.za

STEVENS, L & RULE, S, n.d. Moving to an informal settlement: The Gauteng experience. http://www.egss.uct.ac.za/sagi/gauteng.htm

UNITED NATIONS PROGRAMME ON HIV/AIDS (UNAIDS), 2002. *Report on the global HIV/AIDS epidemic – 2002.* Geneva: UNAIDS.

UNITED NATIONS DEVELOPMENT PROGRAMME (UNDP), 2003. The impact of HIV/AIDS on mortality. Report from Workshop on HIV/AIDS mortality in developing countries. UN/POP/MORT/2003/14.

UNPP, 2000. Population Division of the Department of Economic and Social Affairs of the United Nations Secretariat (UNPD), *World Population Prospects, 2000.*

WEIR, S, PAILMAN, C, MAHLALELA, Z, COETZEE, N, MEIDANY, F & BOERMA, T, 2003. From people to places: focusing AIDS prevention where it matters most. *AIDS*, 17(6): 895–903.

WHITESIDE, A, 1998. How the transport sector drives HIV/AIDS and how HIV/AIDS drives transport. Economic impact: Southern Africa. *AIDS Analysis Africa*, 8(2): 5–6.

Index

Please note: Page numbers in italics refer to tables and figures.

www.ingramcontent.com/pod-product-compliance
Lightning Source LLC
Chambersburg PA
CBHW080926050426
42334CB00055B/2728